ORBÁNLAND

WHY VIKTOR ORBÁN'S HUNGARY MATTERS

ORBÁNLAND

WHY VIKTOR ORBÁN'S HUNGARY MATTERS

LASSE SKYTT

New Europe Books

Williamstown, Massachusetts

Published by New Europe Books, 2022
Williamstown, Massachusetts
www.NewEuropeBooks.org
Copyright © 2022 by Lasse Skytt
Front cover art by Kurt Stengel
Interior design by Knowledge Publishing Services

ISBN: 978-0-9995416-7-8

Cataloging-in-publication data is available from the Library of Congress.

First edition

10 9 8 7 6 5 4 3 2 1

In loving memory of my cousin Lea ♥

"Questions you cannot answer are usually far better for you than answers you cannot question."

—Yuval Noah Harari, historian

Contents

CONTENTS

CONTENTS

Foreword

Lasse Skytt was born in 1987, a year after I moved to Hungary. I learned much from this book nonetheless. He brings to the subject all the verve and curiosity and energy of the recent immigrant, of the newcomer, while nonetheless uncovering insights worthy of a veteran journalist. He puts what has been called "the nationalism of the vulnerable" into a broader, European and global context. And, best of all, from my perspective, he reminds me of myself in my early years here, and that's a good feeling.

For a while, from February 1986, I was the only Western reporter permanently based in Budapest. It was an exciting period, long before the Internet and mobile phones. My sources were personal meetings, and very rarely even the print or broadcast media. Neither the Hungarian Socialist Workers Party (HSWP) nor the government that served it had even a spokesperson. Almost all my reports were exclusives, often informed by Hungarian journalists frustrated by not being able to publish information themselves. Poland had been, with the Solidarity movement from 1980, the first rudder of the changes. From 1985, Mikhail Gorbachev opened the door to change throughout Eastern Europe, though many East Europeans doubted that anything good could ever come out of Moscow. Then, for a period around 1988–89, Hungary led the way, and helped topple the dominos of single-party rule in country after country.

Lasse Skytt arrived in Hungary in 2013. As a Dane, he knew what life in a "small" country is like. By moving to live in Debrecen, in eastern Hungary, rather than the top-heavy capital, Budapest, he could combine his Danish insights with some "provincial" ones—and any understanding of Viktor Orbán and his experiment on the Hungarian people that Skytt dubs, humorously, "Orbánland," must start with the prime minister's own rural origins and charm.

In 1988, when I first met Viktor Orbán, he initiated the meeting. You could say I helped launch his party, whose name was then an acronym, FIDESZ (Alliance of Young Democrats)—since rebranded as Fidesz–Hungarian Civic Alliance. But why report on a bunch of kids starting a new political movement, to rival the Young Communist League (KISZ)? I felt that I was playing a useful role—giving the reformers and revolutionaries in Hungary a platform they would not otherwise have had, and thereby hastening the changes.

Minutes after HSWP leader János Kádár announced his resignation as the party's general secretary in May 1988 after thirty-two years in the job, I bumped into his propaganda chief, Ernő Lakatos, on the stairs.

"Torp úr," he bellowed–greeting me by the Hungarian for "Mister Thorpe." He went on: "If I was your editor, I would promote you to the top of the BBC. But if I was general secretary of the HSWP, I would never allow you to set foot in our country again!" And he carried on down the stairs, guffawing.

Thirty-two years on, I still have Orbán's number in my phone, but he hasn't given me an interview for twelve years, and I suspect he never will—or not so long as he is in power. His team chooses which media he speaks to, and which reporter, very carefully. You don't ask for an interview with him and wait patiently. He selects you, in his own good time, if you're lucky. He's the first Hungarian politician to understand spin, and his team have polished that ball to make it spin so fast that you can hardly see their hands on it.

The book you hold in your hands attempts the impossible: to find some middle ground in a country where the political center has long ceased to exist. That is its author's first act of courage. To do so, he persuades politicians and analysts from both sides of the spectrum to talk—and there are, sadly, now only two sides. He quotes from a wide field of analysts, with many of whom he corresponds. With their help, he seeks to put Hungary in a European, sometimes a global context. His conclusion will be startling for many Western readers: Viktor Orbán is out there in front—if you want to know what happens next, watch this space! Steve Bannon was one of the first to publicize that fact, calling him "Trump before Trump." Geert Wilders, Nigel Farage, and Matteo Salvini were not far behind in recognizing Orban's uncanny skills.

"What's your edge? What are you doing? What have you found?" Craig Oliver, head of the Remain campaign in the 2016 Brexit Referendum, asks Dominic Cummings, his counterpart at Leave, in the feature film *Brexit* (HBO, 2019). In a Hungarian context, this is the task Skytt set himself to answer. As an old hand, I am more interested now in how and when Orbán will fall. As a young one, the author focuses on what still makes him tick.

After observing that Orbán has been shaped by his village origins, Skytt notes that Orbán is also a "rebel"—who transformed himself from anticommunist to antiliberal. He quotes former Fidesz MEP George Schöpflin after Orbán's 2018 election victory, to the effect that "the next chapter of the rebellion against the prevailing liberal ideology in Europe and the West" has begun. This image of Orbán as the "rebel," the "antiglobalist," is another element necessary to understand the man. Because he leads a right-wing party, friends and opponents alike long expected him to be a conservative. But as George Schöpflin himself has pointed out, to "conserve" in Eastern Europe after 1990 would have been to conserve the vestiges of communism. Nevertheless, Viktor Orbán has himself been struggling to name the political product that he has invented. In 2014, he called it "illiberalism." By 2019, he was trying to relabel it "Christian liberty"—a term few could quite grasp. More often than not, he falls back on "Christian democracy," because that is at least a brand that people recognize, even if his own tastes are a little different than what one might find on the supermarket shelves in Germany or Finland.

"I would like to turn Fidesz into a modern conservative party," Orbán told the philosopher of economics Peter Róna in the early 1990s. When Róna gently pointed out that while this was a noble aim, earlier attempts in Hungarian history to do just that had foundered, because when the party got into trouble, the "modern" epithet was quickly jettisoned, Orbán shrugged. "If that happens, so be it," he replied. There is a ruthlessness in the man, one his own friends pass off as "his ability to concentrate."

Hungary is a marvelous country, and at times the future of Europe seems to swing on the Hungarian hinge. One such moment was in 1956, for thirteen days during the Hungarian Revolution. Another was in 1988–89, when Hungary played a central role in bringing down not just its own communist government but also those across Eastern Europe and eventually the Soviet Union as well.

Skytt points out—and I agree—that Orbán, and through him, Hungary, is pivotal again today: a signpost pointing the way all nations should go, say Orbán's friends. A warning to us all, warn his opponents worldwide, about the way their own nations might go. The polarization in my own country, the United Kingdom, can be seen as a spread of the Orbán-effect from Budapest to Bournemouth.

Lasse Skytt's curiosity for what makes Orbán so successful as a politician is the essential prerequisite of a good journalist. The desire to talk with everyone willing to give us the time of day, to ask question after question until we think we understand. To ransack the house of Hungarian democracy in search of both the old and the new crockery. Skytt's great service to the reader is that he shows why so many Hungarians love Viktor Orbán so much. And through that gateway, he strides out onto the bigger political battlefield, to help us understand: why do so many people around the world love *other leaders like Viktor Orban* so much?

Nick Thorpe
BBC News Central Europe Correspondent

Preface

History in the Making
(and a Journalist in Tears)

She had tears in her eyes. We stood next to each other, less than fifty feet from the stage, and I had to do a double-take to be absolutely sure. Was she really crying? She was. Her tears carved a river through the thick layer of makeup on her cheeks and formed a delta at the corner of her mouth. Caught by a light breeze, her blonde hair covered her face for a moment before she tucked it behind her left ear. With the other hand, she surreptitiously wiped away the tears with a napkin.

It was close to midnight, and most of the city was covered in darkness. The reflection of the streetlights along the Danube lit up the slow-moving waters of the river. Up on Gellért Hill, the illuminated Liberty Statue looked as majestic as ever. I wondered to myself whether Budapest had ever looked more stunning than it did at that very moment, on that summery April evening. Perhaps this was why she had tears in her eyes? We did not know each other, but I was well aware of who she was. Earlier in the evening, inside the whale-shaped Bálna (Whale) building, which had functioned as a press center, I had seen her stand in front of the cameras in one of the news studios. She was a journalist—an anchorwoman with the progovernment channel *TV2*. On my way out, I had bumped into her on the stairs, and she had smiled when I told her who I was. And now we both found ourselves on the square, facing the stage. "Orbán will go on stage in a few minutes," she told me.

We were not alone. A crowd of 2,000—maybe 3,000—people had gathered, Hungarians of all ages, waiting for their beloved prime minister to show up. Not surprisingly, the crowd consisted mainly of Fidesz supporters, many of them carrying flags, orange balloons, and banners paying tribute to their hero. For several hours, everyone—including us journalists—had been watching the results from each electoral district tick in on the big screen next to the stage. Slowly but surely it became clear that the night would end up with another landslide victory for Viktor Orbán's party. For the third time in a row, Fidesz had won the election and a convincing two-thirds majority in parliament. "Viktor, Viktor, Viktor," the crowd cheered in unison, encouraging the prime minister to come onstage and address the crowd.

A few moments later, he did. Accompanied by his usual cast of Fidesz loyalists, Viktor Orbán stepped onto the stage, while Roxette's "Listen To Your Heart" blasted through the speakers—a song released around the time Fidesz was founded back in 1988. It was at this moment, as Orbán took center stage, that the tears began to flow down the cheeks of the journalist. "Why are you crying?" I asked. "Because," she responded, clearly moved by the ecstatic atmosphere, "because what we are witnessing here is history in the making. This is truly a historic moment."

After Viktor Orbán's victory speech, in which he declared, "We will continue on this path together," the *TV2* journalist and I went our separate ways. She returned to the news studio in the Bálna building to report on the evening's events. I made my way home to cover the result of the election for a Danish newspaper. As I neared the metro station on Fővám Square, an elderly man on a bicycle approached the crowd of Fidesz supporters I was walking among and he shouted hateful obscenities at them. In response, a few of them ran after the man on the bike and pushed him to the ground. No one helped him up. A mother covered the eyes of her young daughter to shield her from the situation.

In some way, the vicious incident was a stark reminder that the path Orbán wants Hungarians to walk "together" does not lead the same way for everyone. In fact, while 49 percent had voted for the prime minister, the other half of the country had voted against him.[1]

Research shows that Hungary is the most polarized country in the European Union.[2] According to a report on Hungary's polarization, there are ongoing, hostile confrontations between the country's Left and Right. The perceived ideological distance between the two blocs is as wide as the Danube River is long, and liberals and conservatives are "opposing each other in a struggle where the loser is completely denied any influence on policymaking." the report concludes.[3] Meanwhile, Europe—and, indeed, the United States, both during and, still, after Trump—is more politically divided than ever. Another report suggests that the growing divisions in Europe are part of a broader ideological shift in European politics. That's not to mention that comparable divisions in the US are bound up with those of Europe and, more broadly, other global developments. Extreme positions are represented more frequently in European governments, especially those at the far-right end of the political spectrum, including the Orbán government in Hungary. With all this in mind, it would appear sensible to make some attempt at predicting the future of Europe and the US by casting a spotlight on Viktor Orbán's Hungary. Through understanding what is going on in Hungary—and why—perhaps we will be able to predict how the current polarization might shape the future of both sides of the Atlantic.

Welcome to Orbánland

For almost a decade, I have lived and worked as a correspondent in Hungary with the aim of shining a light on a Central European country whose leader has gradually become one of the most decisive—and divisive—political figures on the old continent. I call it Orbánland. I have chosen *Orbánland* as the title of this book—which aims to be an impartial account of the situation in Hungary—to illustrate that we are dealing with a country where the political leader's dominance is so widespread that it reaches almost all elements of society. Many books could be written with similar titles the world over (e.g., *Trumpland* and *Putinland*), and it is safe to say that the election of Donald Trump in November 2016 and the Brexit referendum a few months earlier were both catalysts for me writing this book, and the legacy of these historic events will live on.

Suddenly the changing dynamics I had observed in Orbán's Hungary were happening all over the Western world. The nationalist conservative Jarosław Kaczyński came to power in Poland in 2015. Then came the year of Brexit and Trump. 2017 and 2018 saw electoral triumphs of right-wing nationalists in Austria, the Czech Republic, Italy, and Brazil. Finally, over the past few years, "mainstream politicians" in countries such as France, Germany, and Sweden have come face to face with this new wave of right-wing nationalism.

At the forefront of this trend is Hungary's Viktor Orbán, who came to power in a landslide victory back in 2010.

All in all, it is high time that mainstream politicians and others begin to understand what drives these alternative leaders. Whether nationalists, populists, or antiglobalists, these alternative leaders dominate the political debate. They set the agenda. They often win elections. Viktor Orbán has become the unofficial leader of those who dare to speak out against political correctness. Those who dare to challenge the "1968 elites" and everything those elites and their successors take for granted.

For all of those reasons, I believe it is important to understand why Hungary is changing the way it is.

Given that Europe (read: the Western European states that dominate the European Union) and Hungary are so obviously polarized, it would be of little value for me to contribute to the debate with yet another book in the seemingly endless series of publications criticizing the "fear-spreading, corrupt elite" of Viktor Orbán's self-proclaimed "illiberal democracy." Countless books adopting this angle already exist, such as Bálint Magyar's *Post-Communist Mafia State,* which argues that Orbán is building a "pyramidlike order of obedience."[1] Books focusing solely on Viktor Orbán's role as a pioneer of political ideas that will slowly but surely spread to the rest of Europe are equally plentiful. For instance, Igor Janke's *Forward* deals primarily with Orbán as "a talented leader who has a vision of the future, a clear goal, and who is not afraid to swim against the current in order to achieve it."[2] Both standpoints are valuable in their own right. However, my goal with this book is to provide a broader perspective on Orbán's Hungary and the polarization in Europe and the West.

The migration crisis of 2015 may help illustrate my objective. In the late summer months of that year, Orbán's government built a country-wide border fence to stop the migration flow from the south—a decision that split Europe into two polarized blocs. Many admired Orbán for what they saw as his courage in taking action at a critical time in European history and in protecting the EU's external border, as required by the Schengen Agreement. Others criticized Orbán for having failed to live up to European values by acting selfishly and by greeting people fleeing from war and poverty with inhumane brutality.

If you belong in the first camp, you are likely to support Orbán's "strongman courage." If you subscribe to the other point of view, you will probably back up the criticism of Orbán's "selfish" actions.

Needless to say, this is a simplified way of explaining the current climate—an occupational hazard of many journalists. However, it serves to highlight the current division that prevails everywhere in Europe and beyond: Are you for or against what Trump's USA stood for? Do you agree with the policies of Putin's Russia? Do you believe Orbán's vision for Hungary to be the right way forward?

Whichever stance you take, I don't believe this for-or-against rhetoric to be very beneficial, whether it appears in the media, in parliaments, or at our dinner tables at home. I would much rather present a wider, nuanced take on the situation in Hungary and Europe. It is my hope that this approach will get readers from both camps to better understand each other, and thus to make us able to discuss—on a fully informed basis—what lies behind and beyond the current political trends of Hungary and Europe. This discussion will only become more important and more relevant in the coming years. We might as well start listening to each other.

One of the first things I learned as a young journalist was the importance of being critical. Ask crucial questions. Be skeptical. Never take no for an answer. Be persistent. I found this pillar of journalism relatively easy to adhere to. No matter how the person I was interviewing would try to avert my questions, I could always just follow it up by asking: "But then what about *this*? Have you considered *that*?"

An early lesson from my time at university left me with the conviction that the modern journalist ought to strive for objectivity and leave personal views out of any given story. I still believe this to be the case. However, most journalists—deliberately or not—do express their views in one way or another. This may be through our choice of sources, or in the way we structure an article. In addition to this, I fear that many journalists can—and some of my colleagues have acknowledged that they have—become complacent in their use of the objective method. There can be many reasons for a reporter's lack of journalistic idealism. For some, being a journalist is "just a job." I find this to be quite problematic, and as far as I'm concerned, a journalist is never better than their last story. If we don't actively strive for objectivity, insight, and perspective *every single time* we publish a story, it can damage our own understanding of the world, which is surely to the disadvantage of our readers and the public.

This may sound idealistic. Nevertheless, I have written this book to prove this very point. I firmly believe that the journalism produced today will have a clear impact on tomorrow's actions. If we don't realize our responsibility, the inevitable outcome is that media consumers will become just as complacent. It's not dark yet, but it's getting there, as Bob Dylan once sang.

Moreover, research suggests that poor-quality news media reports result in a "spiral of cynicism and polarization."[3] The incident I earlier related concerning the man on the bike who was pushed over on election night in Budapest illustrates this cynicism and polarization. The tearful journalist proves, to an extreme degree, that some reporters cannot hide their own political bias. The question remains: have we all become too accustomed to switching off content that doesn't fit our existing worldview? To some extent, I believe we have.

People tend to stick to their regular sources of news, and will therefore often only ever see one side of a story. This trend has been reinforced by the algorithm-controlled dynamics on social media: we scroll past or shake our heads at the content we disagree with or dislike—if we are even presented with it in the first place—whereas we tend to actively engage ourselves, as soon as we encounter something that we agree with or "like." We rarely listen to what our opponents *actually* have to say before we move on to what confirms our own bias. There are several terms that seek to define this trend: filter bubbles, echo chambers, confirmation bias.

The consequence is more polarization, more cynicism. Despite the fact that we have never had access to such an astonishing amount of evidence-based information as we do today, paradoxically, we have entered a postfactual era where everyone can have their own truth and where "fake news" is on the rise. Hopefully we can all agree that this is problematic. Can we?

Eight years ago, before I moved to Hungary, I was well-established within my own little echo chamber. The apartment I lived in was located above a fashionable sushi bar, right in the center of the upscale Østerbro area of Copenhagen. It took me but a few minutes to get to the offices of the *Berlingske* news agency, where I worked at the time. Most of my friends and colleagues lived within a two-mile radius. We hung out at the same coffee bars, read the same newspapers, and voted for the same political parties. A few of us even went to New York to complete our master's degrees at the New School, an ultraliberal left-wing university in Manhattan. One of my professors there was the founder of the progressive Occupy Wall Street movement; another was an op-ed writer for *The Guardian*. Barack Obama presided over the White House, and John Lennon's "Imagine" remained everyone's favorite globalist anthem: "Imagine there's no countries / It isn't hard to do / Nothing to kill or die for / And no religion, too." In other words, I was fully prepared to live a life in the fast lane of liberal globalism. Little did I know that my decision to move to Hungary would get in the way of that plan. Today, I am happy it did.

My interest in Hungary was first roused in 2004, when the country joined the European Union. I was in high school back then, and I remember Danish Prime Minister Anders Fogh Rasmussen leading the EU's Eastern Enlargement. Yet it wasn't until I observed Viktor Orbán win his landslide victory in 2010 that I became more aware of this linguistically isolated postcommunist country that had bequeathed the world with goulash soup, Rubik's Cube, the legendary soccer star Ferenc Puskás, and much more. Now, though, Hungary was suddenly labelled "the black sheep of Europe."[4] Judging by the Western media's coverage of Hungarian affairs I had the impression that this was a country the population of which had a markedly different worldview than its neighbors in Western Europe.

I wondered: What could be the reasons for this? Are we really hearing the whole story? What is *actually* going on in Hungary?

Around this time, many of my colleagues began to apply for commercial PR jobs in Brussels, Paris, and London. Meanwhile, the traditional media outlets close to home were forced to cut back on staff. I did not like this development. I wanted something else. I wanted to remain an independent journalist. Moreover, I liked the idea of going East when everyone else was headed West. So that's what I did. I took a leap of faith and moved to Hungary in the summer of 2013.

In many respects, Hungary was a new territory for me. Step by step, I established a dialogue with lawmakers, journalists, academics, and other locals—with Hungarians. Soon I learned that most of the other foreign correspondents based in Budapest had been here since the fall of communism in 1989–1990. Most of them also came from Western countries where the idea of liberal democracy was not something you questioned: the United Kingdom, France, Germany, and the Netherlands. They had witnessed Hungary's development through several decades and all appeared to have a pronounced opinion on the affairs they covered and reported back to their home countries: The Orbán government is corrupt and xenophobic and it is misleading the public with propaganda and undemocratic laws. Not a difficult story to buy into. The evidence was obvious. You only had to pick up any newspaper not owned by Orbán's oligarchs and see for yourself. Still, I wondered if I had just moved from one liberal echo chamber to another, the only difference being that the worldview of like-minded journalists here in Budapest echoed even louder than it had in Copenhagen.

Perhaps the echo was so deafening that it completely drowned out the fact that other people, including millions of Hungarians, might have a different view on the situation?

As I gradually settled into my new surroundings in Hungary—dividing my time between Debrecen and Budapest—I came to see that the international media's coverage of Hungarian affairs did not paint a full—and, thus, a true—picture of Viktor Orbán's "regime" and the country's development. Historians remember better than journalists, I recalled, and was reminded that the former socialist-liberal government of Hungary from 2002–2010 had been a deeply corrupt "regime" that had controlled the media and led the people behind the light; not least its prime minister, Ferenc Gyurcsány, who, in his infamous speech in 2006—to party faithfuls, one of whom was secretly recording it—said that his government had done "nothing for four years" and that it had "lied morning, night, and evening."[5] (Never mind the confusing order of the times of day). This made me wonder: What is the difference between Hungary before Viktor Orbán and Hungary after Viktor Orbán? Who is to decide what is best for Hungary if the majority of the people keep voting for more of the same? Is it just xenophobic propaganda, corruption, and undemocratic laws that keep Orbán in power? Or does he strike the right chord with the Hungarian people on a few crucial subjects? Should journalists be partisan commentators or neutral mediators? And is it even possible for journalists to work "in service of the truth," as one of my old textbooks proclaimed?

It might have been my lack of presence in Hungary before 2013 that led me to these complex questions. Coincidentally, I had ended up in a country increasingly on the global radar. Being a newcomer in Hungary, an outsider, was indeed a challenge. But I also saw its benefits: I could be "the new guy in town," a fresh face to the establishment of Budapest's political and academic elite. I could be the young journalist who tried to grasp a country full of complexities. I could be the open-minded visitor local people would love talking to because I came with no preconceived notions about the Kádár era or the Gyurscány scandal. Furthermore, in all modesty, I was not afraid to take on the role of the innocent child in Hans Christian Andersen's *The Emperor's New Clothes*, blurting out, "He is wearing nothing at all!" to each of the implied camps and their inability to be self-critical. All this—combined with my Scandinavian curiosity and journalistic ideals—would put me in touch with Hungarians who openly would tell me how they looked at their own country. This access, and my conversations with these people, form the foundation of this book.

Eight years on from my arrival in Hungary, I am still asking the same questions: Could there be a way for an increasingly polarized Europe—and America, whose divisions continue in the post-Trump era—to understand itself through the lenses of Viktor Orbán's Hungary? And how do we navigate in such a fragmented world in the years to come? My hope is that this book will bring all of us closer to an answer.

Author's Note

How To Read This Book

First of all, I am glad you made it to this page of the book. It's a good place to begin, actually. Since the book consists of many different elements, as you can see in the table of contents, you might already be wondering: "Should the book be read front to back? Or can I jump around without losing the context?" The answer is that you can do both. Naturally, I have placed each of the chapters where they are because there is a certain structure and progression to the book, starting with the introduction and ending with the conclusion. But especially in Parts II and III of this book, you can jump around between the chapters, and you are more than welcome to begin with the ones you find most interesting—trust me, I know it's important to get a good start. However, promise me to not skip the parts of the book that might at first sound provocative or even irrelevant to you. You see, the whole point is to present you—whatever your political standpoint may be—with views and perspectives that you do not necessarily come across every day. Please hop onboard.

Orbánland is not just a book for "Hungary nerds." It's a book for everyone who cares about the situation in Europe and the West today ... and in the future. Whether you are interested in migration, nationalism, a new world order of Trumps and Brexits, human rights or political correctness, identity politics or European history, family values or the film industry, there will be something in this book for you. Chances are that you will learn something new. Perhaps even change your mind on some issues. Along the way, I will guide you through a polarized landscape of opinions and values in Viktor Orbán's Hungary and beyond. You will meet many different people with often conflicting ideas and agendas. And hopefully, you will be able to better understand what lies behind the current trends of a divided Western world.

In Part I, through historical research and personal observations, I collected my thoughts and learnings on the growing divisions in Hungary and in Europe—focusing on the differences not only between East and West but also between those who sympathize with minorities and their individual rights and those who believe that it's time to pay more attention to the wishes of a society's majority. I learned a lot writing these chapters and I hope you will, too.

In Part II, you will be able to explore some of the journalism I have done here in Hungary over the years. Most of the articles have previously been published in Danish and Norwegian, but here they are, freshly updated, re-edited, and translated into English for the first time. Working as an independent journalist, I have had free rein to write these features exactly the way I wanted. Thanks to my editors, I was given the time necessary to investigate and write in-depth background articles, instead of rushing through the usual breaking news stories of mainstream media.

I am excited to share these features with you. For instance, you can read how the Hungarian film scene suddenly came to win more than a hundred international awards within just a few years. Or why George Soros is the perfect enemy for Viktor Orbán and the like. Or why liberals misunderstand the appeal of nationalism and conservatism. Or what Hungary's political system has in common with the country's most famous invention, Rubik's Cube.

In Part III, you will get to know sixteen individuals with close ties to Hungary, each with their own views on matters like politics, activism, history, and life in general. In the back of the book, under Notes, you will find short biographies on each of them, as well as general references to the sources I have used for the rest of the book—

sources that can also serve as recommendations for further reading. Some of the people I've met are leading members of parliament, left and right, some are famous all over the country, and others are just "ordinary Hungarians" living a normal life in the countryside. They are people from all walks of life.

In reading Part III, I want you to ask yourself: "When was the last time I had an actual *conversation* with—and *listened* to—someone I disagreed with?" My meetings with these people were in fact conversations just as much as they were interviews. Since most of these individuals hold strong political opinions, it would have been easy for me to confront their views with critical questions, counterarguments, and a smoking gun in hand. However, I did not find that to be the right approach for my purpose with this book. So instead, I took a more open-minded, nonjudgmental, and almost anthropological approach to our conversations—listening, learning, and letting the people present their views in full without disrupting them.

I hope you will do the same.

Lasse Skytt
Budapest, 2022

Part I
Essays

"History rarely starts when we think it did,
and it never seems to end when we think it should."

—Sarah Churchwell, author of *Behold, America*

Chapter One
Arrivals in Europe

The Memory Wars

One of the first people I met upon my arrival in Debrecen was a local real estate agent named József. He helped me and my wife to find a place to stay. It took weeks to find something that matched our "Western expectations," privileged and imperialistic as it may sound. Afterward, when József noticed the look on my face, puzzled and perplexed as I was trying to make some sense of my first impression of rural Hungary, he said something that I have heard many times since: "Culture, history, family, our way of living, our traditions—all this means everything to us." By "us" he meant Hungarians, and by "everything" he meant *everything*.

I took note of that fact and accepted the clear differences between Hungary and Denmark. Not that people in Western countries don't consider family and tradition important. People in Central and Eastern Europe are just more actively, often religiously, upholding such values. *Fair enough, we cannot all be the same*, I thought to myself and remained a little suspicious about this "old-fashioned lifestyle" in eastern Hungary. Until a couple of years later, when I realized that in fact something might be rotten in Denmark; or, rather, in Western society as a whole. I came across *Utopia for Realists* by Dutch historian Rutger Bregman, a self-critical book on Western society and its lack of a grand narrative. Reading it finally made me understand that Hungarians do have a reasonable point when they vote for a politician like Viktor Orbán and defend Christian family values and conservative traditions. Bregman writes about Western society that radical ideas about a different world have become almost literally unthinkable: "The expectations of what we as a society can achieve have been dramatically eroded, leaving us with the cold, hard truth that without utopia, all that remains is a technocracy. Driving it all is a force sometimes called liberalism, an ideology that has been all but hollowed out. What's important now is to "just be yourself" and "do your thing." Freedom may be our highest ideal, but ours has become an empty freedom."[1]

Bregman's book made me realize that in Western societies, we are well past the era of the big collectives. The grand narratives. Memberships of churches and labor unions are in decline, fragmented friendships on social media outmatch the traditional family as young people's common ground. Change is the only constant. All we care about is resolving problems so we can enjoy life, and our politicians today are public management consultants more than they are inspiring thinkers. The old truths are falling apart—religion, family structures, and political ideologies—and what do we have left?

Back in Hungary, things certainly look different. Many of the Hungarians I have met through the years do not understand why their conservative political culture is condemned with such hostility by the Western world, especially by the Western media. They are surprised to discover that foreign observers are often patronizing what Hungarians perceive as their "old-fashioned" way of living. Well, guilty as charged.

As I gradually became more aware of this schism and reflected upon it, I wanted to understand the deeper reasons behind this apparent mismatch between, on the one hand, how Hungarians viewed themselves, and, on the other hand, how Westerners looked at them. I found some answers with the Bulgarian political scientist Ivan Krastev. In his book *After Europe*, he argues that there exist two types of Europeans: Those who have experienced oppressive regimes that have fallen apart from within, and those who have not.[2] Thirty years ago, Eastern Europeans were first-hand witnesses to the collapse of communism. In Western Europe, people saw it from the outside without understanding that the fall of communism was not just a liberation from oppression for the Eastern Europeans; it was also the traumatic feeling of experiencing their whole world coming to an end.

The German political scientist Christian Welzel has studied what existential pressure does to people. In his book *Freedom Rising*, he states that in places where the existential pressure has been fading for many decades, such as in Denmark or Western Europe, people are more open-minded. They prioritize freedom over security, autonomy over authority, diversity over uniformity, and creativity over discipline.[3] By the same token, persistent existential pressures, as experienced more recently in Hungary and Eastern Europe, keep people's minds closed, in which case they emphasize the opposite priorities: Security over freedom, authority over autonomy, uniformity over diversity and discipline over creativity. Relatively recent events in Hungary, such as the Soviet oppression and the political and economic disappointments and turmoil since the 1990s—combined with Hungarians' tendency to often articulate their hardships over these events—can explain the fact that many Hungarians show discrimination and hostility against out-groups.

By the start of the 1990s, most people expected Hungary to catch up rapidly to Western living standards. After all, Hungary had been one of the least oppressed countries in the Eastern Bloc, at least since the 1960s, with its pseudodemocratic Goulash communism under János Kádár's leadership. Despite that—or possibly because of that—during the transition to capitalism, Hungary soon came to suffer from unregulated liberalism. In an attempt to boost competitiveness and reduce the country's crushing debt, the country hurried to privatize state-owned companies, which also seemed like a way to adopt capitalism and attract foreign investment. In almost no time, Hungary not only became liberalized—it became more liberalized than most "old capitalist" countries in the West.

Almost overnight, members of the former communist party re-emerged as free-market liberals with a global and elitist worldview of mainstream EU politics. They remained in powerful positions throughout the 1990s and the first decade of the new millennium. At the same time, economic inequality increased between the richer residents of Budapest and the population in much of the countryside, where unemployment was higher. Over the years following the transition from communism, a growing disappointment with the highly anticipated liberal democracy was entrenched all around Hungary: In 2009, just a few months before Viktor Orbán took power, a poll showed that 72 percent of Hungarians felt they had been better off under communism.[4] Evidently, the experience most Hungarians had of liberalism was that it was deeply unsatisfying.

According to the Hungarian-British sociologist Frank Furedi, the political response from Viktor Orbán was clear and understandable, yet controversial: "Since Fidesz emerged as the dominant right-wing party in the late 1990s, Orbán consciously built up an image of the "great Hungarian past" out of second-hand fragments of pre-1944 ideology, while there was little that left-wingers and liberals could set against the emotionally powerful, history-based nationalist agitation."[5]

This idea appealed to millions of Hungarians—hence the aforementioned lack of a grand narrative among liberals—and it also explains, in some respect, the clash of civilizations between the East and the West that we have seen grow larger over the past decade. In the West, 1945 was and still is regarded as the "Year Zero" of European progress. The liberal EU narrative celebrates the post-1945 achievements, while everything that happened before that year is looked upon with great skepticism and fear. In the East, historic events are more recent. Postcommunist countries, including Hungary, did not experience this post-1945 progress, so after the fall of communism in 1989, they had to decide: Which way to go? "Go West!" sang the Pet Shop Boys in 1992. However, the disappointing experiments with Western liberalism up through the 1990s eventually paved the way for Viktor Orbán's conservative—some would say controversial—political alternative, inspired by "the great Hungarian past."

While Western society has grown more and more "historyless" into the twenty-first century, in Viktor Orbán's Hungary the past continues to play a significant role, meaning that most people spend a lot of time dwelling on their nation's bygone days. However, not all Hungarians agree on the government's interpretation of history. For instance, there have been constant disputes regarding the Orbán government's erection of the "Memorial for Victims of the German Occupation" in Budapest's Liberty Square. Critics of the 2014-built monument complain that it points the finger only at Germany for the horrors afflicted on the nation during the war—and that it neglects the fact that Hungarian collaborators also had a responsibility for the war crimes of that era, not least Hungary's fascist Arrow Cross Party. Inside the Great Synagogue on Dohány Street in Budapest, I once met an angry rabbi who was outraged by what he called "Orbán's falsification of history," referring to the disputed monument. In front of the memorial on Liberty Square, hundreds of handwritten notes and other artefacts can be seen criticizing the disregarding of Hungary's own role in the Holocaust. Other memory wars in Hungary include the legacy of the communist dictatorship, the meaning of Trianon (i.e.,, the 1920 Treaty of Trianon, which formally ended World War I and under which Hungary lost much of its territory); and the question of how the 1956 Revolution should be remembered.

Initially, I was somewhat surprised by the intense, constant presence of Hungarian history in most political debates. But I soon learned that this had a lot to do with communism: For more than forty years, Hungarians had been discouraged and often even barred from publicly discussing or reflecting on their past. Therefore, after communism, they had a desire to recover the historical traditions associated with the identity of being Hungarian. Most Hungarians I have encountered over the years—on both sides of the political spectrum—have expressed the belief that there is something distinct about their way of life. Many of them take the view that it is worth preserving their heritage and keeping it very much alive.

The Hungarian Austrian writer Paul Lendvai sums it up like this: "Fears of a slow death for a small nation, and the loneliness of a people with a language unique across the Carpathian Basin, have remained the decisive factors in Hungarian history."[6] The list of Hungary's catastrophes is long: The devastation of a country left in the lurch by the Occident during the Mongol invasion in 1241. The defeat in Mohács in 1526 that resulted in a century-and-a-half of Turkish occupation. The crushing of the struggle for independence in 1848–49 by the combined forces of Austria and Russia. The destruction of historical Hungary with a diktat of the Treaty of Trianon in 1920. Then the four decades of communism after the World War II and the bloody suppression of the October Uprising in 1956. Lendvai continues: "Taken together, these misfortunes have exacerbated the national sense of abandonment. In spite of the centuries of foreign rule, however, the Hungarians have been able to preserve their national identity. It is their passionate love of their motherland that has always given them the strength to survive and to overcome all calamities, trapped, as they believe they are, between the Germans and the Slavs, without any kith or kin and separated by the 'Chinese Wall' of their language."

To many of Viktor Orbán's critics in the West, his focus on the nation's history and identity might sound like "the politics of nostalgia," but it is hard to deny the fact that such sentiments provide a cultural terrain where traditional values are seen to possess meaning. A meaning that is sometimes hard to find for disillusioned, individualistic Westerners without a grand narrative to live by.

Migration Broke the Camel's Back

All of these justifications for the different values between Western Europe and Eastern Europe are quite theoretical. After all, history, identity, and culture are rather abstract concepts, and they can be interpreted very differently, even within societies. And so it was not Orbán's politics of nostalgia, but something far more practical and visible that would come to illustrate the real differences between the East and the West. Something everyone could see with their own eyes: Migration. Hungary was one of the first countries in Europe to experience the palpably increasing inflow of migrants and refugees during the 2010s. Well, small islands like Lampedusa in Italy and Lesbos in Greece for many years had functioned as "unofficial arrival centers" for migrants coming to Europe from the Middle East or Africa. But as the so-called Balkan Route gradually took form around 2013–2014, Hungary was on the forefront as the outermost Schengen country in Europe—belonging, that is, to the Schengen Area, comprising (as of this writing) twenty-six European Union and other states forming a mostly single jurisdiction for international travel without border checks.

In the fall of 2013, I remember going to the Office of Immigration and Nationality, situated a few miles northeast of Debrecen's city center. As an EU citizen working in Hungary, I had to register there. The process took only half an hour, and afterward, before biking back to the city center, I discovered that right next to the Office of Immigration was the Refugee Camp of Debrecen, the largest in Hungary at the time. From the main road, Sámsoni Street, I could observe hundreds of men, women, and children residing in the former military barracks that served as the refugee camp. In front of the light-blue shelters was a wall, no more than six feet tall, and above it I noticed surveillance cameras pointing down toward the concrete ground of the site.

Earlier in 2013, I later found out, there had been an incident in the Debrecen camp when a fight broke out between migrant groups. At least one hundred policemen had to be called to the scene. Already back then, in the summer of 2013, the camp was terribly overcrowded, and according to local media, some of the people in the camp did not have a bed to sleep on. It turned out that things were about to get worse.

A year later, in mid-2014, when I returned from abroad, more and more migrants and refugees kept arriving in Debrecen. The numbers were growing fast. On a few occasions I saw crowds of apparently foreign people (judging from their skin color and the languages they spoke) gathered on the streets and main squares of the city, sometimes by the hundreds. The gate of the refugee camp was open, so most of the people were allowed to leave the camp. Presumably because of the lack of beds in Hungary's largest camp, many migrants and refugees decided to take shelter on the streets of Debrecen.

However, I also observed that most of the local Hungarians barely took notice of the migrants' presence in the city center, for some reason, even though they were almost impossible to ignore. The Hungarians would walk right past them. I wondered why that was. It seemed to me that the locals deliberately tried to look the other way. Tried not to interact with these dark-skinned strangers who had suddenly arrived in their city from afar. I was soon about to find out why they reacted like that.

In the first couple years of that decade, around 2,000 asylum seekers had entered Hungary annually. However, in 2013 this number had grown to 18,900. And in 2014, no less than 42,777 individuals crossed the Serbian-Hungarian border in order to seek asylum in Hungary.[1] The wars in Syria, Iraq, and Afghanistan, combined with the powerful expansion of the ISIS terror group in the Middle East, forced hundreds of families to flee their home country every day, hoping to reach safety in Europe. After weeks of travelling through Turkey, Greece, Macedonia, and Serbia, they would end up at Hungary's border—one of three main entry points to the European Union for irregular migration. In 2014, Hungary granted asylum to nine percent of applicants, even though over 40 percent came from conflict zones such as Syria and Afghanistan. This was the lowest rate across the entire EU, where an average of 45 percent of asylum applications were approved.[2]

2014 was also the year Viktor Orbán had been re-elected prime minister of Hungary. His victory was just enough to secure a new supermajority in parliament for Fidesz, but the government party had seen the far-right opposition party Jobbik win over almost five percent of Fidesz's voter base compared to the previous election. In total, more than 65 percent of Hungarians were now right-wing voters. Throughout 2014 and in the beginning of 2015, Jobbik grew stronger and stronger while the Orbán government faced several political defeats: The antigovernment revolt against the government-proposed Internet tax coincided with a scandal in diplomatic relations between Hungary and the United States. Pollsters were all in agreement that, in the course of just two months, October and November 2014, Fidesz lost 12 percentage points—equivalent to the support of around 900,000 voters. Orbán's popularity plummeted from 48 to 32 percent.[3] The protests continued into 2015, and in just five months, between December 2014 and April 2015, Fidesz lost nine out of eleven regional and communal elections. The most serious setback was the loss of the precarious two-thirds parliamentary majority after the surprising by-election victory of an independent opposition candidate. On the one hand, Viktor Orbán and Fidesz were under great pressure from Jobbik—and, on the other hand, from the growing influx of asylum seekers and migrants into Hungary.

A few days after the *Charlie Hebdo* and related terror attacks in Paris, forty government leaders from across Europe met in the French capital on January 11, 2015. Orbán used the occasion to open up a new front against the external threat to Hungary. Contrary to the statements from most other heads of state, the Hungarian prime minister linked the migration into Europe with the threat of terrorist attacks. In an interview with Hungarian television at the time, he said, "Economic migration is a bad thing in Europe; it should not be looked at as if there were any benefits in it, because it brings only pain and threat to the people of Europe. Therefore, immigration must be stopped. We do not want to see among us a significant minority that has a different cultural background and characteristics from ours. We would like to preserve Hungary as Hungary."[4]

The phrase "to preserve Hungary as Hungary" was—up until that day—something that was more commonly used by the Jobbik camp than by Fidesz. In other words, Viktor Orbán's comments in Paris about migration and terror threats symbolized a radical paradigm shift in Hungarian politics.

Back in Budapest, the moderate conservative political scientist Gábor Török identified the possible motives that may have impelled

Orbán to utilize this type of anti-immigration rhetoric for the first time. On his Facebook page, Török pointed to four possible reasons for this paradigm shift: "1. Orbán said this because he believes it is proper, right, and to be followed. 2. Orbán said this because he was concerned that Jobbik will be able to exploit the situation and, as a result of political calculations, he now considered this to be expedient. 3. Orbán said this because now for him avoiding a further loss of votes is the most important and, according to Fidesz research, the voter base wanted to hear these words in this situation. 4. Orbán said this because he thinks that every sharp "ideological" debate is useful for him now: Especially at home, though even internationally as well."[5]

"All of the above," one could add.

Meanwhile, back in the Debrecen refugee camp, tensions were growing. The facility could handle a maximum of 807 individuals, but in May 2015 at least 1,200 men, women, and children were living in the camp. By then the camp comprised two sections: a section for people who could leave the camp during the day; and a closed-off section, where asylum-seekers could be kept captive for as long as six months, while their refugee status was being contemplated by the Hungarian authorities. According to an ombudsman who investigated the camp during the spring of 2015, the rationale for the detention of refugees was the authorities' demand that they should be "available at all times for speedy decision making."[6] By May 2015, there were sixty-five people in this closed section. All of them, with the exception of one couple, were families with children, from Kosovo.

Outside, in the open section of the camp, which consisted mostly of migrants and refugees from the Middle East, riots broke out the following month, in June 2015. The disturbance began after one migrant ran off with another's copy of the Koran and trampled on it, according to a statement on a Hungarian police website. Several hundred other asylum seekers joined the brawl, which spilled out of the camp as well, onto Sámsoni Street and nearby roads. Shortly after, amateur videos surfaced online with footage of the riots, including one video showing a group of Muslim migrants shouting "Allahu Akbar!" as they set garbage bins on fire and jumped on cars in the parking lot outside the refugee camp. Consequently, riot police fired tear gas to quell the riot and push the group back into the camp.

The whole situation in Debrecen caught even more of my attention when about two hundred area residents, including some local Fidesz politicians, staged a street protest "to show their solidarity with the local people who live in the neighborhood." Viktor Orbán came to Debrecen as well, speaking with mayor László Papp, a fellow Fidesz member, who asked the prime minister to confirm that the refugee camp would not be further developed or expanded, despite the rapidly increasing number of migrants arriving in Debrecen and other Hungarian cities. Orbán confirmed that his government would close the country's largest camp: "What Hungary wants is for no more of them to come, and for those of them who are here to go home."[7] Orbán was backed by Lajos Kósa, parliamentary group leader for Fidesz and the city's former mayor: "Over years past, Debrecen has demonstrated solidarity and humanity by welcoming refugees, but it is time to close the camp. This is a time when Europe must protect its borders instead of setting up camps." Afterward, Mayor Papp thanked the government for its "consistent migration policy," which, indeed, allowed for the refugee camp to be closed down. "The camp posed a security risk for the city," said the mayor, and ultimately, the Debrecen camp would remain a thing of the past.

These events kick-started a historic summer in Hungary—and in Europe. It now became crystal-clear that the Orbán government opposed the permanent settlement in Hungary of any of the more than 150,000 migrants and refugees who had arrived to the country from Serbia since the spring of 2015, although most of them had quickly moved on toward Western Europe. By this time, I was already well aware that migration had become a major political issue in Hungary and beyond.

Migration, if you will, had reached its point of no return.

Still, neither in Debrecen nor in Budapest did I notice any reaction from Hungarian citizens. People kept quiet, looking down or away when passing a group of migrants on the street. The Orbán government's political handling of the migration problem, though, came in several steps. First, in the early summer, the government sent letters containing a questionnaire regarding "terrorism and immigration" to the eight million eligible voters in Hungary. Visiting my downstairs neighbor, Reni—a friendly hairdresser who had received the letter in her mailbox—I learned that the survey contained wording such as this: "There are those who believe that the advance of terrorism is connected to the poor handling of immigration by Brussels. Do you agree with these opinions?" A month later, the Orbán government placed billboards throughout Hungary bearing second-person messages to migrants, such as: "If you come to Hungary you cannot take the work of Hungarians!" The message, it should be noted, was written in Hungarian, so it was clearly targeted at citizens of Hungary.

Then, in July 2015, the Orbán government began the construction of a thirteen-foot-high barbed-wire fence along the entire 109-mile length of the Hungarian-Serbian border in order to prevent migrants from entering Hungary from Serbia at locations other than official border stations. According to the government, Hungary was in fact seeking to live up to its treaty duties by protecting the outer, Schengen border of the European Union, even though the EU insisted that a common agreement must be found to solve the challenge of migration.

While Hungarian prisoners, soldiers, and other laborers worked around the clock to complete the construction of the border fence, thousands of migrants were still entering Hungary every day. Rumors about the recently closed refugee camp in Debrecen seemed to have spread among the migrants, and most of them now walked directly toward Budapest, hoping to board trains heading to Austria and Germany. At the Keleti Railway Station in Budapest, political pressure grew concurrently with the number of people arriving there. On August 23, Hungarian police removed 150 migrants from a train set to depart for Munich. Beginning on this date, the police began preventing migrants who lacked valid visas from boarding trains at the station bound for Austria and Germany. No government officials from the relevant countries offered any explanation for this sudden change in policy. Over the subsequent days, the number of migrants residing in the transit zone located in the underpass outside the Keleti Railway Station rose from a few hundred to a few thousand. Europe was about to witness an unforeseen couple of weeks that would never be forgotten.

Berlin and Budapest became the two main points of interest. On August 31, in Berlin, German Chancellor Angela Merkel used her now infamous phrase for the first time at a press conference, following a visit to a refugee camp near Dresden where local opponents of her refugee policy booed and heckled her. Merkel said: "*Wir haben so vieles geschafft—Wir schaffen das.*" In English: "We have managed so many things—we will also manage this situation."[8] Meanwhile, in Budapest, Hungarian police blocked the main entry to the Keleti Railway Station and prevented migrants from boarding international trains. Syrians and other migrants responded by staging sit-down demonstrations in front of the station, chanting such slogans in English as "Germany! Germany!" and "Let us go!"

By early September, between 3,000 and 4,000 migrants were residing in the station underpass, many of them sleeping on the hard concrete floor without blankets. A few miles away, over in the Hungarian parliament building on Kossuth Square, Prime Minister Viktor Orbán explicitly blamed the European Union—and implicitly Germany—for the crisis at the Keleti Railway Station, claiming that the EU's "defective immigration policies had caused uncontrolled migration."[9] Thousands of migrants, primarily Syrians, then left the station and proceeded through Budapest to the M1 highway to make the 125-mile trip to Austria on foot.

Scenes of migrants walking on highways soon spread to other European countries, including to highways in southern Denmark, where hundreds of migrants were seen marching toward "migrant-welcoming" Sweden. It was interesting for me to observe how the Danish public's interest in the European migration problem had finally become identifiable, as the migrants had now arrived in their own safe, Scandinavian backyard. Suddenly, large news stories and op-ed columns replaced the usual minor press notes on the issue in Danish newspapers. TV crews travelled from Copenhagen to Budapest to follow the events.

"We have been overtaken by reality," said Danish Prime Minister Lars Løkke Rasmussen at a press conference.[10] Everybody was talking about migration, migration, migration. What I had first witnessed two years before, when I discovered the Refugee Camp of Debrecen on Sámsoni Street, had now turned into breaking news stories all over Europe.

A few days later, back in Hungary, Fidesz and Jobbik, still agreeing on the topic, adopted several laws "to handle mass immigration." These included laws that criminalized passing through or damaging border barriers. The Orbán government meanwhile declared a state of emergency in Hungary "due to mass immigration." On September 15, 2015, the laws went into effect and the first new border fence in Europe since the Cold War was completed. "The old Iron Curtain was built *against* us, while this one was built *for* us," said Orbán, adding, "A new legal situation will emerge, another era will begin."[11]

Whatever Orbán's actual motive was, his tactic worked. Domestically as well as internationally. I can sum this up in four categories: Firstly, since Hungary closed its borders to Serbia and later to Croatia with a fence, migration into the country drastically decreased. With more than 150,000 migrants arriving in Hungary during the summer months of 2015, less than 1,000 people entered the country in October, November, and December that year.[12] Secondly, Fidesz ultimately won the political rivalry against Jobbik. According to several opinion polls conducted in the spring of 2015—before the fence was built—Fidesz had been down to 37 percent support, while Jobbik had reached almost 30 percent. However, with Orbán in the lead, Fidesz had managed to turn the migration crisis to its own advantage: By the end of 2015, almost half of the population supported Fidesz, while Jobbik's support had plummeted to less than 20 percent.[13] Thirdly, a public opinion poll by the conservative Nézőpont Institute in mid-2015 showed that 82 percent of Hungarians supported the border fence.[14] This nationwide antimigration support in Hungary has been confirmed by other surveys in recent years.

And lastly, an article in the pro-EU news site *Politico* in September 2017—two years after the historic closure of the Hungarian borders—made it all clear:

> No one in Brussels wants to say it out loud, but Viktor Orbán is winning the migration debate.[...] Look closely at how EU leaders now talk about the issue and the policies they've adopted since the 2015 crisis, and it's clear Orbán's preference for interdiction over integration has somehow prevailed. There was an echo of Orbán's long-standing call for tougher border controls in EU Commission President Jean-Claude Juncker's claim in his State of the Union speech this week that "We are now protecting Europe's external borders more effectively."[15]

A Clash of Solidarities

Back in Budapest and Debrecen, in the months after the borders were closed in 2015, I was curious to find out why most Hungarians saw refugees and migrants as illegal invaders who should be stopped by a barbed-wire border fence. Now that the migration influx to Hungary had diminished and the public opinion on the matter was revealed and well-known, I perceived that more people were open to sharing their views on migrants and migration. Some of the locals who had been walking face-down, eyes closed, as soon as they passed some migrants on the streets of Debrecen or Budapest, were now ready to talk. At least a little bit.

I had conversations with Hungarians from all walks of life—young students, university professors, taxi drivers, pensioners, café owners and bartenders, left-wingers and liberals, as well as conservatives and nationalists. To my surprise, almost all of them said the same thing about the migrants: "We don't owe these people anything." I had not heard that phrase before in this context. In Denmark, and in Western Europe in general, the mainstream approach was almost the opposite. At least back then, around 2015. In the West, people would point to concepts like human rights and the idea of solidarity when asked about their responsibility of the migration into Europe. In the East, once again, things were different: "We don't owe these people anything." However, I soon came to understand that Hungarians and Eastern Europeans do not actually lack the idea of solidarity. For them, solidarity is just something other than what it is in Western Europe.

In his book *After Europe*, Ivan Krastev, the Bulgarian political scientist, argues that the migration crisis not only made Europeans skeptical about their own political model—the migration crisis also bitterly divided the European Union and reanimated an East-West divide that had been bridged after 1989. "What we are seeing in Europe today is not what Brussels likes to describe as a 'lack of solidarity,'" he explains, "but it's rather a 'clash of solidarities': National, ethnic, and religious solidarities are chafing against our obligations as human beings. This clash of solidarities plays out not only within societies but also among nation states."[1]

According to Krastev, the dilemma in Europe is obvious when looking at the continent's demographic challenges. In order to ensure their prosperity, Europeans need to open their borders. Yet, at the same time, such openness threatens to annihilate their cultural distinctiveness. When EU supporters from the West look at Central and Eastern Europe, they see that well under 5 percent of the population in countries like Hungary came from foreign lands, and they wonder: Why is it that these Easterners, more than a decade after they became members of the EU, are still so estranged from the fundamental values that underpin the European Union? Why do they show so little solidarity with the sufferings of others? As Krastev sees it, the "scandal" of Eastern European behavior, as viewed from the West, is not in the readiness to build fences to keep out refugees, but in the claim, "We do not owe anything to these people."

If we are to achieve a fuller understanding of why this is, the historical differences between the countries in Eastern and Western

Europe must be taken into account. As many Hungarians emphasize, their ancestors never travelled to faraway places to conquer foreign people's land, treating them like slaves and forcing them to adapt to their own civilization. In other words, Hungarians and other Eastern Europeans do not have the same collective, postcolonial feeling of guilt and shame as seen in many Western countries.

Another determining variance is the fact that Nazism and Fascism—Western Europe's historical ghosts—were nationalistic movements whose ideologies were built on the idea that Western society should cultivate its own tribe and race. Therefore, today's multicultural and international society in Western Europe is the blissful contrast to our own drawbacks from the past. On the other hand, the historical ghost in Eastern Europe was communism—an internationalist movement. It was not based on national sentiments but on the idea of a global working class. Therefore, from the perspective of Hungary and the likes, internationalism is a historical burden, and a cosmopolitan and multicultural society does not appeal to Eastern Europeans. "In Western Europe, 1968 symbolizes the endorsement of cosmopolitan values, while in the East it stands for the rebirth of national sentiments," Krastev argues with reference to the events in Paris and Prague. He underlines that today's conflict of interests between the East and the West is similar to the conflict between Europe's cosmopolitan urban centers and the rural areas all over the continent, when it comes to diversity and migration.[2]

As an example, Viktor Orbán's point is that the European Union's moral duty is not to help refugees but to guarantee general security. In the West, migration is also a divisive issue—with each terrorist attack increasing the share of people unsatisfied with Germany's open border policy. But while in Germany, almost 10 percent of the population took part in volunteer initiatives aimed at assisting asylum seekers, the public in Eastern Europe remains largely unmoved by the plight of refugees. From Krastev's perspective, the migration crisis has made it clear that Eastern Europe views the very cosmopolitan values on which the European Union is based as a threat, while for many in the

West, it is precisely those cosmopolitan values that are at the core of the new European identity.

In the case of Hungary, many critics have pointed to the fact that good-hearted European countries welcomed thousands of Hungarian refugees in 1956. So why are Hungarians unwilling to show the same solidarity today? The answer is straightforward: Because the current migration challenge is not about ethnic Europeans seeking asylum in other European countries—the migrants are primarily Muslims from the Middle East and African countries with cultures very different from Central and Eastern Europe and its particular conservative, tradition-minded values. As Ivan Krastev puts it: "Although Eastern European hostility toward refugees may be shocking to many, it should not be surprising. It has its roots in history and demography and the twisted paradoxes of the postcommunist transition, while at the same time representing a Central European version of a popular revolt against globalization."[3]

Previously, I mentioned the economic disappointments in Hungary after the rapid liberalization of the 1990s, which did not make the majority of Hungarians as wealthy as they had hoped for after the fall of communism. According to EU statistics, in 2018 Denmark had the highest average salary among member states (€3,270 a month), while Hungary was at the bottom of the list (€635 a month), second only to two more recent EU member states, Romania and Bulgaria.[4] Faced with an influx of migrants and haunted by economic insecurity, Hungarians and many other Central and Eastern Europeans feel betrayed by their hope that joining the European Union would jumpstart prosperity and end their crisis-filled existence. Being more impoverished than Western Europeans, they wonder how anyone can expect them to express spontaneous humanitarian solidarity. Moreover, when they hear Westerners describe mass immigration as a "win-win proposition," their sense of betrayal is certainly not reduced, and neither is their hostility to refugees and migrants. Ivan Krastev sees this in a broader perspective: "The resistance of liberals to conceding any negative effects of migration has triggered the antiestablishment—and particularly anti–mainstream media—reaction that is convulsing political life in democracies in so many places today."[5]

Furthermore, the high rate of emigration from Hungary itself— approximately 500,000 Hungarians are estimated to have left the country since 2010[6]—has resulted in negative feelings among those who have stayed. They feel that their population is rapidly shrinking. The Orbán government has so far responded to this demographic challenge by boosting family subsidies, offering desirable loans to parents who have more than two children.

The demographic challenges are, to some extent, also connected to the fact that for many conservatives, gay marriages signify fewer kids and further demographic decline. Finally, the failed integration of the Roma also contributes to Hungary's and the region's compassion deficit. Hungarians fear foreigners because they don't trust that Hungarian society and its politicians are able to integrate "the others," who have already been part of their country for centuries. "Roma people are among us but they are never becoming one of us," as Krastev sums it up.[7] Surveys and reports on attitudes toward minorities in Europe show that in Eastern Europe, Roma people are viewed less favorably than Muslims and Jews, and, according to Krastev, anti-Roma sentiments in Central Europe have contributed to majorities turning against the rhetoric of human rights: "If in Western Europe the debate around human rights is about 'our rights,' then in Central Europe it is about "their rights." Human rights activists are blamed for ignoring the problems of majorities."[8]

Krastev considers the divide between minorities and majorities as one of the most salient issues of our time. He argues that in the years following 1968, Western Europe had a progressive agenda based on identity politics, fundamental rights for minorities, and autonomy of the individual. However, today we are witnessing a similar wave in society, just with a conservative outlook. Thus, whereas in the 1960s and 1970s progressives were focusing on expanding the rights of minorities, today conservatives all over Europe—but especially in Orbán's Hungary— are attempting to restore the rights of the majorities.

Chapter Two
Another Side to the Story

Is This the End of the End of History?

Growing up in a social democratic suburb of Copenhagen—in the secular welfare state of Denmark—I wouldn't say that I was politically brainwashed. Nonetheless, I will admit that throughout middle school and high school and even at university, I was heavily influenced by one particular textbook; considered "a bible" by history teachers and social science professors alike. Of course, I am referring to *The End of History and the Last Man*, by the American political scientist Francis Fukuyama. In the decades following the fall of communism, this work—which originated with an essay published in 1989—was one of the most—if not *the* most—influential publications in the Western world, whether you asked politicians, academics, or ordinary high school teachers in a Copenhagen suburb. It was the "victory manifest" of the West, proving that "the West is the best."

Fukuyama himself summed it up like this: "What we may be witnessing is not just the end of the Cold War, or the passing of a particular period of postwar history, but the end of history as such: that is, the end point of mankind's ideological evolution and the universalization of Western liberal democracy as the final form of human government."[1] In other words, Fukuyama emphasized that in the aftermath of the fall of the Berlin Wall, the fight was finally over; we had reached the end of history. And there was one winner: Western liberal democracy, which was now "the only (i) deal in town." From here on out, it was only a matter of getting everyone else in the world to follow the example of the victorious West. Over the past three decades, Fukuyama's conclusion has been the dominant intellectual guiding principle in the Western world in general and in the European Union in particular: Humanity will continue to progress toward a more democratic and more tolerant society.

I was fourteen years old on September 11, 2001. It was a Tuesday, and that afternoon I had been delivering newspapers to houses in the neighborhood—my first-ever job, by the way. I came home and found my father standing completely frozen in the living room, as he was watching the World Trade Center twin towers collapse on live television. At the time, I did not comprehend the full impact of these terrorist attacks on American soil, but soon thereafter I realized that I had in fact witnessed an era-defining, historic event. It was also around this time, in the months after September 11, 2001, that I was first introduced to Fukuyama's thoughts in a secondary school history class. Simultaneously, from Washington D.C., President George W. Bush wanted to expand liberal democracy to Iraq and the Middle East. And from Brussels, the EU bureaucrats, headed by the Danish Prime Minister Anders Fogh Rasmussen, wanted to expand liberal democracy to Eastern Europe and so welcomed Hungary and others into the club in 2004. There was no looking back, no time to waste, and the Western world used its momentum to spread the ideas of Fukuyama to the rest of the world.

However, when I was writing a social science thesis in high school a few years later, focusing on the media coverage of the 9/11 terrorist attacks, I came across another political thinker: Samuel P. Huntington. A decade earlier, he had written an article titled *The Clash of Civilizations*, in which he argued that after the fall of communism, Islam would become the biggest obstacle to Western domination of the world. The West's next big war, he argued in 1993, would therefore inevitably be with Islam. The September 11 attacks, and the subsequent War on Terror in the Muslim world, naturally gave Huntington a large following, and his description of post–Cold War geopolitics and the "inevitability of instability" contrasted directly with the influential "End of History" idea advocated by Fukuyama. Huntington summed it up like this: "In the emerging world of ethnic conflict and civilizational clash, Western belief in the universality of Western culture suffers three problems: it is false; it is immoral; and it is dangerous."[2] I was inspired to bring Huntington's thoughts into my high school thesis, but my teacher advised me to just concentrate on Fukuyama's idea, because it was "more widespread and acknowledged in the Western world." Even in classrooms, the Fukuyama train was full steam ahead in those years, and no one could stop it.

Then let us fast forward to today: The world has changed. We have reached what looks like "the end of the end of history." In fact, this has been a three-stage turn of events, beginning with the 2001 terrorist attacks; then the 2008 financial crisis; and, finally, culminating with the 2015 migration crisis. Note, by the way, that these three events were exactly seven years apart. (The next crisis, the coronavirus pandemic of 2020, came a bit early). With each of these crises, Fukuyama's perspective gradually lost its relevance, and today he even admits it himself. "At the moment, it looks like Huntington is winning," he wrote in 2018, recognizing that the world of today is not converging around liberal democratic government, as it seemed to be for more than a generation. "Existing liberal democracies have lost much of their appeal after the financial crises in America and the Eurozone during the 2000s, and are suffering from populist uprisings that threaten the liberal pillar of their political systems."[3]

Despite the heavy influence the "End of History" narrative had on Western society—including on yours truly—it seems like we must now look for other explanations as to why our world is changing again. Most fitting of all might be former British Prime Minister Harold Macmillan's famous phrase: "Events, dear boy, events."[4] In other words, unforeseen events change the course of history, not ideologies or calculated political decisions. Once again, the rug of history has been pulled out from under our feet, and unforeseen events such as the migration crisis have changed Europe from the way it looked between 1989 and 2015, now spiralling into a freefall of doubt and disbelief.

Already long gone is the political distribution of Fukuyama's ideas about liberal progress. According to research by the *Guardian* in 2018, populist parties had more than tripled their support in Europe over the past two decades. Before September 11, 2001, populist parties were largely a marginal force, accounting for just 7-8 percent of votes across the continent. By the end of 2019, one in four votes cast in national elections in Europe was for a populist party.[5] I will get back to the definition of populism—and my problem with that term—but many of these so-called populists are right-wingers, including Viktor Orbán. The Hungarian leader is successful— in getting elected again and again, and in capturing the world's attention—partly because he was one of the first politicians in Europe to realize that Fukuyama's ideas had come to an end. And, more than anything, the events of 2015 came in very handy for Viktor Orbán and his entourage. Not least because the EU and the liberal elite of Europe came too late in its handling of the evident migration crisis. As Ivan Krastev puts it, "It was liberalism's failure to address the migration problem, rather than the economic crisis or rising social inequality, that explains the public's turn against it. The inability and unwillingness of liberal elites to discuss migration and contend with its consequences, and the insistence that existing policies are always win-win, are what make liberalism seem to so many synonymous with hypocrisy. This revolt against the hypocrisy of liberal elites is fundamentally reshaping Europe's political landscape."[6]

That the world would not develop the way Fukuyama assumed was predicted by another American political scientist, Ken Jowitt. Already in 1992, he argued that the Cold War's end was hardly a time of universal Western triumph. It was rather the return of ethnic, religious, and tribal identities, as Jowitt describes in his book *New World Disorder*.[7] If we look at Eastern Europe, this has particularly been the case in Hungary and Poland, where the rapid liberalization of the 1990s led to disappointment and frustration. Here, the dissatisfying liberal approach was eventually replaced by the Orbán and Kaczyński governments, in which religion and ethnicity today play a major political role—something that would have been unheard of just a decade ago, even by postcommunist standards.

From my perspective, the recent political turn in these countries is what makes more and more Westerners interested in knowing who someone like Viktor Orbán is. Krastev, the Bulgarian political scientist, explains it like this: "Today, many Western Europeans are asking: what is going on in Eastern Europe? That was certainly not the case ten years ago. Back then, Westerners did not find Eastern Europe interesting at all, because they knew where we came from and they knew where we were heading: toward the West."[8] As we know today that this was not the case.

Personally, as a correspondent based in the old Eastern Bloc, I am happy for this new curiosity from the West. After all, this interest is my livelihood, if you will, and the interest in Hungary has skyrocketed in the past few of years. Suddenly, initiatives and tendencies that started in Eastern Europe can now be seen in Western Europe. For instance, one thing that spread from East to West recently—from Hungary to Denmark—was the comeback of border control and barriers between European nation states. The pandemic lockdowns did not change that course; on March 16, 2020, Hungary was the first European country to close its borders, and soon other states followed suit.

As I have been a music fan and a writer for many years, the current shift in politics reminds me of the musical counter-movements throughout the twentieth century: After psychedelic hippie harmonies came dark underground melancholy. After progressive rock operas came rapid punk. And so on. We see a similar dynamic on the political scene during these years, with nationalism, populism, and conservatism poised to take over and replace the dominance of universalism, globalism, and liberalism. After a period of liberal democracy, favoring minorities such as homosexuals and immigrants, we now see a countertrend, with citizens accepting the majority's demands to be prioritized.

The hundred-dollar question: Is the pendulum of history swinging back to the other side? The million-dollar question: Will the three decades after 1990 go down in history as the once-upon-a-time highlight of liberal democracy? Have we really entered a new world order in which all the old rules are being rewritten? Or are we witnessing an up-in-the-air decade of chaos before Western liberalism returns to its previous dominance?

To be able to answer those essential questions, we must first understand what we are talking about. So let us take a look at some of the divisions. Globalization really took off in the 1990s, and it began primarily as an economic project. Bill Clinton became one of the leading promoters of the global financial order when he, as newly elected president in 1993, presented his economic idea of a "global economy in which we will compete with nations *all around the world*."[9] At the end of that year, Clinton signed the North American Free Trade Agreement (NAFTA), which eliminated nearly every trade barrier between the United States, Canada, and Mexico, creating the world's largest free trade zone. Furthermore, the ideological line between Left and Right was blurred.

The British sociologist Anthony Giddens developed his theory of the Third Way, a position akin to centrism that tried to reconcile right-wing and left-wing politics by advocating a varying synthesis of some center-right economic and some center-left social policies.[10] British Prime Minister Tony Blair, who came into power in 1997, joined forces with President Clinton, and in a speech in Chicago in 1999, Blair launched what became known as the "Blair Doctrine"— the ultimate liberal world order agenda for an international, globalist community: "We live in a world where isolationism has ceased to have a reason to exist. By necessity, we have to cooperate with each other across nations. Many of our domestic problems are caused on the other side of the world. [...] These problems can only be addressed by international cooperation. We are all internationalists now, whether we like it or not," Blair said.[11] Toward the end of his speech, he explained that the so-called Third Way was "an attempt by center and center-left governments to redefine a political agenda that is neither Old Left nor 1980s Right. In the field of politics, too, ideas are becoming globalized."

Globalization, the *economic* project, had now expanded into globalism, the *political* project. With no significant opponents to question the idea of globalism, Blair, Clinton, the EU, and various transnational institutions experienced a historic tailwind in the two decades following the fall of communism, praising Fukuyama's idea of the End of History as their universal gospel.

Today, as mentioned before, the world is a different place. Globalism and liberalism now stand face to face, once again, with nationalism and populism. Real politics has returned; alternative political ideas are once more up for debate. In 2016, another British prime minister, Theresa May, gave a speech, shortly after her country had voted to leave the EU. May's tone was almost the complete opposite of what Blair's had been: "Today, too many people in positions of power behave as though they have more in common with international elites than with the people down the road, the people they employ, the people they pass in the street. If you believe you are a citizen of the world, you are a citizen of nowhere. You do not understand what the very word 'citizenship' means."[12] Clearly, globalism is no longer an irreversible, progressive idea—neither in the Western world nor anywhere else. To many people, the globalist idea is simply not desirable at all.

The Anywheres Versus the Somewheres

In the introduction, I mentioned that Brexit and the election of Donald Trump inspired me to write this book, because I observed that some of the dynamics seen in Orbán's Hungary were now echoing all over the world. Two main groups—the globalists and the nationalists—today symbolize a new kind of civilizational clash. Not between different religious beliefs or different ethnic identities, but between different social viewpoints and identities. The British editor and journalist David Goodhart used the case of Brexit to describe the different social viewpoints that led to a divided Britain, a nation now leaving the European Union. In his book *The Road to Somewhere*, Goodhart distinguishes between two rival groups within society: The Anywheres and the Somewheres.[1]

The Anywheres are the well-educated, mobile elite who are not bound to one particular place but have the whole world as their "playground." They see open borders as an enormous advantage because they are basically able to work from anywhere due to their high educational skills and flexibility. According to Goodhart, the Anywheres account for 20-25 percent of society, and they dominate the media as well as academic and cultural institutions. They value openness, diversity, and tolerance. And, like most people do, they prefer to hang out with people who are like them. For that reason, the majority of their friends also went to university and belong to the upper middle class, if not the upper class.

Thus, they do not have much contact with the Somewheres, who, according to Goodhart, represent around half of the population. The Somewheres generally did not go to university, and if their education continued past high school, it was a relatively short one. They are deeply rooted in their local community, and they prioritize safety and knowing who their neighbors are. In most European countries, including in Hungary, around 60 percent of the population lives within twenty miles of where they grew up.[2] Many of them are Somewheres who do not really care about free movement because they themselves are not going anywhere. Goodhart adds that the remaining 25-30 percent of the population are Inbetweeners, representing a bit of both worlds.

Today's conflicts between Anywheres and Somewheres—between globalists and nativists or nationalists, between open societies and closed ones—have, at least to some degree, replaced the old Left-Right political spectrum that used to shape voters' identities. Broadly speaking, these are the differences I meet when I leave Budapest and go to Debrecen and out in the countryside. Among Hungarians, the Anywheres reside mainly in central Budapest, or abroad in Western Europe, whereas the Somewheres live outside the capital in smaller cities, towns, and villages.

In 2018, on March 15, one of the national holidays in Hungary, I stood on Kossuth Square in Budapest, where Viktor Orbán was about to give a speech in front of the parliament building. In the middle of the square, I was surrounded by thousands of Orbán supporters. Thousands of Somewheres who had travelled to the capital from Debrecen, Miskolc, and other provincial areas of Hungary. Hundreds from Székely Land, a distinctly ethnic Hungarian region of Romania, and even a large group of Orbán fans visiting all the way from Poland. With less than four weeks until the parliamentary elections, the Fidesz campaign was in full swing. Since the opposition was fragmented and almost invisible, in order to stir up the battle Orbán and his government had made the Hungarian-born billionaire George Soros—the man behind the Open Society Foundations—their main enemy, although the liberal financier was not even running in the elections. Well, from the Fidesz perspective, he was, at least symbolically. In his speech that day, Viktor Orbán launched an ambiguous attack against Soros, the globalists, the liberal elites— a warning against the Anywheres: "We are fighting an enemy that is different from us. Not open, but hiding; not straightforward, but crafty; not honest, but base; not national, but international; that does not believe in working but speculates with money; that does not have its own homeland but feels it owns the whole world."[3]

As a young, liberal-minded law student in Budapest, Viktor Orbán was seen by many people as an idealistic hero of the anti-Soviet student-resistance movement in Hungary at the end of the 1980s. In 1989, he attended Oxford University on a scholarship with support from George Soros's Open Society Foundations. From England, Orbán watched the revolutions unfolding across Eastern Europe in Czechoslovakia, East Germany, Bulgaria, and Romania, and then broke off his studies to hurry home to Budapest to make sure he was in the front row of his own country's time in the spotlight. In Oxford, he could have ended up as more of an Anywhere, but the sudden return to his homeland instead put emphasis on his Somewhere background as a Hungarian country boy.

In Hungary's first democratic elections of the postcommunist era, in 1990, Fidesz won a respectable nine percent, but slipped to a disappointing seven percent four years later. After the death of conservative Prime Minister József Antall, however, Orbán saw a gap opening on the political right and seized it, dragging his liberal Fidesz party to the conservative side, although several of his closest friends quit in protest. Inspired by Germany's long-serving center-right chancellor, Helmut Kohl, from 1995 onward Orbán set about gathering everyone in Hungary who was right of center under his own flag. And in 1998, at the age of only thirty-five, he became Prime Minister of Hungary. The road to power was tough in the crowded political landscape of 1990s Hungary, and along the way, Viktor Orbán understood that he had to stick to his roots. Already in his first years in politics, Orbán confronted some of his university friends, many of them belonging to the inner Budapest elite.

Orbán himself had grown up in a poor family in the countryside, and his encounter with Oxford academics and Budapest intellectuals made him realize that conflict was inevitable. During the first electoral period of the newly democratic Hungary, Fidesz and Orbán were in an open conflict with the Alliance of Free Democrats (SZDSZ), a liberal party. To understand the conflict—which eventually helped Orbán drag Fidesz in a more conservative direction—the differences in personalities and social status have to be taken into account. The Hungarian author Paul Lendvai describes it like this: "The leading Free Democrat politicians were overwhelmingly left-wing intellectuals—philosophers, sociologists, economists who had broken with Marxism and often came from ex-communist, bourgeois, sometimes Jewish families. They were well read, open to the world, and fluent in foreign languages. In contrast to the first generation of Fidesz politicians, predominantly lawyers with practical knowledge, who came mostly from a rural or small town background."[4]

Already back then, Orbán was well aware of this divide, which has obvious similarities to the "Anywheres versus Somewheres" theory. In his own words, Orbán considered himself to be a resolute person, as he explained in a 1993 interview: "I like rational arguments and also that style of politics in which resolve is an important element. My mentality also offers a target in the sense that by origin, I am not a sensitive intellectual of the twentieth generation, and this throws up some questions of style. There is in me perhaps a roughness brought up from below. That is no disadvantage, as we know that the majority of people come from below."[5] For those who follow Viktor Orbán, they know that these personal traits are still very present in his character today. He knows where he is coming from, and he tells it like it is.

Another person who is not afraid to present inconvenient truths to the public is the conservative British writer and commentator Douglas Murray. In March 2018, Viktor Orbán posted a photo on Facebook of himself reading Murray's book *The Strange Death of Europe*, and a few months later, the two met in Budapest. In his book, Murray describes the dispute between Orbán and George Soros at the height of the migration crisis—a conflict that highlights the divide between globalism and nationalism. Murray refers to an email that Soros sent to *Bloomberg*, in which he argued that his Open Society Foundations were seeking to "uphold European values" while he accused the Hungarian prime minister of trying to undermine those values. Soros went on to say of Orbán: "His plan treats the protection of national borders as the objective and the refugees as an obstacle. Our plan treats the protection of refugees as the objective and national borders as the obstacle."[6]

So who has the most sustainable plan? Not the most humanitarian, but the most realistic plan? In Murray's view, no one except Anywheres and globalists would sign up for Soros's plan to solve the migration issue. In September 2015, George Soros elaborated on his solution in an article, which was later used in the Orbán government's anti-Soros campaign. Soros wrote: "First, the EU has to accept at least a million asylum seekers annually for the foreseeable future."[7] Less than two months later, the whole conversation in Europe shifted when, on the evening of Friday, November 13, Paris was rocked by three hours of coordinated terrorist attacks. Murray writes in his book: "Yet, two days after the Paris attacks, the president of the European

Commission, Jean-Claude Juncker, insisted at a press conference that 'there are no grounds to revise Europe's policies on the matter of refugees.' Whether he liked it or not, public and political attitudes were shifting."[8]

In the subsequent months, a dozen European countries followed Orbán's initiative—including Norway, Denmark, Germany, and France—and introduced border controls or began to build fences or other barriers. Nevertheless, leading EU bureaucrats continued to ignore or downplay the will of the majority of Europeans. In a 2017 opinion piece in *Politico*, EU Commissioner for Migration Dimitris Avramopoulos wrote, "Europe's migrants are here to stay. [...] At the end of the day, we all need to be ready to accept migration, mobility, and diversity as the new norm and tailor our policies accordingly. The only way to make our asylum and migration policies future-proof, is to collectively change our way of thinking first."[9] According to Murray, the financial crisis and the migration crisis killed the idea of globalism, and antiglobalism is no longer a marginal phenomenon—it is the mainstream: "The utopian 'consensus' of globalism is over, and we will again see that politics means decisions where not everyone can be satisfied," Murray writes in his book.[10]

One result of the migration crisis is that the rights of migrants and refugees—which developed in the 1960s and 1970s and peaked in the years after 1989—do not have the same significance when we discuss and seek consensus on the issue today. Instead, security is topping the agenda. As pointed out before, Viktor Orbán's argument is that the European Union's moral duty should not be to help migrants and refugees but to guarantee general security.

On December 10, 2018, the United Nations celebrated the seventieth anniversary of the *Universal Declaration of Human Rights*. However, the celebration was largely overshadowed by the growing resistance to human rights. The reason seems to be Europe's ideological awakening. As a matter of fact, the idea of human rights is largely a Western project. That means that the majority of Western citizens grew up with human rights, and to many people, the rights can help measure whether a state behaves properly. To be against human rights seems almost incomprehensible in the Western world—if not plainly malicious. But the truth is that it is a legitimate political point of view to not care about them a whole lot. Why? Because the human rights declaration is ideological in its nature. Article One of the declaration states: "All human beings are born free and equal in dignity and rights. They are endowed with reason and conscience and should act toward one another in a spirit of brotherhood."[11]

Now, it may seem obvious that the phrase "all human beings are born free and equal" is primarily a liberal parole. At least, very few self-respecting conservatives would agree that all people are born equal, or at least that they should all be raised with equal opportunities. And harsh critics of human rights argue that the declaration was a way for the postwar liberals to institutionalize their ideology and make it universal. That went well for many years because the West, despite changing its national governments from time to time, was essentially liberal. Not anymore. The Western world has again become an ideological battlefield. Liberalism is no longer the only deal in town.

This also goes for the *UN Refugee Convention*, first created in 1951 for the definition and protection of refugees. Later, in 1967, it was extended to also include asylum seekers from all countries of the world.[12] Thus, the treaty was made long before globalization. Its original aim was to give rights and protection primarily to dissidents and political leaders on the run—not teeming masses fleeing war and poverty to come to Western countries. Around the globe, almost eighty million people are displaced from their homelands as of this writing, and their internationally enshrined rights have become practically unrealistic for the Western world to live up to. As a result, several countries—including Hungary—have demanded a revision of the *UN Refugee Convention*. They claim that the conventions instill false hopes for the refugees and therefore must be redone. In June 2018, President Trump withdrew the United States from the UN Human Rights Council (in a move reversed by the Biden administration in 2021). Later that year, the UN presented its *Global Compact for Migration*. The aim was to set out "a common understanding, shared responsibilities, and unity of purpose regarding migration."[13] Initially, Viktor Orbán was the only political leader to indicate that his country would not adopt the agreement. He called it a "flawed document," adding that "whoever signs it presents a serious risk to their own citizens."[14] In the end, one third of EU member states—including Hungary, as well as the United States, Israel, and Australia—did not sign the migration agreement.

All this turmoil around migration and global agreements does not necessarily mean that human rights are dead and gone. But it is a reminder that rights are political and not definitive truths. If you are in favor or of a liberal Europe and the associated conventions and declarations, you can no longer just sit back and say to yourself that whatever is right is right. Seventy years after the 1948 UN declaration, we must once again acknowledge that there is political opposition to human rights, and for those who care, it is time to find the good arguments and win the political battle. An open border policy is no longer a sign of freedom but a symbol of insecurity. When EU leaders like Juncker and Avramopoulos problematize nationalism and xenophobia—instead of the migration itself—the support for people like Orbán will only grow larger. The reason is that people who prefer security and safety to freedom, diversity and open borders, do not feel represented in the EU. They are "the unrepresented Somewheres." Therefore they tend to vote for parties and politicians opposing globalist arguments.

Viktor Orbán gladly takes credit for the fact that the migrant flow into Europe has been largely reduced since 2015–16. And Hungary's initial vigilantism with its border fence *did* have an impact. More substantial, though, was the EU's agreement with Turkey and later with Libya to let those countries take care of the problem by holding back migrants on their way toward the European continent. However, such agreements make it easy for Orbán to point to the EU's double standards: "In the public, you preach globalism and solidarity with the world's victims of persecution. In reality you are paying the Turkish leader Erdoğan and Libyan clan rebels to physically block the route for the migrants."

The EU's actions ring ever more hollow, from Orbán's perspective, when the EU attacks Hungary for what some EU leaders consider that county's problems with the rule of law. That makes it easy for Orbán to criticize transnational institutions such as the European Union and the United Nations when they, in his eyes, have not accomodated their views to the current reality. Perhaps the EU and the UN must admit as soon as possible that they are acting in a situation of force majeure, and that the international rule of law must be renegotiated and adjusted to the realities of the twenty-first century. But instead, the counterarguments from the globalists point to the fact that the nationalists are less educated, and therefore ignorant of the situation. But that is a very dangerous strategy.

It is correct, also in Hungary, that people voting for nationalists or populists are mostly living outside of the large cities, and that they rarely have university degrees. After all, they are the Somewheres. But what exactly is the point of that argument? That their vote should count less? Forget about it. A citizen is a citizen, a vote is a vote. Democracy is to accept that. And then to play by the rules if you want to change the situation. This goes both ways. As long as the old political elite does not have a better answer than the antiglobalists to the challenges of our time, then the support for parties like Fidesz and politicians like Viktor Orbán will continue to grow.

We Need to Talk about Populism

Have you ever met a hipster who admits that he is a hipster? Me neither. Well, with my full beard, my style of clothes, and my taste for rare vinyl records, I myself might in fact be considered a hipster in some people's eyes. But I would of course never admit to that.... The hipster never calls himself a hipster, and in that, he has a lot in common with the populist. Have you ever met a populist who admits that he is a populist? Both "hipster" and "populist" are social labels that society uses to define certain groups of people. Both labels have a mostly negative connotation; both the hipster and the populist are subject to a lot of skepticism and sometimes hatred from the mainstream. We could say that hipsters and populists are both antimainstream—they tend to go against the (main) stream. Furthermore, we could add that they are often first-movers in society, acting in ways that other people will copy a few years later.

There is just one problem. The term "hipster" comes from the word *hip*, meaning modern or cool. The term "populist" comes from the Latin word *populus*, meaning people. In other words, the hipster is cool and modern and the populist is someone who represents the people. You see, that could be almost anyone, depending on whom you are asking. Most politicians would say they are trying to represent the people. A common framework for interpreting the populist—or populism in general—defines populism as an ideology, which presents "the people" as a morally good force against "the elite," who are perceived as corrupt and self-serving. However, there is still a problem: For instance, Viktor Orbán is often called a populist by political scientists and opponents alike, and Orbán also likes to say that he fights for the people against the elite. But isn't Orbán part of the elite himself, having been at the top of Hungarian politics for three decades and surrounding himself with rich business owners and global leaders? Isn't András Fekete-Győr, the political founder of the Momentum Movement, then also a populist when he speaks against "the corrupt elite" in Hungary and says that he will represent the (young) people? Is Emmanuel Macron a populist? Was President Obama a populist?

The point I want to make here is to question way we use the term "populist." In my opinion, the definition is too vague, because it is dependent on who uses it. The same goes for the term "hipster," although that discussion is far less important here. If we don't know exactly what and who were are talking about when we use the word "populist," I think it might be better to use another, more precise word. The people we talk about—people like Viktor Orbán, Donald Trump, Jair Bolsonaro, Matteo Salvini—came to power mostly because they are *against* something. What they have in common is that they are against globalism, represented by the liberal Anywheres as described before. Therefore, if we should call Orbán, Trump, and the like anything, we should call them *antiglobalists*. But then, please note that antiglobalists are not necessarily right-wing politicians. Left-wing politicians such as Bernie Sanders in the US, Jeremy Corbyn in the UK, or Yanis Varoufakis in Greece have all promoted themselves as antiglobalists, criticizing globalization for benefitting only the elite. The important distinction, though, is that the left-wing antiglobalists are fighting globalization, the *economic* project, while the right-wing antiglobalists are also fighting globalism, the *political* project.

According to the French economist Thomas Piketty, the current uphill battle for the Left is due to the fact that over the past decade or two it has gradually changed its voter base. From once representing those with low education and low income back in the more class-based systems of the past, today the Left has more appeal among those with high education and high income. "The left wing has basically left the poor in the lurch, while at the same time, globalization has led to increased inequality," Piketty said in an interview with the Danish newspaper *Information*.[1]

His point is that right-wing antiglobalists are supported not only by those who oppose immigration—the Right has also won over a large part of those once–left-wing voters who oppose economic globalization. Those who feel left behind because their jobs were outsourced and their wages undercut as a consequence of globalization. Because right-wing antiglobalists appeal to these people, claiming that they can make their country great again, they are the ones who have won some key elections and have grown in popularity.

Let me try to explain this development by looking at the history of music. In the early 1970s, John Lennon wrote political songs that appealed to the same group of people: The liberal left-wing, embracing both hippies and hard workers. The first song, "Working Class Hero," contains these lyrics: "They hate you if you're clever and they despise a fool / Till you're so fucking crazy you can't follow their rules / A working class hero is something to be." According to Lennon, the song was a warning to working class individuals about being processed into the middle classes, exploited into the "capitalist machinery." Today, many of these working class people feel let down by left-wing politicians who have not been able to address their problems. The working class hero of today is a Somewhere who votes for a right-wing antiglobalist politician he feels can take his problems seriously.

Another Lennon song, "Imagine," contains these lyrics: "Imagine there's no countries / It isn't hard to do / Nothing to kill or die for / And no religion too / Imagine all the people living life in peace / You may say I'm a dreamer / But I'm not the only one / I hope some day you'll join us / And the world will be as one." According to Lennon, this was just a song about peace. However, according to many conservative critics, the idea of a nationless, borderless, religionless world where an individual is defined not by traditions and roots but only by a global goodwill aligns perfectly with the globalist idea of the Anywheres. This is still the case today. Fifty years ago, these two songs—"Working Class Hero" and "Imagine"—symbolized the unity of the Left. Now they symbolize the polarization of Western society: The working class Somewheres and the imaginary-minded Anywheres.

In 1991, George Soros organized a conference in the Polish city of Krakow. The initiative was inspired by the liberal concern that "former members of the Warsaw Pact were historically disposed toward the embrace of highly volatile and irrational forms of ethnic nationalism," according to the Hungarian-British sociologist Frank Furedi.[2] In a speech at the conference, a Hungarian intellectual touched on this concern. The speech was titled "Return to Tradition – What Tradition?" Furedi describes the speech as an early example of the typical globalist's "lack of empathy and sensitivity toward the meaning that national tradition and sentiment could have for large sections of society."[3] Luckily, Furedi adds, the German editor of *Die Zeit*, Marion Gräfin Dönhoff, attended the conference and understood that in Eastern Europe, national conscience was far from fleeting. After the conference, Dönhoff wrote: "There, in Krakow, I realized that nationalism, which Westerners regard with a lot of skepticism, had been indispensable for the survival of the Eastern Europeans. That was the only way they had been able to fight for their identity and finally achieve freedom."[4]

Since then, we have experienced that nationalism indeed possesses an important meaning for a lot of people in Hungary as well as in other postcommunist and even in Western countries. And while the left-wing intellectuals' idea of global liberalism gradually came to sound more and more hollow to the majority of Hungarians, right-wing nationalism only grew stronger.

One example is the so-called Trianon Trauma, referring to the 1920 Treaty of Trianon, under which Hungary lost two-thirds of its geographical area and at least one-third of its inhabitants. Since the return of nationalism after 1989, the Right has kept the Trianon Trauma on the political agenda, while the Left has swept it under the carpet. As the Hungarian author Paul Lendvai puts it, "As a consequence of the increasingly aggressive rhetoric of the Right and the passivity of the Left, the right-wing interpretation of Trianon has prevailed among the adult population in the last decade."[5] One of Viktor Orbán's first measures when he rose to power in 2010 was to establish a national memorial day on June 4 to mark the anniversary of the day the treaty was signed in 1920. Since then, Orbán often refers to the infamous treaty to play on the sense of victimhood, boost national pride, and lambast Western European nations. In 2017, he said, "Since Trianon, we have never been so close to bringing our nation back to self-confidence and vitality as we are now."[6]

On the other hand, the Hungarian Left has preferred historical amnesia to remembrance, in an attempt to avoid public debate about the controversial historical event. According to Furedi, the same dynamic is seen when the Left calls on the EU and Western governments to help fight Orbán and Fidesz in domestic battles in Hungary. However, with this alliance, the Left isolates itself from Hungarian society because it places its faith in transnational Western cothinkers rather than attempting to appeal to and mobilize Hungarian public opinion. The polarization grows because the Left and the EU promote diversity and minority rights as a counterpoint to the authority of the nation. Furedi writes, "From their standpoint, minority rights are de facto logically prior and morally superior to the principle of nationality."[7]

Viktor Orbán has criticized Angela Merkel for her "moral imperialism" during the migration crisis, and he has called liberalism a "tyranny of political correctness." In a 2016 speech, Orbán said about the identity politics of the Left:

> When we dared to speak about the nation, we were branded nationalist. When we started talking about matters related to the creation of human existence, we were dismissed as clericalist, feudalist, and medieval. When we started talking about the family, and we said that we were taught in school that the natural order of things is that there is a man and there is a woman who together form a couple, and they will have children, we were branded sexist and homophobic. So I, for one, did not see this political correctness as some self-imposed restraint, or as a synonym for right-thinking, fair, decent, and honest behavior, but rather as political oppression; because those who did not share this outlook were branded, shamed, and blacklisted, and there were attempts to ostracize them. This is the truth. Political correctness as a mode of speech was one of the most obvious tools for the intellectual oppression of the world."[8]

On the other side of this contemporary culture war, it is important to note that Fidesz is also "guilty" of identity politics with its nationalistic, Christian, family-based political agenda. Identity politics on the Right embodies the same feelings of outrage and victimhood as seen on the Left. The only difference is who the victims are: On the Left, they are women, homosexuals, and transsexuals, Roma (Gypsies), refugees, migrants, and asylum seekers, and those who speak on behalf of these groups. On the Right, the victims are the "Hungarian citizen," white males, the nuclear family, "the people," and Christians, and those who defend these groups. What the Left and Right have in common is a belief that their own identity is vital—and much more important than beliefs and ideologies—because their own identity determines who is right and who is wrong.

Identity politics is essentially a means to resistance. To claim sovereignty in a situation where you feel suppressed. As long as someone feels they don't have the same rights as others, there will be a basis for identity politics. And the fact is, different identity groups will never come to agreements that will erase their differences. The paradox of identity politics is that the goal is for everyone else to be the same as oneself. Identity politics is a Gordian knot created by two types of logic, leading to two fundamentally different ways of perceiving the world. It is utopian to think that one of the logics suddenly will discover that the other one was in fact better and then end the discussion. That is not how extraordinary political battles function. And this is indeed the extraordinary political battle of our time.

Chapter Three

Stuck in the Moral Matrix

The Tables Have Turned

We live in a time with many similarities to what happened in Europe and in the United States in 1968 and in the following years. The protests of 1968 comprised a worldwide escalation of social conflicts, predominantly characterized by popular rebellions against conservative bureaucratic elites. Now, it seems, the tables have turned. More recently, at least to some extent, conservatives like Viktor Orbán, Matteo Salvini, Jair Bolsonaro, and Donald Trump took over the role as society's rebels—a role that in the 1960s and 1970s belonged to leftists. As sociologist Kim Lane Scheppele pointed out when I interviewed her right after Viktor Orbán's election victory in 2018, "Just think about the message that we should get rid of political correctness and defend freedom of speech. Those ideas used to belong to the left wing, but now the right wing has completely adopted them. Conservatives have spent decades trying to break through with their message to the people, and now it is finally happening. Meanwhile, the leftists are at a complete loss as to what to do. They do not even understand why their message of universal rationalism and humanism does not appeal to everyone."[1]

I believe we are witnessing a critical moment in politics and in history, though I am not sure whether "the era of liberal democracy is over," as Orbán phrased it shortly after his third consecutive win.[2] Nevertheless, I am convinced that the liberals and the leftists are facing an uphill battle in the years to come, and the first question they must confront is this: What did we do wrong? This is not an easy realization to come to but it is an essential one nevertheless. To continue to claim that the antiglobalists are the root cause of Europe's problems, I believe, will only confirm voters in their decision to turn away from mainstream political parties, which, in their view, have not yet fully recognized the problems.

The solution is not necessarily to be parroting the antiglobalist rhetoric. But the first important step for left-wing and liberal politicians is to acknowledge that they need trustworthy answers to the challenges in a globalized world. Even if the antiglobalists disappeared, the real problems would still be there. The liberals need a new narrative to compete with the nationalistic narrative of Viktor Orbán, who says, "Rather than try to fix a liberal democracy that has run aground, we will build a twenty-first-century Christian democracy."[3]

In July 2018, precisely four years after he first used the infamous phrase "illiberal democracy," the Hungarian prime minister elaborated on his interpretation of the much-discussed expression in a speech at the annual Bálványos Summer Open University: "A Christian democracy is not liberal. It is illiberal, if you like. Unlike liberal democracy, Christian democracy rejects multiculturalism and immigration while being anticommunist and standing for Christian values. We are facing a big moment: We are saying goodbye not simply to liberal democracy, but to the 1968 elite."[4]

We can discuss the real meaning of "illiberal" to the end of time, and we can certainly keep debating Viktor Orbán's ideas, but there are other, vital angles to consider as well.

Today's polarization should in fact be easily understood. As the ultimate winner of the Cold War, the modern Left had an easy run against an intellectually weak Christian Right up through the 1990s. With Fukuyama's End of History "bible" in hand, it was easy for the center-left to declare that the Culture War was finally over. However, the lack of real opponents made them retreat into a bubble of self-righteousness, political correctness, and a no-need-for-discussion approach. Little by little, the modern Left has thus effectively become what conservatives were until the 1960s, and what it once rebelled against: the establishment.

As we now know, it took the conservatives many decades to get back into the game. The question is: How long will it take for the liberals?

The liberal house of cards was demolished in four rounds—September 11, 2001; the financial crisis of 2008; the 2015 migration crisis; and the COVID-19 pandemic—and now all the cards are lying there on the table, in one big mess. Who will pick up the cards and start playing the game? The praiseworthy goals the Left fought for in the postwar decades, including equal rights for men and women, acceptance of homosexuality, and combating institutional racism, created better and freer societies in the West. No doubt about that. But especially for people on the conservative side of the political spectrum, it is a striking paradox that by claiming ownership for words like "inclusiveness," "tolerance," and "diversity," the modern Left, time and again, manages to display a zero-tolerance for dissent and the only diversity that really matters: diversity of opinions.

Having a debate is how such opinions are exchanged. My view is that the culture of public debate back in Denmark is healthier than in many other Western countries. It might be because the political spectrum in a small Scandinavian welfare state is more narrow and homogenous than in much larger states such as Germany, the United States, and the United Kingdom. However, it is worth noting two key political events that have shaped and influenced the culture of public debate in Denmark during the twenty-first century.

The first one happened in 2001, just a couple of months after the 9/11 attacks. Before the national elections, Denmark's social democratic prime minister at the time, Poul Nyrup Rasmussen, had declared that the emerging right-wing nationalist Danish People's Party would "never become respectable [*stuerene*, in Danish] enough, no matter how much effort is made." However, Rasmussen then lost the elections, and the new center-right government instead went on to include and cooperate very closely with the Danish People's Party in most of the years since that election. By 2015, the party's support had grown to around 20 percent.

On the other side of Øresund, in Sweden, establishment politicians have taken a different approach toward the country's right-wing nationalist party, the Sweden Democrats. Instead of including them on the political stage, both the center-right and the center-left governments as well as the mainstream media excluded and sometimes even boycotted the Sweden Democrats and their opinions from the public debate. Along the way, popular support for the party also grew to around 20 percent. In Sweden, from my point of view, the debate climate is unhealthy, both because one-fifth of the electorate is excluded and because social problems and political extremism are relatively pronounced. In Denmark, there are definitely disagreements, too, but at least to some degree, all voices are heard in parliament as well as in the media.

My view is this: Exclusion leads to extremism, inclusion leads to insight and understanding. That is a true diversity of opinions.

The other important event shaping the Danish debate culture in the twenty-first century was the Muhammad cartoons crisis. It began when the newspaper *Jyllands-Posten* published twelve editorial cartoons on September 30, 2005—most of which depicted Muhammad, the principal figure of the religion of Islam. The newspaper announced that this was an attempt to contribute to the debate about criticism of Islam and self-censorship. Muslim groups in Denmark complained, and the issue eventually led to protests around the world, including violent demonstrations and riots in some Muslim countries. Relating the whole story here is not my aim, but suffice it to say that the ensuing intense and protracted debate over issues such as self-censorship, political correctness, Islam, and freedom of speech provided Danish society with a familiarity and a perspective on such topics. Topics that became even more relevant a decade later, as a consequence of the migration crisis in 2015 and everything that followed.

According to Canadian psychologist Steven Pinker, restricting a debate, or making certain ideas taboo, is really dangerous. He argues that if people who stumble upon a contentious idea—for instance, that Muslims are invading Europe—are completely alienated from mainstream intellectual life, radicalism may result:

> If a certain idea never gets discussed out in the open, then some people might jump to extremist conclusions. Any idea needs a pushback, contextualization, counterarguments, and critical questions. If these people are never even challenged with the controversy of their idea in the first place, then within this like-minded community, the group sometimes jump to the most extreme conclusions. Whereas if you put them out into the open, give them a platform, and facilitate the debate, then you can put the idea into perspective. Sunlight is the best disinfectant.[5]

So, what about the debate climate in Hungary? As mentioned before, Viktor Orbán should get credit for instituting a broader debate on critical and sensitive issues such as the European Union elite, political correctness, and the implications of migration. If Orbán and his government had not put their finger on these delicate topics in the first place, one can only wonder how Europe would have developed over the past few years. Perhaps someone else would have said it, perhaps no one would have listened. We do not know.

Having said that, Viktor Orbán should not get much credit at home for his contribution to the debate climate in Hungary. Or the lack thereof. The fact is that Fidesz barely ever engages in political debates if they risk a defeat or negative exposure, particularly not Orbán himself.

As of this writing, Hungary has gone through four national election campaigns—2010, 2014, 2018, and 2022—with Viktor Orbán refusing to engage his opponents in any televised debates. Something that was otherwise common practice in Hungary until 2006—and still is in nearly every other country that holds democratic elections. Ever since performing poorly against then Prime Minister Ferenc Gyurcsány in 2006, Orbán has avoided all domestic debates with his opponents.

The explanation could be, as many observers suggest, that Orbán is a better orator than he is a debater. But as a government official said in 2017, "Nobody has earned the right through their political achievements to have the prime minister in office stand up to debate with them,"[6] Besides, according to same official, a debate is always more beneficial to the challenger: "It helps those more who are smaller and weaker."[7]

It does not seem to be in the interest of the Orbán government to ever create the perception that there are alternatives to the country's current ruler and that Orbán has any legitimate opponents. "The homeland cannot be in opposition," as Orbán has put it.

But Hungary needs these political debates, and it needs Fidesz to participate in them. Furthermore, rarely does Viktor Orbán grant interviews to journalists who will pose critical questions or push back on his responses. Personally, thus far all my requests for an interview with the prime minister have been rejected. I will keep trying. On Fridays, Orbán gives a relatively uncritical radio interview on the state-run Kossuth Rádió's *180 Minutes* morning program. On Thursdays, the government's spokesperson, Zoltán Kovács, hosts a press conference where the press can direct questions to the head of the Prime Minister's Office, most recently Gergely Gulyás. So it's not that the government doesn't talk to the press, but that most of the time Viktor Orbán seems to be "protected" from having to deal with critical questions.

For a long time Hungary's largest media outlet critical of the government was the online news site *Index*—well, at least until the dismissal of its chief editor in July 2020 sparked the mass resignation of much of its staff after a pro-Orbán businessman gained control over the firm controlling its advertising and revenue. The last time *Index* managed to interview Viktor Orbán was in 2007. That is a long time ago. In May 2018, when *Index* tried to catch the prime minister for a quick question at a public event he was attending, Orbán refused to answer, referring to the outlet as a "fake news factory."[8] But then, suddenly, at the beginning of January 2019, the prime minister unexpectedly showed up for the weekly press conference next to his spokesperson, Zoltán Kovács. And for more than two hours, Orbán made himself available for questions from both progovernment and government-critical media outlets. During the press conference, the prime minister explained why he never gives interviews to critical outlets: "I am not willing to go on a bullfight with a journalist. I will not go into situations where there is an ill-meaning person on the other side of the table asking questions filled with prejudice."[9]

At that press conference, Orbán also repeated his mantra that Europe is at a turning point: "The determining historical viewpoints, dominant assessments of political situations, and the governing sets of values all stemmed from liberalism. Today, Europe has a dominantly liberal interpretation of the world. This is a historical legacy, but this era is now over." He added, "Migration is going to shift this balance of power in the world of politics and hopefully in the world of media as well."[10]

A few weeks earlier, in December 2018, the prime minister had signed a decree exempting the newly formed progovernment media conglomerate from scrutiny by media or competition authorities. As a move of "strategic importance at a national level," the decree attempted to justify the controversial merger of over four-hundred progovernment media outlets under one giant umbrella organization, the Central European Press and Media Foundation.[11] The foundation's assets include cable news channels, Internet news portals, tabloids, sports newspapers, and all of Hungary's county newspapers, as well as several radio stations and numerous magazines. At the same time, news media outlets that have been critical of the government have faced major challenges in recent years, culminating in the sudden closure of the largest left-leaning opposition newspaper, *Népszabadság*, in 2016, political pressure on *Index* (that led to its 2020 mass resignations) and *Klubrádió*, and more.

How Should the Left Fight Back?

Since Viktor Orbán came back to power in 2010—and especially since Brexit and Trump—we have seen an expanding group of right-wing nationalists proclaim that they will give back to the people the voice that has been captured by the "elites." What the right-wing election winners understand is that politics is always partisan and requires an "us versus them" confrontation. Furthermore, they recognize the need to mobilize the realm of emotion and sentiment in order to construct collective political identities. They have a strong and simple narrative, unlike the existing establishment. By drawing a line between the "people" and the "establishment," the right-wingers openly reject the postpolitical consensus of the West and "Third Way" globalist politicians like Tony Blair and the Clintons. On the other hand, these globalists only consider rational debates acceptable, owing to their consensual concept of politics and the rationalistic view that passions must be excluded. This explains their hostility to what they call populism, a phenomenon they associate with demagogy and irrationality.

As post-Marxist Belgian philosopher Chantal Mouffe wrote in the *Guardian*, referring to Hillary Clinton's degrading description of Donald Trump's supporters in the 2016 US election campaign, the challenge of right-wing nationalism should not be met by "stubbornly upholding the postpolitical consensus and despising the 'deplorables.'" [1] Mouffe emphasizes that it is vital for the center-left to realize that the moral condemnation and demonization of right-wing nationalism is nothing but counterproductive:

> It merely reinforces antiestablishment feelings among those who lack a vocabulary to formulate what are, at core, genuine grievances. Classifying right-wing populist parties as "extreme right" or "fascist," presenting them as a kind of moral disease and attributing their appeal to a lack of education is, of course, very convenient for the center-left. It allows them to dismiss any populist demands and to avoid acknowledging responsibility for their rise." [2]

Mouffe's advice is, more precisely, that left-wingers should instead get these feelings out of their systems as soon as possible and then start fighting back in a more constructive manner. From

Mouffe's perspective, the Left's battles require establishing a bond between social movements and a new type of party to create a "people" fighting for equality and social justice. Such political strategy, Mouffe adds, can be found in movements such as Podemos in Spain, with Bernie Sanders in the US and also in British politics in the name of Jeremy Corbyn, whose endeavor to transform the Labor party into a popular movement, working "for the many, not the few," initially was succeeding in making it the greatest left-wing party in Europe. "I am convinced that in the next few years, the central axis of the political conflict will be between right-wing populism and left-wing populism, and it is imperative that progressive sectors understand the importance of involving themselves in that struggle," Mouffe concludes.[3]

One relevant approach for the Left can actually be to analyze what Viktor Orbán did while he was in opposition. And then maybe try to copy his strategy. After four years as prime minister, Orbán's defeat in 2002 was "traumatic," because he had expected a clear victory. He felt he deserved it, according to John O'Sullivan, director at the Danube Institute in Budapest: "Orbán disappeared to a mountaintop, communed with nature, and returned with a new political strategy. Having been defeated because most of the institutions of society, privatized industry, and media in particular were, as he thought, in postcommunist hands, he determined that Fidesz would have to build up its own institutions—think tanks, media, universities, civic bodies—to give it something like equality in the political struggle."[4] As it turned out, after Orbán also lost the next election in 2006, he ended up with a total of eight years in opposition. That is a long time in politics. Because of his vigor and determination, however, Orbán remained leader of Fidesz through all those years. And he did not waste his time. Not only did he create an entire parallel political organization in opposition to his postcommunist rivals, but at times he even skipped sessions of parliament because he was busy ringing doorbells out in the countryside—where he himself originated from—targeting the votes of those "left behind" in the transition from communism.[5]

If we look at the liberals and the Left in Hungary today, few of them seem to spend much time in the rural parts of the country. Undoubtedly, Budapest is a wonderful place to spend your time. But it is the home for only two million of Hungary's ten million people. Center-left politicians seeking a return to power would be well advised to leave the complacent and liberal Budapest bubble and win back some of the rural territories. With Fidesz usually getting support from less than half of the electorate, trying might just work. The 2019 municipal elections in Hungary showed that by coordinating their strategy, opposition forces were able to win two handfuls of the larger cities, including the mayor's office in Budapest, hoping to continue the success in the 2022 parliamentary elections.

Over the past few years, Hungary has seen several semisuccessful antigovernment demonstrations, including some small ones in the countryside. But protesters often lose stamina after a week or two. Before these protests reach a level of noteworthy momentum and impact, the opposition stops believing that it can manage to mobilize Hungarians enough to stir "revolutionary sentiments." The explanation is, obviously, that the opposition has been fragmented into a handful of different parties, competing in what essentially is supposed to be a two-party system like in the UK or the US. The opposition—which is at least united in its anti-Orbán sentiments— has been lacking a charismatic leader, one the masses are willing to follow, in order to challenge the Orbán government. Ahead of the 2022 elections, the opposition parties held their first-ever primaries, and elected—to the surprise of many—the political outsider Péter Márki-Zay, a conservative father of seven and the mayor of small-town Hódmezővásárhely. "Our project is to dismantle the system, so that nobody in Hungary's future can hijack democracy like Orbán has," said opposition leader Márki-Zay6, a former marketing expert who lived in Canada and the United States before returning to Hungary and beating Orbán's candidate in the 2018 mayoral race in the decade-long Fidesz-stronghold.[6]

If no one does anything, nothing will happen.

Why Nationalism is Here to Stay

Liberals and left-wingers may dream of defeating nationalism, just as nationalism itself helped defeat communism. However, as we have learned over the past few years, such hope is fast turning into political tragedy. Nationalism, it appears, is here to stay. While communism was a radical political experiment based on abolishing private property, nationalism or conservatism is an organic part of any democratic political scene. Acknowledging this must surely be part of addressing its growing influence.

Research over the years, including New York University's report *The Secret Lives of Liberals and Conservatives*, has shown that in industrialized nations, nationalists, social conservatives, and religious fundamentalists possess psychological traits that tend to predispose them toward prejudice.[1] For instance, the valuing of conformity and the desire for certainty. Meanwhile, liberals and the nonreligious tend to be more open to new experiences, a trait associated with lower prejudice. So one might expect that conservatives and Christians should be inherently more discriminatory on the whole. Thus, the political Left might consider itself more open-minded than the Right. But Dutch-American professor of social psychology Mark Brandt has conducted research lately revealing that liberals are *just as prejudiced* against conservatives as conservatives are against liberals: "While liberals and the nonreligious sometimes defend themselves as being intolerant of intolerance, they can't claim this line as their own. Our study shows that bias on both ends is largely driven by seeing the opposing groups as limiting one's personal freedom."[2]

Another way to understand the differences between liberals and conservatives is by looking at the research pioneered by American psychologist Jonathan Haidt. As revealed in his 2012 book *The Righteous Mind*, people tend to arrange their values along six different areas, or domains.[3]

What are these six domains? The first—care versus harm—concerns people's empathy and desire not to see others hurt. The second—fairness versus cheating—is concerned with justice and rights. According to Haidt, liberals tend to see fairness as an issue of equality, while conservatives see it as an issue of proportionality. That helps to explain liberals' desires to see a large social safety net versus the conservative attitude that people should get what they work for and no more. Liberals derive their values largely from the first moral domain, empathy, though they also care about the second one, justice. Liberals also worry about the third domain—liberty and oppression—which motivates people to stand up against bullies and fight for individual liberties.

What is important to know here is that conservatives care about these values, too. But they *also* care about three other moral domains that liberals tend to shrug off. These include: Loyalty versus betrayal, which concerns patriotism and group identity. Authority versus subversion, which includes deference to social hierarchies. And sanctity versus degradation, which concerns disgust and beliefs about the desecration of the body.

With these basic concerns driving people's political beliefs, it is easy to see how the Left and Right see issues very differently. For example, a conservative might be disgusted by gay marriage, believing that homosexuality desecrates the body. A liberal, on the other hand, would not worry about the sanctity versus degradation domain; his or her concerns would involve causing the least harm to gay couples, falling under the domain of harm versus care.

Once people join a political team, they get ensnared in what Haidt calls "the moral matrix." They see confirmation of their own grand narrative everywhere, and it is difficult—perhaps even impossible—to convince them that they are wrong if you argue with them from outside of their matrix. In his book, Haidt suggests that liberals might have even more difficulty understanding conservatives than the other way around. Why? Because liberals often have difficulty understanding how the foundations of loyalty, authority, and sanctity have anything to do with morality. Liberal critics of Viktor Orbán, for instance, might argue that loyalty to a group shrinks the moral circle and that it is the basis of racism and exclusion. They would see Orbán's authority as oppression. And for the liberals, the Fidesz focus on Christian sanctity is religious "mumbo-jumbo" whose only function is to suppress female sexuality and justify homophobia.

Now, Haidt is not suggesting that conservatives are superior to liberals. He points out that conservatives like Viktor Orbán's supporters tend to value order even at the cost of those at the bottom of society, which can result in morally dubious social implications. Liberals, however, often desire change even at the risk of anarchy. Haidt explains that conservatives often feel that the Left has won the culture war and controls the media, the universities, and the education of everyone's children. "Many conservatives think they are the victims," he observes. "They are fighting back against powerful and oppressive forces, and their animosities are related to that worldview."[4]

Some people, of course, will refuse to accept Haidt's explanation of moral reality. This is not surprising. As Haidt puts it himself, "The human inclination is to believe in one's own understanding of morality, and many people will live their entire lives without seriously attempting to understand their ideological counterparts."[5] These people, Haidt adds, reside on both sides of ideological spectrum. They exist in a moral matrix.

If you think that half of the Hungarian electorate vote for Viktor Orbán because they are blinded, then Jonathan Haidt's message to you is that you are trapped in the "moral matrix": "You can either take the blue pill and stick to your comforting delusions. Or you can take the red pill, learn some moral psychology, and step outside your moral matrix."[6]

So what to make of all this? I must say, despite its complexity, I find Haidt's explanation quite insightful. It certainly helps explain our contentious and polarized culture. His point is that even many intelligent and reasonable people, after all, will have a difficult time agreeing on anything if they view the moral underpinnings of society through vastly divergent lenses.

Part II
Features

"In any dispute, each side thinks it's in the right
and the other side is demons."

—Steven Pinker, psychologist

Chapter Four

What Does Viktor Orbán Really Want?

One Solution: Orbán's Solution

There was something symbolic about Viktor Orbán's encounter in 2014 with Ernő Rubik, the Hungarian inventor of the Rubik's Cube. It was at an official event celebrating the fortieth anniversary of the world-famous toy, and on the table in front of them, a cube had been solved, so the colors on each of its six sides had been put in order: red, white, green, and so on. Invented in 1974, the Rubik's Cube is a physical manifestation of logic. It is an object with only one final solution. But while the philosophy behind the cube is beautiful in theory—and in toy stores—it also symbolizes a frightening political idea: the idea of absolutes, of one truth, one way of doing things.

As the Rubik's Cube was lying there on the table in its absolute form, it somehow signaled how Orbán himself, since gaining power in 2010, had built an absolute political system that does not allow for alternatives. This extreme trend has surfaced in Hungary again and again for more than seventy years. In 1944, the Arrow Cross Party took power in Hungary as Nazi Germany's puppet government. Months later, the Soviets "liberated" Hungary, dissolved the parliament, and before long installed a government that enforced four decades of communism under a one-party state. Hungary swung from absolute Right to absolute Left with little room for argument. At both ends, much of the Hungarian population faced deportation, imprisonment, and death.

In recent years, two Orbán critics have written two different books, arguing from quite different perspectives that today's Hungary may have installed a new absolute political system. In *The Hungarian Patient*, sociologist Péter Krasztev—with contributions from a number of other professors in Hungary—diagnoses the nation's current situation in light of a hundred-year "history of diseases."[1] Following the mantra "You must know your past in order to understand your present," Krasztev's 2015 book addresses primarily the antiauthoritarian movements and activists who have attempted—with no success—to resist Orbán's regime because they have failed to renew themselves.

Furthermore, the book also tells the story of a country that has some deep historical wounds. Wounds that have never healed, for there was no consensus on the meaning of historical events. For instance, the meaning of the Trianon Treaty in 1920, when Hungary lost two-thirds of its territory and one third of its inhabitants to the neighboring countries. Or Hungary's role during the World War II, when the regime, hoping to restore ancient grandeur by siding with the Germans, lost again. Or the meaning of the 1956 Revolution, which began as a fight for freedom from Soviet rule but ended up as yet another bloody defeat.

When I interviewed Krasztev, he called for a reasonable discussion that could lead to a higher degree of historical consensus among Hungarians—instead of always letting the strongest force push through its own version of an absolute truth. "As a representative of those who actually want to deal with the horrors of the past, Viktor Orbán makes a lot of Hungarians feel that his values are the true Hungarian values. History can mobilize the population and be used politically, and Orbán exploits Hungary's history to back up the national conservative values he stands for," Krasztev adds that, especially on the Right, there is a common interpretation that Hungary has been badly mistreated throughout history. "The tendency to blame others instead of looking inward is dominant among much of the Hungarian population," the sociologist says.

Drawing on ideas advanced by Russian historian Alexander Achiezer, Péter Krasztev also argues that Hungarians have a divided mindset, that they interpret the country's tragic history through a mental duality. "Hungarians have not processed the fate of the past because the country's progress has always been interrupted by new tragic events. Their two coexisting, and often completely contradictory, interpretations of the same events, create a polarization in society. And with perfection, Orbán takes advantage of this game." Krasztev points to the prime minister's speech on the March 15 National Day in 2016, in which Orbán presented an absolute interpretation of the country's history. To explain his view to the Hungarians, Orbán divided the population into "us"—patriots, nationalists, and moderate freedom fighters—and "the others": internationalists, EU supporters, and "foreign mercenaries" present during communism.[2]

Krasztev elaborates: "During his speech, Orbán blurred the lines between the EU and the former Soviet Union by calling both 'internationalists that invaded our nation state.' But in reality, the ambiguous historical narrative and Hungary's inability to face its own imperialist, Nazi, and communist past have never really been debated or discussed." He acknowledges that *The Hungarian Patient*, which was published both in Hungarian and in English, failed to create a platform for such reflection: "It was primarily activists and intellectuals who reacted to the book, whereas political leaders and other decision-makers were completely silent, even though they received the book. Thus, there was only a quiet discussion of the book, which did not lead to anything."

Krasztev adds that the dual mindset has also shaped Hungary's framework of public and other institutions, within which there are two sides of virtually all levels of society. In the field of art, in the health sector, and in the police and judicial area, there is always an official *and* a semiofficial or alternative way of doing thing; and sticking to the official version is rare. "Hungary is a 'two-in-one country,' and its two sides know less about each other than they know about the rest of the world," Krasztev concludes.

Another Orbán-critical book, *Post-Communist Mafia State* (2016), is by sociologist and former liberal politician Bálint Magyar.[3] He analyzes and criticizes Viktor Orbán's politics from a different perspective than Krasztev, focusing on each of the elements in the machinery of Orbán's self-proclaimed "System of National Cooperation." Magyar claims that Orbán's Hungary is the only country in Europe that lives up to the term "mafia state," stressing that a mafia state is different from both a dictatorship, an autocracy, or an oligarchy, but that it features traits from those kinds of governance.

Magyar, contrary to Krasztev, does not believe that the current situation can be traced further back than to the fall of the communism. When I interviewed him, he argued that the situation of today cannot be compared to anything we have seen before. "The development is mainly due to the failure of the socialist-led governments in the period 1990–2010, widespread corruption, the financial crisis in 2008, a failed welfare policy, and the absence of liberal political parties," he says. "Fidesz is a political movement that has taken power over the state. It all takes place within an adopted political family, and it is a cultural pattern in which the actors do not feel obliged to create a better Hungary. Solidarity is only shown to the family who are loyal to the 'Godfather.'"

For example, Fidesz has nationalized the education system and created a system in which all school principals are appointed by politicians. Observes Magyar, "There are 5,000 schools in Hungary, so there are a huge number of principals, and none of them have independence when it comes to hiring the school's teachers. If someone criticizes the government, that person can easily be tracked and he or she will never again get a job anywhere in Hungary."

Teachers have been among the sharpest critics of the government since Fidesz came to power, and initially, it was often the teachers who organized demonstrations and protests against government cuts in education. "But now teachers are afraid to participate in demonstrations," says Magyar, "and this dynamic has spread to other professions, such as nurses, doctors, and other public-sector workers."

At the time of publishing the book, Bálint Magyar experienced a lack of will to discuss and criticize Hungary, similar to what Péter Krasztev experienced. Bálint Magyar was one of the founders of a leading liberal political partym the Alliance of Free Democrats (SZDSZ), and he served as Minister of Education on two occasions.

1996–1998 and 2002–2006. Naturally, he cannot run away from his political past, but despite his book's more than one hundred detailed examples and well-argued criticism of Fidesz's corrupt methods, *Post-Communist Mafia State* was completely rejected by the right-wing as "lying propaganda" with an "exclusively political agenda."

On the Left, the parties have, according to Magyar, been busier criticizing each other than finding a common way to fight Orbán. "We are moving further and further away from being able to change the system. If you are a Christian and you see the pastor stealing money from the church, then it requires extraordinary courage to expose him, because he is such a great authority with the power to punish you," says Magyar, whose book failed to spark a broader public discussion in Hungary of the long-term consequences of Orbán's so-called mafia state.

Magyar concludes that it was the 2008 financial crisis that finally paved the way for Hungary's government to morph into a highly centralized powerhouse whose approach to politics is significantly different from—and almost the opposite of—the classic "give-and-take" approach typically seen in democracies.

And thus, we can end the story where we began, with the Rubik's Cube, as Magyar concludes: "Today, it seems that there is only one solution to Hungary's problems, and that is Orbán's solution."

How Liberals Misunderstand the Appeal of Conservatism

In April 2018, Fidesz once again painted the map of Hungary orange—the party's color—winning a new supermajority in parliament for the third time in a row. Apart from three constituencies outside of Budapest, the country looked like a sea of orange with a multicolored capital in the middle. According to György Schöpflin, a longtime Fidesz member of the Europeaan Parliament, who passed away in 2021, Budapest had "turned left" and is, hence, out of synch with the rest of the country. "The Budapest elites should ask themselves why the rest of the population rejects them," Schöpflin wrote on Twitter, adding that Orbán's victory was more than just a Hungarian event. It marked the next chapter of the rebellion against the prevailing liberal ideology in western Europe and, more broadly, the West. "Fidesz's clear victory is a rejection of the hyper-liberalism that claims a hegemony over European politics," the nationalist conservative MEP concluded. " It is time for the European Left to start a rethink."

With his latest victory, Viktor Orbán manifested his role as the dominant force of the European Right. In recent years, he has attacked the "liberal" West and not least its "moral imperialism" and the "tyranny of political correctness" of Brussels bureaucrats. But the criticism of liberalism does not come only from conservatives like Viktor Orbán. Even some liberal academics have called for progressive forces in Europe to look inward.

One of them is Jonathan Haidt, professor of political psychology at New York University. Since the release of his *The Righteous Mind* in 2012, Haidt has argued that the economic narrative of "the losers of globalization" is not the full explanation of why many of these people have voted for nationalist, conservative politicians like Orbán and Trump. Morality and political psychology play an equally important role in their choices, Haidt argues, explaining that the Left has a tendency to look down on moral order, hierarchies, and tradition—all of which are essential values for the conservative citizen. "Conservatism and authoritarian tendencies can best be understood as reactions to a left-wing going too far," the American professor writes.[1] It happens, for instance, when progressives focus intensely on gender, minority rights, race, and environmental policies. According to Haidt, the concept of political correctness is what creates the counterreaction on the Right.

Haidt's points are backed by another liberal academic, professor George Lakoff from UC Berkeley. In an email interview, he argued that many on the Left believe, to their own political detriment, that their values are universal and thus apply to everyone. "Therefore, the Left believes that it just needs to present facts and suggestions on how to realize those values. Conservatives, on the other hand, have a different view of values and morals: They know that morality and values are not shared equally by everyone. You have to fight in order to impose your own morals," Lakoff points out, adding that conservatives are winning because they talk about morality, while progressive are losing because they talk about politics and procedures.

At Princeton University, sociologist and longtime Orbán critic Kim Lane Scheppele recognizes Haidt's and Lakoff's theories. When I talked to her shortly after Orbán's 2018 triumph, she explained that conservatives to some extent have taken over the role as society's rebels—a role that in the 1960s and 1970s belonged to the Left;

> Just think about the message that we should get rid of political correctness and defend freedom of speech. Those ideas used to belong to the left-wing, but now the right-wing has completely adopted them. Conservatives have spent decades trying to break through with their message to the people, and now it is finally happening. Meanwhile, the leftists are at a complete loss as to what to do. They do not even understand why their message of universal rationalism and humanism does not appeal to everyone. [...] I believe that people in less-favored positions in society, including many Orbán, Brexit, and Trump voters, adopt the perspective that the African American scholar W. E. B. Du Bois articulated as a "double consciousness." He noted that black people had a double consciousness—they could think like both white and blacks. It was a survival skill if you had little power or self-determination. I believe that conservatives feel they have suffered from a lack of power and therefore have adopted a similar perspective. They are able to understand both sides of the political spectrum, at least better than liberals are.[2]

Scheppele thinks that, in general, the West has underestimated Viktor Orbán:

> Initially, in the first couple of years after his 2010 victory, he looked like a tin-pot dictator in a remote location—why

should the West care about him? But now that Europe has more experience with him, everyone can see that he is clever, ruthless, and efficient in exploiting cracks in the liberal façade. Migration policy in the EU is now set by Orbán. He was the one who proposed making deals with third countries to get them to stop the refugees before they came to Europe. He was the one who cracked down on asylum seekers and insisted on the enforcement of the Dublin Regulation, which the European Court of Justice has certified. Orbán has become not just a Hungarian politician but a European politician, and I think that Europe did not see this coming.

Scheppele believes that the West has misunderstood how powerful nationalism has become, particularly when a financial crisis was followed by an immigration crisis:

This twin assault on the self-confidence of the less economically advanced groups has produced a backlash that takes an illiberal form. We see the strains everywhere across Europe, but only in Hungary did a government—not just an opposition party—make the bet that it could rally people [who are] nervous about their precarious status to undermine everything that Europe has defended.

At the University of Kent, Hungarian-British sociologist Frank Furedi thinks that the outlook of the West toward Eastern Europe is guided by values and impulses that fundamentally diverge from those of Eastern Europe. He wrote in an email to me:

There is an imperious impulse that insists that Eastern Europe should take it or leave it. That they must fall in line with the Brussels consensus, otherwise they will be ostracized from civilized life. This is very much a case of willful understanding. In turn, a lot of Eastern Europeans do no not understand why they are pathologized, and why they cannot be left alone..

According to the conservative sociologist, it is important to understand that different societies are influenced by different values that help them to make sense of their lives: "Instead of demanding that everyone speaks from the same scripts, it is better to allow different people to express their dreams and hopes in accordance with their own experience and worldviews. It does not work to force others to adopt the same view of the world." He adds that journalists also play an important role and must be careful not to become politically biased in their coverage.

In addition, Kim Lane Scheppele notes that most Western journalists are liberals in a particular sense—they believe in civil liberties and checks on governmental power. "They do not all vote for the same parties. But the accusation of liberalism sticks because journalists do not want to be seen taking sides, and so they are nervous about loudly proclaiming the basic values of self-sustaining democracies. But what are journalists doing if they don't believe in free speech, evidence-based knowledge, democracy, and more?"

Scheppele believes that the accusation of "liberal bias" of the media merges two different things: Firstly, the defense of the very institutional set-up that makes journalism vital and so protected in democratic societies. And secondly, the defense of particular parties and candidates. According to Scheppele,

[I]t is easy to overstate how different right-wing people are from the Left. Conservatives by and large want the same thing liberals do: A better life for their kids, a government that shares their values and is not corrupt, a life of dignity in which others do not look down on them. Liberals might be surprised if they spend more time with conservatives at how much they share.

The sociologist underlines that the two sides need to spend more time talking to each other.

> Polarization means that few right-wing conservatives have liberal friends and vice versa. Journalists and social scientists have a professional excuse to break the ice with "the other side." We must talk to people with whom we disagree to do our jobs. Our professional training means that we need to know what they think and how they see the world. Let us hope that journalism and social science are both not killed off trying to do this work.

Can Hungarians Save Their Country by Having More Children?

Csók means "kiss" in Hungarian. But in Hungary, CSOK is also the name of the government's family policy. Through economic benefits, it encourages Hungarians to have more children. A friendly kiss from Prime Minister Viktor Orbán, if you will.

One of the families that has welcomed the invitation is the Adamecz family from the industrial city of Veszprém. The family consists of the father, Zoltán; the mother, Eszter; and their five children, of whom the youngest is two years old at the time of my visit. They have expanded their house on the outskirts of the city thanks to a state subsidy that only parents with more than two children can receive. Explains Zoltán Adamecz, the owner of a construction company in Veszprém with more than twenty employees, "With the help of the CSOK support, we can give each of our children their own room, and now we also have a larger garden where we can keep pets and grow vegetables. In that way our children can learn how to take responsibility for other living creatures and how to turn the resources of nature into food on the table." The fifty-year-old father is not religious, but he gives the traditional family an almost religious value. "The family is and remains the core unit of society, and it gives you an opportunity to raise your children in the most secure environment. Belonging to a community is a basic need for all people in society, and the family is the most natural community."

All across Europe, the aging populations entail that the continent will be facing major demographic challenges in the coming decades. But while the populations of most northern and western European countries is steadily growing as a result of immigration and a slightly increasing birth rate, the populations of most central, eastern, and southern European countries are in decline. This is due mainly to the fact that many people emigrate from their home countries, while immigration rates are low and women generally give birth to few children.

According to Tomás Sobotka, senior researcher at the Wittgenstein Center in Vienna, central, eastern, and southeastern European countries have lost 12–15 million inhabitants since the fall of the Berlin Wall—particularly due to their persistently low birth rate and emigration to richer parts of Europe. "The poorer parts of Europe must find a way to deal with emigration," he says. "Potentially they may have to make it more attractive for the emigrants to return to their home countries, and many of the eastern countries are already working on it. But in addition, a family policy where the government encourages its citizens to have more children can also help to reduce the challenges that will arise with a declining population."

According to the United Nations, Hungary is tenth on the list of countries with the most declining populations, and the organization estimates that by 2050, the Hungarian population will be down to 8.3 million inhabitants. If so, that would be nearly 2.5 million fewer than in 1981, when Hungary "peaked" with 10.7 million inhabitants. Today, the population is already one million fewer than back then, about 9.7 million.

"We need a population turnaround," Viktor Orbán said at a 2017 family-themed convention in Budapest.[1] "As many children as possible must be born, because if there are children, there is a future." The prime minister later proclaimed that Hungarian women who give birth to more than three children will be exempted from paying income taxes, and they won't have to repay their student debt. Furthermore, Orbán announced at the convention, parents with more than two children will receive tax benefits and get a deduction in their housing loan. "Where there is room for two children, there is also room for three—or even four." Orbán, himself a father of five, added, "Braver families may even find room for five," He continued: "The more we support our families, the more children will be born. With little support, only a few more children; with more support, many more children."

Actually, there are indications that Hungary's proactive family policy may have resulted in what could be called a "CSOK effect" over the past few years. At least the statistics show that the Hungarian birth rate—which was 1.2 children per woman when Orbán came to power in 2010—as of 2020 has grown to 1.5 children per woman. The government's goal is to raise the birth rate to a stabilizing 2.1 by 2030. As Szílard Németh, a long-time Fidesz lawmaker, himself a father of three children, bombastically remarked in 2017: "Those who pump the world full of babies will rule the earth."[2]

Today, virtually every European country has some kind of family policy aiming to support families or help them with childcare, curb poverty, eradicate social inequality, or promote women's job opportunities and gender equality. But more direct support for the birth of more children—currently most dominant in Viktor Orbán's Hungary, in Vladimir Putin's Russia, and in Aleksandar Vučić's Serbia—could essentially be successful if the policy genuinely addresses the real problems that families and couples are facing. Tomás Sobotka explains: "Think of families with a generally low income and inadequate housing conditions. For them, any direct or indirect support increasing their income or improving their housing will help them decide whether to get the extra child that they want."

However, Sobotka warns, a family policy supporting the birth of more children may also have certain disadvantages. For example, if the policy primarily reflects the wishes and ideas of the government instead of the actual wishes and needs of the families. Or if it focuses primarily on financial incentives rather than building a stronger infrastructure to support families, such as childcare. "A policy encouraging the birth of more children can also increase the social inequality with regards to fertility," Sobotka notes, "because poorer and lower-educated women in rural areas typically will respond more positively to new economic incentives." He also emphasizes that this kind of family policy, in the short term, can make birth statistics look nicer than they really are. "Part of the impact of financial incentives for families is due not to the fact that parents get more children, but that they get their children *earlier* than otherwise, because they may fear that the economic benefits could be gone soon," the researcher explains. Some governments, he adds, are "unrealistic" when it comes to state-funded initiatives. Such schemes can run the risk of being rolled back when the economy requires cutbacks on the state budget. That happened in the case of the so-called "baby bonus initiative" in Spain, from which mothers received about €2,700 for each newborn child. The scheme was launched in July 2007, but it did not survive long and was scrapped in 2011 due to savings during the financial crisis in Spain.

Tomás Sobotka elaborates that political ideologies of multiple childbirths often can stigmatize those people who cannot or do not want to have children, including voluntary childless couples as well as gay couples. He refers to one of the ethical principles that was formulated in 1994 at the UN's Conference on Population, which academics and politicians still bring up to today: "All couples and individuals have the basic right to decide freely and responsibly the number and spacing of their children and to have the information, education, and means to do so."[3]

In Budapest, the young activist and photographer Zsuzsanna Simon has created attention and a furore on social media after she posted pictures of her own and other women's bare bellies with this blood-red inscription: "I will not give birth until the government changes!" She is radically opposed to what she says is the Orbán government's interference in the family plans of Hungarian citizens. Speaking to *Euronews,* she said, "With my activism, I try to make people aware of this insulting policy, ordering us how many children we should have. Why do the politicians stick their noses into this? This is our private sphere, they should not make rules about the number of children we should give birth to,"[4]

However, as is often the case in Hungary, attitudes in Budapest are very different from those in rural areas, where two-thirds of the Hungarians live, including Zoltán Adamecz from Veszprém: "Of course, someone may think that it is a private matter, but if you look at it from the perspective of society, the country's birth rate is not a private matter. It actually matters how many babies a nation brings to the world. A country's declining population is a sad death spiral."

Viktor Orbán seems aware that his family policy is a sensitive topic. In comments in 2018 before launching a new national consultation on family issues with questionnaires sent to all Hungarians, he said, "We must admit that the decision to have children is the most personal public affair—and one that only women can decide. Therefore, we must hear them."[5]

One of the few female politicians in Orbán's male-dominated Fidesz cabinet is Katalin Novák, former minister of state for family and possibly the next president of Hungary. In recent years, she has become more outspoken when talking about family composition and the family's role in society. In an announcement prior to the 2018 Budapest Pride Festival she said something that was later adopted into the Hungarian constitution:

We support the traditional family structure with a *man* and a *woman*. Some are fighting for the rights of a small minority, but the danger is that we then forget the majority. When discussing traditional values, people are often cautious because they are afraid of being accused of homophobia, even though they are just talking about the most natural ties. [,,,] Every child has the right to have a father and a mother. Every family needs a woman and a man, and only one woman and one man. The family's role is to continue life, and thus, the family is the foundation of the nation's survival.[6]

In 2020, the Hungarian government ensured that this was added to the nation's constitution: "The mother is a woman, the father is a man." And that gay couples were prohibited from adopting children. Back in Veszprém, Zoltán Adamecz agrees: "It is in the family that the parents, contributing with the different strengths of their sexes, work together to achieve a common goal: To raise and educate their children." Although it may be difficult to talk about fertility, the family man from Veszprém believes that the Orbán government's efforts to get families to have more children is the right way to go:

> You have to recognize the importance of taking responsibility for society by having children. We live in a time where society tends to prefer solutions that are safe and convenient for the individual, rather than prioritizing solutions that are valuable but demanding for everyone.

A Superstar Conservative Comes to Town

On the front row sits Paul Feher, an American with Hungarian roots. He is wearing a green T-shirt with the Hungarian coat of arms on his chest, and he has flown in all the way from Florida, where he runs a shelter for military veterans like himself. He is holding on to his crutches. "I am a proud Christian Republican who has fallen in love with my family's old homeland," says the sixty-year-old veteran whose Hungarian parents emigrated to the United States after the 1956 uprising. Paul Feher has come to Esztergom—a picturesque Roman-Catholic town near the Slovak border on the banks of the Danube —to see his political icon, Tucker Carlson. The same holds for the majority of the approximately one thousand people attending the event. Most of them are Hungarians living here, but some American immigrants, expats, and tourists are present as well.

What they all have in common is being on Tucker Carlson's side. They are Viktor Orbán supporters, and now it is time to hear the naked truth. "Tucker and Orbán don't wrap it in, they say it like it is," Paul Feher explains about his two conservative idols.

A moment later, Tucker Carlson takes the stage. A group of cheering spectators unfolds a huge Stars and Stripes banner by the front seats. "This is by far the strangest thing I have ever done. But I enjoy being here," says the protagonist up on the stage, obviously baffled by his presence in what surely feels to be an obscure European town, far from the FOX News teleprompter in his TV studio back home in Washington, D.C. A middle-aged man wearing black Aviator sunglasses jumps up from his seat so everyone can see his T-shirt with its caption "CNN Fake News." Tucker Carlson notices him immediately and reacts: "Sadly, I couldn't agree more."

Tucker Carlson is a polarizing figure in the purest sense of the word. He is a famous host on the FOX News channel, and his political talkshow is one of the most-watched American television programs in recent years, with three million viewers every night. According to his opponents, Tucker Carlson is a highly controversial manipulator who spreads conspiracy theories about immigrants, vaccines, and the storming of Capitol Hill.

"Here's the man who helped create Covid-19 to begin with," he ones said of Anthony Fauci, the White House adviser on infectious diseases. Carlson has also suggested that the FBI was involved in the invasion of the Capitol on January 6, 2021. Right-wing proponents rather argue that Tucker Carlson is in fact just telling the unfiltered truth—a truth that the politically correct liberals just do not dare to talk about.

There is little doubt that the fifty-two-year-old American divides the crowd. But he does make an impact. *Time Magazine* and the BBC have called him "the most influential conservative thinker in the United States,"[1] and some consider him a future Republican presidential candidate. A rebellious heir to Donald Trump.

I want to find out what brought Tucker Carlson to Hungary. For a week, he has been staying at the luxurious Matild Palace Hotel in Budapest and using its roof terrace to air his daily shows on FOX News, bringing his audience the lessons from Viktor Orbán's Hungary that Americans should learn from: That you can keep immigrants away by closing your southern border with a fence. That you can provide security for Christian families and let them raise their children in accordance with old norms and traditions. That you don't have to surrender to "woke capitalism," but that it is possible to strive for an alternative to left-wing liberalism.

"America is the best country in the world—that's what I've always thought. But it is not a freer country than Hungary," according to Tucker Carlson.

Viktor Orbán has dubbed his own project "illiberal democracy." He first did so in a speech in 2014, and since then, according to critics, Hungary has dismantled the fundamental (liberal) principles of the rule of law—including freedom of press, academic freedom, and independent courts. According to Orbán himself, however, the concept of "illiberal democracy" must be understood more simply as a society that is not, as in the West, governed by the one-sided ideas of liberal democracy. Later, aware of the toxic connotations of "illiberalism," Orbán has been trying to rebrand his vision of democracy as "Christian liberty."[2]

On the stage in Esztergom, Tucker Carlson elaborates that it is in fact the "oh so tolerant liberals" on the left who do not tolerate any counterarguments to their worldview. "What they are imposing on us is illiberalism, the opposite of liberalism. It is the totalitarian idea that everyone behaves the same, everyone reads from the same catechism, the same list of slogans, and that everyone obeys," says Tucker Carlson, and the audience applauds him.

During his visit to Hungary, Tucker Carlson visited the infamous southern-border fence and produced a fifteen-minute solo interview with Viktor Orbán—a man who otherwise never participates in such sessions with outside journalists, and certainly not in English. In the interview, Orbán tried to explain his political approach, which he feels is often ridiculed by Western leaders, including President Joe Biden. "Liberals in the West cannot accept that there is a national conservative alternative within the Western civilization which is more successful in everyday life than the liberal. That is why they criticize us," the prime minister argued.[2]

According to critical commentators from American media such as NBC News and the *Atlantic*, the fact that an American TV host chooses to spend a whole week "whitewashing Viktor Orbán's regime" has created a lot of furore on both sides of the pond. Opinions have been about as polarized as they often are in the "Divided States of America."

The criticism hit a homerun spot when a journalist from the *New York Times* discovered that the Orbán government had deleted a particular passage in the government's transcript of Orbán's interview with Tucker Carlson. The deleted passage concerned Chinese President Xi Jinping, who, according to Carlson, has "murdered many of his political opponents." Carlson's blatant exposure of China's leader reflects badly on Orbán's government, which is already widely condemned for working closely with the regime in Beijing. After the embarrassing attempt of censorship was discovered, the Orbán government felt forced to republish a complete, unedited transcript of the interview to the public.[4]

Tucker Carlson is far from the first Western conservative to set course for Hungary. In recent years, there have been numerous occasions at which Viktor Orbán welcomed people that rarely get exposure in the Western mainstream media. Those who have met with Orbán include Trump-adviser Steve Bannon, author Douglas Murray, psychologist Jordan B. Peterson and even the liberal French philosopher Bernhard Henri-Lévy. In addition, two recently deceased gentlemen—Scottish historian Norman Stone and English thinker Roger Scruton—belonged to Viktor Orbán's intellectual inner circle for many years. Moreover, former Margaret Thatcher speechwriter John O'Sullivan now heads the Danube Institute, a think tank in Budapest which is supported by the Orbán government. The institute's most recent fellow, a conservative American author named Rod Dreher, is said to have been instrumental in Tucker Carlson's visit to the country. "I am amazed by the courage that Viktor Orbán shows. He just does not care what the West thinks," Rod Dreher said when I met him in Esztergom. "It is time for intellectual depleted Anglo-American conservatives to take a fresh look at Hungary," he argued. But what does he think of people who criticize Orbán's lack of respect for democracy and the rule of law? Dreher acknowledges that he certainly does not like Orbán's corrupt and authoritarian aspects. "There's a lot to criticize, just like there was with Trump. But in the cultural struggle of our time, Orbán is an important voice. Had Trump only had half of Orbán's intelligence and drive, America would be somewhere else today," Rod Dreher said.

In the government-critical media in Hungary, several political commentators have highlighted what they describe as double standards among the conservative pilgrims in Orbán's Hungary. One of them is political scientist János Szilárd Tóth, who wrote in *Válasz Online*: "There is a roaring inconsistency with these guests. They are outraged by the West's politically correct language police, but they do not have one bad word to say about the fact that the Hungarian government has destroyed several media outlets over a decade, or that it has forced a university out of the country."[5]

After Tucker Carlson left the stage in Esztergom, I contacted a man named Boris Kálnoky in help me put it all into perspective. The Hungarian-born, former correspondent for *Die Welt* nowadays heads the media school at the Mathias Corvinus Collegium (MCC) in Budapest. This heavily government-backed conservative-minded university recently received $1.7 billion from the Hungarian state, equivalent to 1 percent of the country's GDP. MCC expects to admit 10,000 students over the next three years and expand their presence in Hungary and neighboring countries to thirty-five branches. It was the main organizer of the Tucker Carlson event, which in addition to Carlson's performance consisted of three days of debates, music and lectures. A political festival for conservative Hungarians.

According to Boris Kálnoky, there is "something big going on" in the environment surrounding the Hungarian prime minister. "Orbán is intellectually trying to unite conservatives from around the world. A significant development is that many American and Western European thinkers are realizing that conservatives have lost their traditional bases in Western society: big business, think tanks, even the military. They understand that it would be wise to regard the state itself as the foundation for their ideas, and here they feel that they can learn from Orbán," explains Boris. He elaborates that the MCC has a fundamental principle of being "patriotic, but not ideological." The cultural dominance of the left must be broken— here in Central Europe, the conservatives of the future must be fostered and trained. "Brain drainage has been Hungary's biggest problem for years. Now we want to reverse the trend," says Boris Kálnoky. I ask him whether imposing government-backed, conservative politics into the academic world does not only lead to further polarization ? "Polarization? Nonsense. You cannot create more polarization than we already have in this country. We are just trying to balance the views. If there is anyone who polarizes, it is the liberal left with its empty claims. I am absolutely certain that when they come to power in Hungary—perhaps as early as 2022—they will act in the same way."

A few hours after Tucker Carlson has left Esztergom, the Hungarian analyst Péter Krekó is participating in a political debate with Rod Dreher on one of the other stages of the festival. The theme is the ongoing culture wars of the West. Krekó is a professor of political science and leader of the liberal think tank Political Capital, and he is the only nonconservative debater at MCC's political festival. This he gets to feel onstage, as several people in the audience boo at his arguments and shout "lies" after every other sentence.

The professor still has sweat dripping from his forehead when I meet him after the debate. "Many American conservatives are dazzled by Viktor Orbán's rhetoric. But in my opinion, as was the case with Donald Trump, Orbán does not even believe in his own narrative— he just uses it to overshadow the stories of corruption and autocracy. What is better than having a world-famous man like Tucker Carlson come and pay homage to your narrative? I suspect these people are in fact acknowledging Orbán's autocratic sides," argues Péter Krekó.

The event has now come to an end. Paul Feher and all others are leaving the festival's beautiful surroundings with new memories, but with their worldview intact. What a day in Esztergom.

Chapter Five

Attacking the Opponents

The Man Who Became the Symbol of Europe's Polarization

"Don't let George Soros have the last laugh!" For almost an entire year, that message from the Orbán government dominated the public space in Hungary. Thousands of state-funded billboards and full-page media ads appeared across the country in 2017 and 2018, depicting a smiling George Soros next to the above-mentioned warning. Today, hardly any Hungarians don't know who Soros is and what he stands for. Especially not after a questionnaire appeared in the mailbox of all Hungarian households in 2017. The questionnaire was signed by Viktor Orbán, who in this national consultation called on his compatriots to take a stand on the so-called "Soros Plan" —a divisive plan with the supposed goal of undermining the Orbán government, influencing the decisions in Brussels in a more liberal direction, and bringing more refugees into Europe. At the end of the nationwide anti-Soros campaign, on World Refugee Day in 2018, the Hungarian parliament passed the equally divisive "Stop Soros Law," which narrows the scope for action by NGOs, making their workers liable for jail terms for helping migrants to seek asylum when they are not entitled to it.

But who is he, this heavily debated scapegoat of the Orbán government and other nationalist conservative forces?

George Soros was born in Budapest in 1930 to well-educated Jewish parents. After surviving World War II, he left his homeland in 1947 for England, where he began studying economics and philosophy at the London School of Economics. There Soros met a professor who would be of great importance to his later efforts: the Austrian-born philosopher Karl Popper, author of *The Open Society and Its Enemies* (1945).[1] The encounter inspired Soros so much that he wanted to devote his life to spreading Popper's idea that an open society is a cure for any authoritarian, closed-minded rule.

But in order to become influential, it helps to become rich first. And so George Soros did. As of 2020, Soros had a personal wealth of $8.6 billion and was among the world's thirty richest people. He made his first big earnings in a British bank before moving to New York in 1956, where he established himself as a hedge fund currency speculator, with great financial success and new enemies to follow. In 1992, George Soros became a hated man in many circles because he earned more than a billion dollars by speculating aggressively against the British pound, causing England to step out of the then European Monetary System, the ERM, and devalue the pound. George Soros was later known as "The Man Who Broke the Bank of England."

Along with building up his fortune, Soros began funding NGOs, social projects, universities, and free media outlets in in former dictatorships, including in his city of birth, Budapest, where he opened the liberal-minded Central European University (CEU). Simultaneously with Hungary's anti-Soros campaign, this institution came under threat of closure following legislation pushed through by Orbán's government. Eventually, in December 2018, the university opted to move some of its programs to Vienna.

Clearly inspired by his onetime teacher Karl Popper, Soros founded the Open Society Foundations in 1993, an international grantmaking network offering financial support to civil society groups. Over the years, the network has used Soros's many billions to spread the idea of open society. "Starting the foundation was actually very rewarding, because it gave me a motivation to keep on making money," he once said in a speech.[2]

But just as he has been accused of shady business methods, some have come to consider his foundation's charitable work in the former East-Bloc as such. From the beginning, George Soros was rather controversial. Former Czech leader Václav Klaus has called him a "colonizer." and the political battle between Klaus and Soros forced the CEU to relocate in 1993 from Prague, its initial location, to Budapest. Across Eastern Europe, the general attitude of conservatives and nationalists is that they would do much better without the help of George Soros, who, as they point out, does not have a political mandate to interfere with internal affairs of sovereign nation states. Soros himself describes his project as "political philanthropy." As a consequence of the Orbán government's continuous pressure against his projects, Soros decided to move the Open Society Foundations from Budapest to Berlin in summer 2018.

This decision only confirmed Viktor Orbán in his view that George Soros is a liberal globalist who settles where he wants to without caring about national sentiments or borders. As Orbán said in his speech on March 15 National Day in 2018, "We are fighting an enemy that is different from us. Not open, but hiding; not straightforward, but crafty; not honest, but base; not national, but international; an enemy that does not believe in working but speculates with money; that does not have its own homeland but, rather, feels it owns the whole world."[3]

This was an obvious attack on George Soros in particular, and on globalists in general. Moreover, according to some critics, these exact sentences had an anti-Semitic undertone. One of the critics, Guy Verhofstadt, Belgian leader of European Parliament's liberal group, said that the billboard campaign of a smiling Soros "brings back memories of the darkest period of recent European history. It has an anti-Semitic sentiment, is full of lies, and is unworthy of a democratic European country." In right-wing media outlets, such as *Breitbart News*, some have even linked George Soros to the 1930s prejudice about the Jewish "squid" controlling the world as a puppeteer. Nevertheless, the Orbán government repeatedly rejected all accusations of antisemitism. But Orbán has openly accused Soros of leading a network of EU bureaucrats, including the aforementioned Verhofstadt and the left-wing media, all working to "create a multicultural Europe and condemn Hungary's opposition to it." as he put it in a 2018 radio interview.[4]

As emphasized by the Hungarian government time and time again, George Soros did actually describe how he wanted to bring more immigrants to Europe in the wake of the 2015 migration crisis. In an article published on *MarketWatch* in September 2015, shortly after Hungary sealed its southern borders, Soros wrote, "The EU has to accept at least a million asylum seekers annually for the foreseeable future."[5] Later, however, he downgraded the number to 300,000.[6] After that, Soros remained more or less silent for more than two years, until he had had enough of the hateful campaign against his person. In late 2017, he broke the silence and shared his views on the campaign in the *Financial Times*: "It is a tragedy for Hungary that its government seeks to stay in power through hate-mongering and misleading the population."[7] Soros followed up with a nonverbal response by transferring most of his wealth to the Open Society Foundations—a move suggesting that he would not change course anytime soon despite constant criticism by the nationalist-conservative Right in Hungary and beyond.

All in all, the Orbán government's ongoing crusade against George Soros, and the growing support for the resistance, proves that the rising confrontation between liberals and nationalist conservatives in Europe is here to stay. George Soros symbolizes the status quo of the liberal world order, and thus could be no further from the illiberal, nationalist conservatism that Viktor Orbán stands for.

Is Academic Freedom in Decline in the Old East Bloc?

It was something both researchers and students at the Central European University in Budapest had feared for a long time. Nevertheless, the news hit them as an early April Fool's at the end of March 2017. But it was not a joke: A new amendment to the National Higher Education Law, submitted by the Orbán government, would make it almost impossible for the university to continue its existing operations as a liberal-minded higher education and research institution in Hungary.

The bill was passed in the Fidesz-dominated parliament only a few days later and signed by the Hungarian president. It required non-European universities such as the CEU—which is registered in the United States—to reach an agreement between the government of Hungary and the country of registration. In addition, the bill required universities operating outside of the European Union to have a campus in their other country of operation. At first, it seemed financially and practically impossible for the CEU to set up a campus in the United States on such short notice, but the university did actually succeed in setting up a new campus in the New York State just six months later.

However, despite doing everything necessary to meet the requirements of the new university law in Hungary, no deal was made. Therefore, in December 2018 the university announced that it would relocate the majority of its operations to Vienna, as a consequence of the Orbán government's refusal to sign the agreement allowing it to continue teaching its US-accredited programs in Hungary. Less than one fifth of CEU's programs would remain in Budapest. CEU President Michael Ignatieff, former leader of Canada's Liberal Party, argued, "The law is targeted and discriminatory, attacks the CEU, and is an unacceptable assault on our academic freedom, and the academic freedom of Hungarian higher education in general."[1] Viktor Orbán responded in a radio interview that the CEU had enjoyed an "unfair advantage due to its unclear legal situation." The prime minister continued: "A Hungarian university can issue only one degree, a Hungarian one, yet there is a university that operates in Hungary that issues two degrees, a Hungarian and also an American one."[2]

The dispute led to large protests in Budapest, and hundreds of academics all over the world, including twenty Nobel laureates, spoke out against what they said was an attack on academic freedom—symbolized by the CEU, which is ranked among the top

100 universities in the world in the fields of politics, social policy, sociology, history, and philosophy. More than anything, though, the government's amendment to the law seemed to be a direct attack on the Hungarian-born financier George Soros. He founded the CEU in 1991 as part of his Open Society project, whose stated purpose was, and still is, to strengthen democratic values in those parts of Europe where openness, freedom, and tolerance are under pressure. In the aftermath of communism, after many decades of censorship and state control, there was a strong need in Hungary and the other postcommunist countries to rebuild the study of the humanities and social sciences at universities. The Open Society idea and the founding of the CEU were not only a philanthropic project but also a political one—Soros himself has called it "political philanthropy"[3]—and it was all established on a liberal basis.

On the other hand, Viktor Orbán has declared that he wants to see Hungary develop into an "illiberal democracy."[4] His enemies are liberal intellectuals, and their stronghold is the CEU, which he likes to call "the Soros University."

But the attack on the Soros University was just the beginning. In July 2018, Orbán announced that major cultural and intellectual changes were in the works, adding that his landslide victory a few months earlier was "nothing short of a mandate to build a new era."[5] One of the government's first moves was to stop the financing of gender studies in Hungary. "The Hungarian government is of the clear view that people are born either men or women," the government's chief of staff Gergely Gulyás explained. "They lead their lives the way they think best, but beyond this, the Hungarian state does not wish to spend public funds on education in this area."[6]

Although the expression *társadalmi nem* ("social sex") has been introduced, the word "gender" does not really exist in Hungarian. Using the English word "gender" in the least anglophone EU country can be confusing for many Hungarian people—which may come in handy to those who want to demonize it. In general, Orbán and his supporters want a shift toward conservative values in order to end what they describe as a dominance of leftists and liberals in the arts, the sciences, and education. The move against gender studies was one of the first specific such government policies. Others included a move to reduce the independence of the Hungarian Academy of Sciences in the allocation of public research funding.

To understand these developments, I interviewed Anamaria Dutceac Segesten, professor of European Studies at Lund University in Sweden. She explained that the Orbán government's interfering with academia is similar to the "dictatorial attempts of the past to control ideas and adapt them to the political goals of the regime."

In the communist era, the one-party states of Central and Eastern Europe suppressed academic freedom in varying degrees. Cross-border communication between researchers in many fields was limited, and researchers' participation in international conferences and memberships of professional organizations were subject to considerable state control. Segesten points out that Marxism-Leninism was a comprehensive ideology that included science in its worldview. In Romania, for instance, the situation was extreme. Dictator Nicolae Ceaușescu completely removed psychology and social sciences from the universities, and those who spoke critically against the regime or who had divergent opinions were subject to imprisonment or forced into exile.

In the 1970s and 1980s, a Danish professor of political science, Søren Riishøj, participated in academic trips to Central and Eastern Europe, where he had contact with many of the region's researchers. There were certainly limitations in the social sciences back then, he told me, "particularly the part that dealt with international politics, which is my field. Political science and especially sociology were not in favor in many Eastern European countries, because the research in those fields often fell outside the scope of the Marxist-Leninist doctrine." However, sociology did exist in Poland, and several researchers from that field also became active in Solidarity, the independent Polish trade union founded in 1980. According to Riishøj, Hungary was also a country where academia had certain "breathing spaces," but many sensitive topics were taboo, including the 1956 uprising, the relations with the Soviet Union, and the Warsaw Pact, as well as Comecon, the economic organization of the Eastern Bloc. Riishøj observes that there were some changes after Mikhail Gorbachev came to power in the Soviet Union in 1985, but in the 1970s and into the 1980s it was "tough," as he puts it.

After the collapse of communism in 1989, such severe state control of universities ceased, and many private educational institutions, including the CEU, were founded. Since then, as Anamaria Dutceac Segesten explains, the state's role has been reduced to the task of checking that private education lives up to certain standards. "This does not mean that everything suddenly became much easier for Central and Eastern European researchers," she says. "Instead of ideological or political constraints, they now had to relate to economic constraints." The transition to capitalism meant that public budgets shrank, and higher education and basic research were given low priority due to the poor economies of postcommunist states. From 1989 to the present day, the biggest problem for academics in Central and Eastern Europe has not been censorship, but a lack of funding. Riishøj recalls that after 1989, the spread of academic freedom happened rapidly. "The first years were largely a learning process in which experienced economists, sociologists, and political science scholars from the West acted as mentors and contributed to building up the research areas in the East," he explains.

The Czech cultural historian Veronika Pehe, from the European University Institute in Florence, adds that Central and Eastern Europe has had a strong intellectual tradition ever since the nineteenth century. The region's "scientists and intellectuals are respected and credible characters who should participate in public debates when their knowledge is relevant," she says. However, as elsewhere in the world, the influence of experts and research-based knowledge is declining in Central and Eastern Europe after a decade of increased commercialization and cutbacks in higher education funds. "In a system where researchers early in their careers have to spend most of their time applying for the next limited scholarship, it is no surprise that they cannot find time to actually do high-quality, thorough research. The low status that facts have had in recent years, both in society and in academia, confirms the ongoing distrust in experts and intellectuals," explains Pehe, who believes that researchers in postcommunist countries are facing many of the same challenges as their counterparts in the West.

Søren Riishøj observes that social science has again come under pressure, not only in Central and Eastern Europe but also in the West. Alternatively, Anamaria Dutceac Segesten sees the current pressure on academic freedom in postcommunist countries from a slightly different angle:

> In short, researchers in countries such as Poland, the Czech Republic, and Romania are free to research the topics they want. They are free to express their opinions in the public debate and free to criticize the government's actions throughout the region. In the Czech Republic, Poland, Slovakia, Romania, and Bulgaria, the largest constraints are economic. There is a lack of money to support research in a broad sense.

In Hungary, however, the situation is different, Riishøj adds. There, artists and academics have been under threat, almost ever since Viktor Orbán came to power in 2010. In addition to the recent cases with the attacks on the CEU and other institutions, Fidesz previously accused several government-criticizing academics—including the late Ágnes Heller, one of Hungary's best-known philosophers—for misusing public research funds. The academics were later cleared of the accusations, but all in all it seems like the illiberal direction of Orbán's Hungary has somehow restored the need to control scientists and intellectuals in the country.

Politically, the Polish government has moved in a similar direction but, according to Segesten, without influencing academic freedom:

In Poland, there is an intense public debate on ideological matters related to national identity. For example, with the dispute over a World War II museum in Gdansk, many academics are actively participating in the debate. The contrast to Hungary is striking. Academics who are critical of the Hungarian government's policy and ideology risk being punished by the state power, which is not afraid of using undemocratic methods. This is possible because Fidesz has a supermajority in parliament, making it able to change the laws accordingly. In Poland, the Law and Justice Party does not have the same amount of nationwide support, and the Polish population is almost equally divided between conservatives and progressives.

Segesten's words are echoed by Tomasz Sawczuk, professor at the University of Warsaw and a member of the liberal think tank Kultura Liberalna. He does not want to put all the postcommunist countries in the same basket when it comes to academic freedom: "What is happening in Hungary right now is worrying, but not surprising. I would say that academic freedom in Poland is generally the same as in any other EU country, and so far I have not heard of any direct political influence on academic life in Poland."

Back in Budapest, Hungarian historian András Mink, from the disputed Central European University, agrees that researchers in Hungary are likely to face a difficult future: "Harder times are ahead of us. Perhaps the golden age of liberal progress has come to an end, or at least temporarily halted. But the situation is never hopeless. As a historian, I would argue that the elder generations of the last century had to cope with far more dangerous, fatal, and damaging developments." Mink encourages all researchers who find that academic freedom is under pressure to keep calm and carry on: "Instead of being shocked, the best thing academics can do is to invest more efforts in order to understand why we see a growing distrust in democratic institutions."

Trianon Trauma: A Wound That Keeps Bleeding

"Out with the Hungarians, get out of our country," the Romanian hooligans shouted as they invaded a cemetery in eastern Transylvania, where ethnic Hungarians had gathered to commemorate their fallen heroes of World War I. The episode took place in 2019, and since then furious provocations have been sent back and forth over the 448-kilometer-long border between Hungary and Romania. Viktor Orbán responded by posting a controversial image on social media of a globe in his study showing the old Greater Hungary, as it looked in the country's heyday a century ago. At that time, the Hungarian Kingdom stretched all the way from the coast of Trieste to far into present-day Romania.

"Every nation has a history book in which they themselves are the bravest people," says Leo Constantin Cocos, a middle-aged man born in Romania who knows much about the hatred between the two neighboring nations. He grew up in the west-Romanian city of Timișoara, where as a young man he helped set off the 1989 revolution against the country's dictator Nicolae Ceaușescu. Later in life he got married to a Hungarian woman and he has lived most of his adult life on the other side of the border, in the east-Hungarian town of Debrecen. "Many Romanians perceive Hungarians as if they are living their lives in a distant past. On the contrary, many Hungarians regard us Romanians as some erratic troublemakers who are setting the streets on fire and who are always just following the way where the wind blows," says Leo Constantin Cocos who for years has worked in the region as an independent haulier, driving back and forth across the border every single week.

Viktor Orbán's outdated world map on Facebook was felt as a provocation across the region, including Hungary's neighbor to the southwest, Croatia. "In our cabinets and archives there are numerous historical cards and maps that show our homeland much bigger than it is today (…). Don't share them and put them on your profile— they are not relevant or effective today, and more importantly, they are endlessly annoying our neighbours. Learn from history, but look into the future," wrote Zoran Milanović, the Croatian president, on Facebook[1].

The conflict results from an event occurring June 4, 1920. On this day, after the defeat in World War I, Hungary was ordered by the Allied Powers to hand over two thirds of its territory to its neighboring countries. A decapitation for Hungary, initiated by Western politicians, without any referendum, at the Baroque style château Le Grand Trianon near Versailles in France.

In Hungary, the controversial Treaty of Peace is known as just "Trianon," and these seven fateful letters send a shiver through many Hungarians even to this day. A monument in the border town of Békéscsaba depicting a guillotine cutting Hungary into small pieces embodies this historical trauma. From a Hungarian perspective, Trianon was and is an extremely unfair demarcation, which has turned three million ethnic Hungarians into an outcast, and sometimes oppressed, minority—especially in Transylvania and in the Szekler part of Romania, but also in Ukraine, where 150,000 ethnic Hungarians are no longer allowed to be taught in their own mother tongue at local schools. A dispute which has led to years of diplomatic crisis between Hungary and Ukraine.

According to Viktor Orbán, one can draw direct parallels between 'Trianon' and the current migration to Europe. "They want to take our country away. Not with the stroke of a pen as 100 years ago at Trianon. Now there are those who want us to voluntarily hand over our land to others. Strangers who do not speak our language, and who do not respect our culture, our laws or our way of life," as Orbán put it in a speech a few years ago.[2]

Of course, this is rhetorical twist, but according to historian András Mink, the trauma of Trianon is nonetheless essential in order to understand today's nationalist, EU-skeptical uprising in Hungary. "If you want to trace the roots of the anti-Western and anti-liberal mood in Hungary, then you have to go back to this time in history, to June 4, 1920, when the lesson for many Hungarians was that the idea of freedom and self-determination applies only to the Western powers," explains András Mink.

For a long time, the Hungarian left has stayed passive, while conservatives have managed to spread the narrative of the victims of Trianon. Recently, however, liberal Gergely Karácsony, major of Budapest, tried a new approach. He called Trianon "disgraceful and unfair" because the Western signatories had "trampled on the sovereignty of nations." He added: "If our goal really is to process the past for a better future, we need to address the shadow of Trianon. We must admit that Trianon does not belong to the right. It belongs to all of us, Hungarians."[3] The liberal party DK also recognized the injustice that happened 100 years ago, but urged its Hungarian compatriots to move forward. No successful nation has ever been built on grief and pain, argued party leader and former prime minister, Ferenc Gyurcsány. "Trianon was a polarized event, and its truth depends on the eyes that see. In Romania, the meaning is the opposite than what it is in Hungary. What counts is what the law says about the borders today. The rest is political rhetoric and emotions," he said.[4] Since Gyurcsány was in charge of Hungary in the 2000s, the former prime minister has been heavily criticized for opposing the idea of allowing dual citizenship for ethnic Hungarians—an idea that the Orbán government quickly turned into reality when returning to power in 2010. With the citizenship came the right to vote in Hungary, which more than one million ethnic Hungarians living in neighboring countries have done. Of those, approximately 95 percent have voted for Orbán's Fidesz party[5], which has given the support for the government a significant, but also controversial boost.

Back in the borderland, Leo Constantin Cocos recalls his youth in Timişoara when he lived in the same apartment building as a German and an ethnic Hungarian. The three of them became friends and spoke the same language—Romanian—when they went out together. "Not so anymore. Today, people prefer to speak their own language everywhere, even if they learn both Hungarian and Romanian in school. My hope is that the young generation will start to be more interested in their neighbor's language," says the Romanian. He believes that better language skills can be a shortcut to peaceful coexistence. "We have to open the borders. Not between our countries. We have to open the borders between the mentality of our people," he concludes.

Chapter Six
A Colorful Past

Hungarian Film in the Spotlight

Moving through Budapest is like walking around inside a huge movie set. On an oval-shaped expanse of pavement, close to the buzzing Vaci Street with all its many shops, lies the charming Café Gerlóczy, which in 2005 imitated a Parisian café in Steven Spielberg's *Munich*. Not far from here we have Andrássy Boulevard, a mile-and-a-half avenue resembling 1950s Buenos Aires so much that *Evita* was filmed here in the mid-1990s. And if we cross the Danube River via the Liberty Bridge, we can see Hotel Gellért at the foot of the Buda Hills, an iconic building that gave Wes Anderson visual inspiration for his 2014 film *The Grand Budapest Hotel*.

However, over the past few years, the story of Hungary as a film nation has taken a new, remarkable turn. Now it is not Budapest's role as a backdrop for expensive Hollywood productions, but Hungary's own movie scene that attracts attention and gives international recognition.

The recent success of Hungarian film really took off in 2014, when director Kornél Mundruczó's *White God*—a movie about rebellious street dogs—won the prestigious *Un Certain Regard* award at the Cannes Film Festival. In 2017, Mundruczó was back in Cannes with his tale about a magic migrant, *Jupiter's Moon*, which was nominated for the *Palme d'Or* main prize. Also in 2017, director Ildikó Enyedi won the *Golden Bear* award at the Berlin International Film Festival for her dreamy romantic movie *On Body And Soul*, and

Kristóf Deák won the Oscar for Best Short Film for *Sing* about a competitive children's choir.

The ultimate culmination of Hungary's recent film wave, though, came in 2016 when debut director László Nemes and his Holocaust-depicting *Son of Saul* won first a *Golden Globe* and then an *Oscar* for Best Foreign Film. In total, more than one hundred film awards have ended up in Hungary within just a few years.

Some may find it peculiar that a conservative government with a self-proclaimed illiberal approach can put something as liberal as film culture so high on its political agenda. But the fact of the matter is that the movie industry's recent success is—at least to some extent—due to a very determined effort from Viktor Orbán. The prime minister himself believes that culture—and sports—can unite the nation and help restore ancient grandeur in Hungary. "If we unite our efforts, if there is support, if we have the determination it takes, we can take on any nation of the world, including those bigger than us, be it in the field of science, culture or sport," Orbán said in a 2016 speech.[1]

So far, sports, and in particular soccer, have received the largest portion of government funding in the cultural field. For instance, the government has helped finance the construction and renovation of twenty-eight modern soccer stadiums, despite the fact that relatively few Hungarians care about attending the national league matches. Furthermore, large funds were spent on preparing Budapest to host the 2024 Olympic Games, until the government reluctantly had to withdraw the candidacy in 2017 as a result of a successful anticorruption campaign organized by the opposition.

With the international applause for Hungarian cinema in recent years, the government's commitment to film culture now appears to be the most fruitful priority. Since 2011, the Orbán government has tripled its support for the film industry, and Hungary is now the EU country that spends the most money per capita on its national film industry. In 2016, the industry's total turnover was approximately €400 million.[2]

In order to find out how Hungary came to compete among the world's greatest on the big screen, we must leave downtown

Budapest's beautiful setting and take the S-train to the suburb of Zugló. Here, between communist-era apartment complexes and a newly renovated hospital, is Hungary's national film fund—*Magyar Nemzeti Filmalap*. Since its founding in 2011, the film fund has been the only organization providing financial support to Hungarian films, and its government-appointed leader, the late Andy Vajna, played an essential role in the booming Hungarian film industry. "Making the Hungarian film industry a success is not a sprint, it is a marathon," Vajna explained shortly after welcoming me into his colossal office on the top floor of the film fund's industrial building. "We are not even halfway there." (My interview with Andy Vajna took place in June 2017; he died in January 2019.)

Back in 1956, Andy Vajna fled the uprising in Hungary and ended up chasing the American dream in California. From the late 1970s onward, he established himself in Hollywood as a producer of big budget action films like *Rambo*, *Die Hard*, and *Terminator*. However, with several United States tax cases hanging over his head, Vajna came close to ending up in prison because he was accused of tax fraud and debt in several of his American companies. He decided to return to his homeland, after his close friend through many years, Prime Minister Viktor Orbán offered him a leading position in the newly created national film fund. "Bring Hollywood to Hungary," was Vajna's ambitious slogan upon his return to Hungary. One of his first moves was the implementation of a favorable tax rebate, to make it even more financially attractive for Hollywood crews and others to make their movies in already low-budget Hungary. More importantly, the scheme meant that the revenue, as well as the professional experience with skilled Hollywood crews, could benefit Hungarian film productions.

Half a decade later, the results of Andy Vajna and the film fund speak for themselves: Budapest is today the second most popular European film city after London, and the Hungarian film industry has finally had its global breakthrough with prizes from Los Angeles to Sydney. However, Andy Vajna's entry into the Hungarian film industry can easily be characterized as controversial. The film fund's building in Zugló is located next door to the government-friendly media house *TV2*, which was owned by Vajna. And the roulette table in Vajna's office was a reminder that he also owned the rights to most casinos in Hungary. While criticism came from several sides, for an oligarch in a country with oligarch-owned media, it quickly faded.

Throughout the interview, Andy Vajna was smoking a thick cigar, which made me think of the cigar-smoking Danish film mogul Peter Aalbæk Jensen, but Vajna's voices sounded more like Donald Trump's. He spoke almost in tweets: "Before there was chaos. Now we have created a direction. The goal is to make better movies. Much better movies," So said Vajna, blowing the cigar smoke over to the office bookshelf, on which the block letters HASTA LA VISTA BABY literally spelled out his glorious past as the producer of several Schwarzenegger films in Hollywood. Another of Vajna's initial decisions as director of the film fund was to close all other existing film organizations in the country, thereby streamlining and systematizing support for the Hungarian film industry. "I know there is a difference between arthouse films and so-called audience films." he told me. "But a good movie is a good movie. The hope for the future is that there is only one category, the 'good movie' category. *Son of Saul* was not the typical audience movie, but because of all the awards, it made a wide audience interested. I love that. To make a mix of an art film and entertainment."

Getting more Hungarians to go to the cinema to watch Hungarian films is a big motivating factor for the Orbán government, as it was for Vajna and as it still is for his film fund. In a country with a population of just under ten million, 400,000 moviegoers may not sound like much, but nevertheless, the film *Kinscem* beat the national record in 2017, as it became the most watched Hungarian movie in the nation's cinemas of all time. "We like to beat records, but this is just the beginning," Andy Vajna said when asked about the Hungarian blockbuster, which at the same time was Hungary's most expensive film production ever, with a total budget of more than €10 million. *Kinscem* is about a beloved Hungarian racehorse, Kincsem, during the days of the Austro-Hungarian Empire.

In 2017, the film fund had a total pool of €20 million to be distributed over approximately eighteen Hungarian feature films.[3] One of the highlights, according to Vajna, was the Ferenc Török–directed *1945*, which follows the trail of *Son of Saul* and the World War II theme, in this case zooming in on life in a small Hungarian village to which a couple of surviving Jews return after the war. "We like to make films dealing with historical issues here in Hungary," explained Vajna, who himself was responsible for the production of the 2006 film *Children of Glory*, which commemorates the freedom fighters of Hungary's Revolution in 1956 and the Olympic "Blood in the Water" match later that year.

And there is more to the story than meets the eye on the big screens: In Hungary, there are solid political disagreements over the country's past, including the cooperation with the Nazis during the World War II as well as the decades under Soviet rule until the fall of communism in 1989.

But Andy Vajna did not want to answer the question of whether the government was bent on influencing the narrative of Hungary's variegated history through its state-funded film fund. "I am not a politician," he told me, "I don't want to be a politician. I am not on any side of the political rainbow. I just want to make good movies."

According to Vajna, it is the directors' close collaboration with his film fund that has ensured the success of the recent Hungarian films. The way it works is that a committee of five people early in the process decides whether a project should receive financial support or not. The funding comes directly from the state budget and is only given to film directors who agree to cooperate with people from the film fund's script development department. "This is to ensure that the money is not wasted on projects that are not finalized," he explained, "Our manuscript department ensures that, to avoid finding out too late in the process that a movie is completely unworthy."

This approach has led several of Hungary's most famous film directors to criticize Vajna's business-oriented course. The most obvious critic has been the Béla Tarr, the guru of "slow cinema" and probably Hungarian film's most respected director of all time.

Among other things, Tarr has created stylistic and philosophical masterpieces such as the more than seven hours long *Sátántangó* (1994) and the melancholic mystery *Werckmeister Harmonies* (2000), both black-and-white films. In 2011, Tarr retired after releasing his last film, *The Turin Horse*, another black-and-white drama shot in just thirty long takes. For a few years, Tarr was leading one of the independent film organizations that Andy Vajna closed upon his arrival in Hungary. The famous art film director believes that Andy Vajna's government-supported film fund marks a shift from a cultural to an economic focus of Hungarian film. "The film fund prevents filmmakers from making their own decisions in the process," Béla Tarr, who left Hungary for Serbia in 2014, wrote to me in an email, "If people want to make movies, they have to compromise on the system." In Serbia, he created the Film Factory workshop before going on to become the head of the Chinese film festival First. Back in his Zugló office, Andy Vajna's response to Tarr's comment was even more terse: "Béla Tarr is no longer part of the Hungarian film industry."

Whereas older Hungarian directors such as Béla Tarr, István Szabó, and Miklós Jancsó preferred to make films about historical periods and events from a philosophical point of view, the current generation of Hungarian directors is more concerned with social realism, often focusing on the quirky characters and those at the bottom of society. And although recent movie successes like *Son of Saul* and *On Body and Soul* cannot be characterized as mainstream, they are still a bit more in that direction compared to the antimainstream works of Tarr and Jancsó.

Moreover, a common theme in many newer Hungarian films is the "fear of the stranger": There is the antisemitism against two returning Jews in Török's countryside drama *1945*. There is the suspicion of the local Roma community in Csaba M. Kiss's *Brazilians*. And then there is the distrust toward immigrants in *The Citizen* and *Jupiter's Moon*.

A ten-minute taxi ride north of Zugló, the Origo Film Studios can be found on the edge of Budapest. The large studio has hosted many of the recent Hungarian movie triumphs as well as dozens of Hollywood productions, including Ron Howard's *Inferno* and *Blade Runner 2049*, starring Harrison Ford and Ryan Gosling. The studio's head of production, Mihály Korom, has followed the development closely over the past decade, where Hungary's film scene rose to fame. "The current Hungarian film scene is a very fast moving one," Korom says. "It is a lot more dynamic than before Andy Vajna's arrival. A new genre of movies was born that are easier for people to identify with. We always had great drama directors like István Szabó and Béla Tarr, but we never had, for example, thrillers and historically accurate dramas." He emphasizes the talents of Kornél Mundruczó, László Nemes, and Ildikó Enyedi

The latter's award-winning *On Body And Soul* depicts the prejudices against people who are different by telling the story of a middle-aged man and a younger woman both working in an industrial slaughterhouse on the outskirts of Budapest. By chance, they find out that they dream the same dream every night, and with each of their odd personal traits they try to come closer to each other in real life. Enyedi told me by phone that she is happy for the general success of the Hungarian film scene, but that she does not feel like she is part of any wave or movement. "Making movies is a form of self-therapy. The difference is just that we directors get paid for it … if we are lucky."

That was the extent of Enyedi's comments on the subject, and for their part, Kornél Mundruczó and László Nemes also declined the opportunity for a broader discussion on the current Hungarian film industry.

To be able to draw a general picture of the successful Hungarian film directors, therefore, we must speak to an "outsider" with in-depth knowledge of the country's movie culture: Gabór Dettre is himself a Hungarian-born film director, but has lived abroad for many years, teaching at New York University. Over a Skype connection from Manhattan, Dettre points to successful Hungarian directors' international backgrounds and mentalities as a common feature. Most of them are trained outside of Hungary or have worked on films abroad. Additionally, he points out that Hungary has—with its language unrelated to any nearby linguistic families—always been an isolated island in the European sea of Slavic, Germanic, and Romance-speaking cultures. And this still affects Hungarians today, even when making movies, explains Dettre: "Hungarians have always been—and always wanted to be—unusual. Both to protect their distinctive culture, but also because they are disgusted with the idea of being part of a wave and, not least, by making something that others have done before." He adds, "So, as was the case with older Hungarian films, many of these newer, successful Hungarian films still contain unique experiments and different approaches to the art of filmmaking." He highlights the "shoulder angle" in *Son of Saul* and the flying refugee in *Jupiter's Moon* as noteworthy examples of the unique style.

Gabór Dettre does not believe that the success of Hungarian films is a new phenomenon. But the recognition of it is new, he added. "The successful Hungarian filmmakers of recent years all grew up after the fall of the Berlin Wall. The time after communism has matured them but also made them less courageous." Referring to Andy Vajna's approach of mixing arthouse cinema with box office entertainment, he adds, "They are able to—and willing to—make films that are closer to the mainstream European cinema than their predecessors." With the exception of László Nemes, who was thirty-eight years old when *Son of Saul* was released, the majority of recent years' award-winning Hungarian film directors are closer to fifty. Though Dettre welcomes the recent international recognition of Hungarian films, he notesthat this is the result of a more commercial, less artistic approach. "The Hungarian film scene has renounced parts of its artistic freedom to become more successful abroad. Hungarian artistic sovereignty has suffered damage, but on the other hand, it has become more widely accepted and internationally successful."

Back in central Budapest, the award-winning director Roland Vranik is hanging out at a café in the hip Jewish Quarter. He is back in his hometown after travelling the world for six months with his 2017 film *The Citizen*. Vranik explained that his primary inspiration for the film comes from legendary filmmaker Rainer Werner Fassbinder's *Fear Eats The Soul* (1974), whose portrayal of prejudice and intolerance is also seen in *The Citizen*. Vranik's film centers around the African refugee Wilson, who really just wants to integrate into Hungarian society but is constantly met by conflict from the country's bureaucracy and in his personal, romantic life. "I want to show that refugees are also people," Vranik said, "That they are not dangerous. Here in Hungary, you rarely see anything other than white Hungarians, and that is a problem." He lowers his voice a bit and leans in over the café table: "Especially when politicians play on the fear of the foreigner."

Vranik explains that *The Citizen* just made the cut through Andy Vajna's film fund committee, with three votes for and two votes against. The film focuses on issues such as integration and immigration—issues the Hungarian government sees very differently. "I never really thought that a movie like this could get support from the state's film fund, but I think the government is aware that it should not censor artists like us," he said, noting that he is strongly against Viktor Orbán's migration policy. "It would add fuel to the fire."

In 2016, another Hungarian film director, Gulya Nemes, had to deal with a controversial clip in his political film *Zero*, focusing on topics such as globalization, pollution, and capitalism. The film fund demanded that a clip showing the face of Viktor Orbán on a watermelon next to Vladimir Putin and Silvio Berlusconi be removed. Otherwise the fund would pull the film's funding. In a sarcastic tone, Nemes clarifies: "Well, it was not censorship, because there has been no censorship at all since the fall of communism. So I do not know what to call it." Orbán's face ended up being crossed out in the clip, so no one could see that it was him.

Back at his top-floor office in Zugló during our 2017 interview, Andy Vajna rejected any form of censorship in Hungarian films. "We base our decisions not on a political matter. We base our decisions on talent and story. And the filmmakers are not working in a political environment;, they are working in a very free environment. We don't have censorship. We make movies that are not in the best light if I wanted to promote the country politically. We have total freedom of speech. If we think a movie has a point of view or something realistic to say, and in an entertaining way, then we will make the film. We don't have to go for any kind of government clearances."

Licking the Wounds of Communism

The reporter Zsigmond Gordon steps out on Rákóczi Street. He begins walking with determination through the city while digesting the breaking news story about the death of Hungarian Prime Minister Gulya Gömbös. As Gordon passes a rainy Erzsébet Square, the cold October breeze from the Danube River hits his face, and he continues to the police station on Zrínyi Street. There he stops—and so begins *Budapest Noir*, a best-selling Hungarian crime novel by Vilmos Kondor.[1] The plot takes place in 1936, but the book was published in 2008. The novel is based on an actual historical event; namely, the Hungarian prime minister's death in 1936, which back then became the starting point for some rather chaotic and gloomy years in the nation's history. And the locations in the book are also historically accurate, including the above-mentioned police station in central Budapest.

In Hungary, *Budapest Noir* is widely considered the country's first crime novel success. It was written only a decade ago, suggesting that the genre has had a relatively late breakthrough compared to, for instance, Scandinavia's so-called "Nordic Noir" crime wave. Moreover, the book's translation into English and other Western European languages in 2012 also reveals an increasing interest in the Hungarian crime novel genre outside the country's borders. Gergely Huszti, editor of the Hungarian publisher Libri Kiádo, explains: "A book like *Budapest Noir*, as well as the other books in the series, is quite characteristic of what is happening in the growing market for crime novels from Hungary and the rest of Eastern Europe nowadays. The historical sites and events in the region have enormous significance for how the crime novels are told and unfolded."

Apart from the author's eternally curious reporter Zsigmond Gordon, the city of Budapest is the main protagonist in all of Vilmos Kondor's novels. The detailed descriptions of Budapest illustrate the story—both Gordon's actions and Hungary's decay. This is also the case in the rest of the books in Kondor's series, which unfolds in other fateful Hungarian years, such as 1946 and 1956. Vilmos Kondor's research for the books was made by wandering the streets, following in the footsteps of the fictional Zsigmond Gordon and the factual Budapest. The Hungarian capital has survived several wars and bloody attacks, yet it has remained intact. The streets look much as they did 150 years ago, and many of them still have the same names. For that reason, it was possible for Vilmos Kondor to find out what was in certain buildings sixty or seventy years ago. Police stations, pubs, and law offices. "Old newspapers are a very rich ground for a fertile mind," the Hungarian author explains to me about his research. "One article can lead to a story, and a series of articles can lead to a whole novel,"

Kondor hopes that the geographical and historical background of his novels can contribute to broader public knowledge about the past—and thus make it easier to understand the present. "World War I ended a century ago, yet we still have not been able to talk about what happened. Crime stories set in a historical context might help readers understand that we have the same roots, that we are friends and neighbors and relatives and colleagues of each other, and that the current state of affairs is our own doing."

In Hungary, though, crime novels have not yet initiated any noteworthy debate about the past, according to editor Gergely Huszti. "Even though Vilmos Kondor 'killed' our prime minister on the first page of *Budapest Noir*, the genre has not sparked any debate in this country," he says.

Elsewhere in the region, however, it is a different story. According to Michael Stein, someone like Zygmunt Miłoszewski has had more success in generating a debate: "*A Grain of Truth* has certainly contributed to a controversial debate on Poland's history of antisemitism and its role in the Holocaust. Just as his previous novel, *Entanglement*,[5] which dug into the country's communist past, but with less controversial repercussions." Stein adds, "What might be most interesting now is how writers in increasingly authoritarian countries will reflect the recent developments in their works. There are a frightening number of parallels to the 1930s in today's Central Europe. This is terrible for life, but it could be a fantastic source for the crime novelists, whether they want to set their work in the present or in their nation's past."

The Return of Jewish Life

On a hill in the northeast corner of Hungary, there are grapevines on one hillside and gravestones on the other. If you like, you can interpret this place as a kind of life cycle: Something lush grows from beneath the soil and becomes alive—then eventually, life becomes death and ends up in the same soil. Suddenly, a red Mercedes arrives at the hilltop's parking lot and interrupts my philosophical stream of thought. Out come three men in dark coats and with long-curled side locks, *payos*, appearing from under a black hat. Three generations of a Hasidic family—a young, a middle-aged and an older man. Shortly after, a woman wearing a *tichel* headscarf and a long dress also steps out of the car. She follows the three men while their driver, a Hungarian man, remains seated behind the wheel of his Mercedes. "I'll be waiting here," the driver tells them, but they do not understand his language.

Today, the hilltop cemetery near the village of Bodrogkeresztúr is a place of pilgrimage for Hasidic Jews from all over the world—from New York to Tel Aviv. In the tabernacle temple by the cemetery, where the three men go in to pray, a famous old rabbi lies buried. His name was Rebbe Shaya'la, and he lived in Bodrogkeresztúr in the early twentieth century. At that time, 5,000 people lived in the town by the hill, and 1,000 of them were Jews. From all over Central Europe, Hasidic Jews came to Bodrogkeresztúr to listen to the rabbi's wisdom, even after his death in 1925. The miracles attributed to the rabbi make up three thick books and range from healing sick children to saving marriages. "The soul lives forever, whoever will come to me to pray after my death, I will help," Rebbe Shaya'la predicted.

World War II ended in horror for the Jewish population of Hungary. In 1944, when the fascist Arrow Cross Party had come to power, hundreds of thousands of Jews were deported to the camps up north. The terror of the Holocaust was then followed by over four decades of communist rule, which meant that many of the old synagogues were razed to the ground or used for nonreligious purposes. The demographics of the region changed forever, and for almost 70 years, there were no Jews in Bodrogkeresztúr and the surrounding area. Until a few years ago. Suddenly, orthodox Jews began travelling to the region. In big numbers. "Four or five years ago, a few thousand started coming every year. Today we are no longer able to count the arrivals. I would estimate that in 2019, we topped 100,000 visitors, and even during the pandemic, the numbers have still been in the tens of thousands. They keep coming, more and more of them," explains Mariann Frank, a Hungarian woman from the area. She is not religious herself, but has studied Hebrew and now runs a recently opened Jewish visitor center in the neighboring village of Mád, which is also filled with Hasidic history. When Jews from Williamsburg or Tel Aviv are planning their pilgrimage to Hungary, Mariann Frank is the one they call. "On a busy weekend, more than 20,000 religious pilgrims come to this small village, which has only 1,000 inhabitants. It is obvious that this huge influx presents certain challenges," Mariann Frank points out.

Hasidism is movement within Judaism that originated in western Ukraine in the eighteenth century. From there, it spread rapidly throughout Eastern Europe, including into Hungary. Hasidism is typically known for its religious and social conservatism, where the Hasidic Jews are living closely together and often isolated from the society around them. Many are dressed in distinct religious outfits and speak the Yiddish language. Almost the entire Hasidic population of Eastern Europe was wiped out during World War II, and today, most Hasidic Jews live in Brooklyn and elsewhere in the United States, London, or Israel. It is estimated that there are between 500,000 and one million Hasidic Jews worldwide, and they constitute about 5 percent of the global Jewish population[1].

A five-minute drive from the hilltop, down on the village's main street, you will find the miraculous rabbi's old home. It has been converted into a Jewish house, offering accommodation, free meals and places to pray. The place is buzzing with life. Next door the old synagogue is being restored, and out on the main street, several Mercedes vans are parked. A group of Hasidic Jews who speak only Yiddish is getting ready to jump into one of the vans. They are heading uphill to visit the grave of Rebbe Shaya'la, says a *tichel*-wearing woman who speaks a somewhat broken English. The woman claps her hands: "We have come all the way from Israel," she whoops. In front of the house, I meet a middle-aged American named Jon, who is visiting from Brooklyn. He is Jewish, but not an Orthodox Jew. He has short blonde hair, wearing an ironed white shirt and a *kippah*. "Look around you. People have come from far and wide," he says. Several daily flights are connecting New York, London and Tel Aviv with Hungary—most of them to Budapest, but also some to Debrecen in the east, which is closer to Bodrogkeresztúr. "Some people stay for an extended weekend, others come for several weeks. And then there are some, like myself, who have bought a house in the area. The Hungarian government really supports us," says the American Jew and adds that he has Hungarian roots. "To tell you the truth, we feel more secure here in Hungary than we do in Western Europe."

His view is confirmed by a study by the EU Agency for Fundamental Rights in 2018. European Jews were asked whether they feared violence and harassment because of their Jewish background. In France, Germany and Belgium, about 70 percent responded they did. In Hungary, which was lowest on the list, only one in five Jews had such concerns.[2] Outsiders might think that Hungary wouldn't be a particularly inviting place for Jews to travel—especially not when arriving in large herds as is happening now in Bodrogkeresztúr. For many decades, hatred and distrust toward Jewish people has manifested itself in parts of Hungarian society—from right-wing extremist political statements to government posters with anti-Semitic undertones. The statistics on the issue speak their own, clear language. A report by the Central European University, CEU, estimates that at this very moment, about 30 percent of Hungarians have anti-Semitic views. According to the Jewish organization Anti-Defamation League the share of Hungarians with anti-Semitic views is 42 percent—one of the highest shares in Europe.[3]

So what is the American Jew talking about when he talks about feeling safe and secure here in Hungary? In Western Europe, there has been an "alarming rise in anti-Semitism" in recent years, as the Council of Europe warned in several European newspapers in 2021: "Synagogues have been vandalized and Israeli flags burnt. The incidents present a heightened threat to Jewish life in Europe and Jewish citizens continue to fear for their security."[4]

However, in eastern European countries like Hungary, distrust does not lead to physical assaults or hate crime in the same way it does in Western Europe, Mariann Frank points out. She won't deny that this has something to do with the fact that are very few Muslims here in Hungary. "But for me, it is important to nuance what is actually going on in Hungarian society. Yes, there are certainly genuine anti-Semites here, but in my opinion, no anti-Semitic policy is pursued, nor do I want to call the Hungarians anti-Semitic people. But many Hungarians are distrustful of everything that is foreign to them—Jews, Muslims, black people, foreigners in general. They are against what in their worldview is not perceived as Hungarian," explains Mariann Frank. She elaborates that this view has been widespread in Hungary throughout the years since the Holocaust and World War II. "In other words, these views have spread during the years when there were not very many Jews or other 'foreigners' in the country."

The critically acclaimed Hungarian film *1945*, released in 2017, tells the fictional story of two Orthodox Jews who return home after the war to a small village just like Bodrogkeresztúr. As the villagers hear about their return, rumors begin to swirl: "Have they come to reclaim the properties that we have stolen from them while they were away? Are there more Jews on their way?" A similar mix of skepticism and shame is present in today's Bodrogkeresztúr. A fifty-one-year-old local resident named Annamária says she is afraid that the pilgrimage will turn into a more permanent presence of the Hasidic Jews in her hometown. "They fill in the street scene, but still keep to themselves and do not speak the language. They are buying up the city bit by bit, and we have only seen the beginning," she argues. At the same moment, an elderly Hungarian man is cycling past the rabbi's old house, putting a finger to his temple and shaking his head at the Jews outside. The man's body language speaks for itself. "It's a very sensitive issue," Mariann Frank admits when I ask her about the locals' views of the Orthodox Jews in Bodrogkeresztúr. She tells me about an episode from last year when more than 80 young Hasidic men from Brooklyn wanted to have a big party. One of the town's largest eateries offered them a place to stay, and the young Jews had a great time. But when the party was over, they left the place without cleaning up after themselves, as had otherwise been agreed. Such episodes affect the attitudes in a small village community. "Now people in town call them 'the dirty Jews,' and this is exactly the kind of incident that just cannot happen," says Mariann Frank.

She understands the local concerns that the influx is affecting property prices and the demographic composition of the local community. As a poor town, situated in an isolated corner of Hungary with few opportunities for education and work, Bodrogkeresztúr has been largely depopulated over the last decades. Many houses are empty or for sale, and often it is the Jewish pilgrims who strike a deal. Mariann Frank explains that more than 30 buildings have already been bought over the past year by Jews from abroad. "This has caused prices to rise tremendously. For those who want to sell, it is a good development. But for young couples who want to buy a house here, it is suddenly almost impossible due to the demand and high prices," she says. Every month Mariann Frank get calls from Jews in the United States or in Israel who ask her if she knows about any houses for sale. "They ask me, 'How much, how much?,' and they ask me what a dollar is in Hungarian forints. It can get pretty wild," she says. From her perspective, the influx of pilgrims into eastern Hungary will soon have to be regulated in some way. "To be completely honest, I don't know how this will all end. The Hasidic Jews are really starting to move here and buy even more houses ... Right now, it's spinning out of control, so something has to be done by the authorities," she argues. However, if it is managed well, Marian Frank sees a bright future for Bodrogkeresztúr and the surrounding area. "It could become a culturally revived area where the story of the returning Jews adds another dimension for curious tourists who are visiting the famous wine region here in Tokaj." She adds: "Imagine all these places… For more than 70 years, there were no Jews. Now they are returning. I cannot think of any other places in Europe where Jewish life was removed and where it is now being brought back to life. There is something very beautiful about that," Mariann Frank.

When the Pope Came By

It had already been eventful weeks for Zsuzsa Mézesné Makó, a kindergarten teacher from Debrecen. A few days prior, she inaugurated a new Catholic kindergarten in her hometown, which aims to give the Hungarian children "a spiritual upbringing in a chaotic age," as she puts it. A week before that, she stood in front of Debrecen's Catholic Church, St. Anna's Cathedral, where a bronze statue of Pope John Paul II was erected to commemorate the 30th anniversary of his historic visit to Debrecen. Back in 1991, Zsuzsa Mézesné Makó had been present herself, and even though she was just 10 years old at the time, she remembers how the Polish-born pope diligently tried to unite Hungary's two Christian faiths—the Catholics and the Calvinists—by holding an ecumenical worship service in the city's Reformed Church. "At that time, great changes were taking place in the country. Unprecedented changes that I did not fully understand yet, but I felt it would make a huge difference. We Hungarians felt that everything was getting better and that we could finally become part of the West. It was in this hopeful uncertainty that the Holy Father came to Hungary in 1991. He came to bring us the encouragement of Christ and said: Fear not," explains the now 40-year-old Catholic.

Today, on a sunny Sunday in the early autumn of 2021, Zsuzsa Mézesné Makó is standing on Heroes Square in Budapest. She's accompanied by her husband and their two sons. Along with about 100,000 other Hungarians, the family from Debrecen is waiting for Pope Francis—or Ferenc pápa, as he is called around here—to step up on the podium and share his Christian message with Hungary and the surrounding world. Zsuzsa Mézesné Makó is excited. "I have brought my children with me because I would like them to experience what a tremendous experience such an event can provide; what strength and encouragement a shepherd can provide to his flock," she says.

The pope has come here to conclude the 52nd International Eucharistic Congress—a global convention of the Catholic Church, held every four years. Budapest is hosting for the first time since 1938, and in Hungary, expectations are particularly high, as the event had to be postponed by a year due to the pandemic. Meanwhile, Hungary experienced the highest corona death rate in Europe. For almost two years, many train stations and tram carriages have sported banner ads inviting to "meet Jesus in Budapest." Now the time has finally come; or at least, the Vicar of Christ has arrived. "The pope's visit will be a great sign of hope, after a year and a half of pandemic. A sign of openness, of rebirth, and also a sign that divine providence does not leave us alone," said Péter Erdő, Archbishop of Esztergom-Budapest and primate of the Catholic Church of Hungary.[1]

In 1938, Hungary had been an "island of peace in Europe," as the archbishop stated. Budapest experienced silence before the immanent storm in a world on the brink of a world war. In 1991, again new changes were underway when the Polish pope came by as Hungary struggled with its transition to Western democracy. And now, in 2021, doubt and uncertainty is once again spreading in Christian Hungary. Prime Minister Viktor Orbán is making the role of Christianity in Central Europe a political topic, and he is paying gigantic sums to Hungarian churches, hoping that Christian Hungarians will return the favor with a vote on Fidesz.

Orbán himself is a Calvinist, and as a young politician, he was a strong advocate of secularization. Later, according to his own statements, his political views have become "Christian Democratic." Together with his Catholic wife, Anikó Lévai, the Prime Minister has five children, and family values are a key pillar of Fidesz's political program. "Our task is to defend the great achievement of Christian civilization," Orbán said in an interview with the country's semi-official Catholic newspaper, *Magyar Kurír*.[2] "The world around us is hostile. There is currently a cultural, even civilizational, struggle going on—the struggle for the soul and future of Europe," Orbán said.

According to a 2019 Eurobarometer survey[3], 62 percent of Hungarians perceive themselves as Catholic, while 20 percent have no religion, 5 percent are Calvinists, and 8 percent are "Other Christians." 1 percent are Jews, and 2 percent belong to other faiths, while 2 percent are undeclared.

Another survey, conducted by Pew Research in 2018, showed that just 14 percent of Hungarians feel that religion plays an important part of their lives. 17 percent answered that they attend worship services at least once a month.[4] Furthermore, a study from 2020 compared the beliefs of young Hungarians (aged 15-29) today with those from 20 years ago. Back in the year 2000, 10 percent answered that they were practicing Christians. In 2020, the percentage dropped to only 5 percent. On the other hand, 49 percent of young people today answer that they are religious "in their own way."

In government-critical media, one can sometimes read human interest stories claiming that some Hungarians—and especially Catholics—feel uncomfortable with Orbán's "Christian Democratic" project. Such attitudes, however, most often remain inside the confessional, if you will, as many church leaders have much to lose by publicly criticizing Fidesz. "The government's church policy is definitely polarizing," theology professor David Baer, who has written several books on religion in Hungary, explains to me. "By pulling the churches into a general culture war, Orbán has made the churches into a kind of a political football. It's hard to believe that's good for the churches in the long run," argues the professor.

Hungary's annual church budget of 130 million dollars in 2009 had more than quadrupled to 570 million dollars by 2016, according to the business news site *G7*.[6] In 2020, despite an economy decimated by the pandemic, the churches received a record subsidy of 590 million dollars. Most of that money goes to large construction projects—usually lacking transparency and benefiting government-allied entrepreneurs—but the money also covers the salaries of church officials, both inside Hungary and beyond its borders, as reported by *Balkan Insight*[7].

From David Baer's perspective, the policy to legally privilege churches in Hungary, including the Catholic Church, has largely been co-opted by the government. "Orbán has created a system of public financing of churches that makes them completely dependent on Orban's good will to sustain the majority of their activities," he says, adding that public financing of churches in Hungary is based on a patronage system: "Instead of developing a neutral and transparent system for distributing public support to church activities, most government funding of Hungary's churches is determined through individual, discretionary agreements. This means the government can reward churches and bishops that support the government, and it can withhold money from churches or bishops that are critical of the government," David Baer explains.

As the editor of the Catholic magazine *Szemlélek*, father István Gégény shares his criticism as one of the few outspoken priests: "Political interests are hard to reconcile with Christian values. Priests should preach instead of making politics, and politicians should do politics instead of preaching."[8]

At the Heroes Square in Budapest, Zsuzsa Mézesné Makó, the Catholic kindergarten teacher from Debrecen, is waving at Ferenc pápa when he finally arrives in his open-sided popemobile. She agrees that politics and religion should not be mixed. However, she fully agrees with Viktor Orbán's view that Europe is facing a crisis of values: "Individualism, self-realization, the immodesty of consumer society have turned the hearts of Europeans away from their roots, from Christian values, from God. Some forces are trying to shatter the foundations of Christian society. This will result in more and more vacant lives with desperate people left alone, left behind, and will lead to the emergence of new ideologies. This threatens the family image that is the foundation of society. I fear this re-ideologization of real values, such as goodness, beauty, truth," Zsuzsa Mézesné Makó explains.

For weeks prior to the event, the media had been reporting about a "worldview clash," claiming that the "liberal" Pope Francis allegedly hesitated to meet with the "illiberal" Viktor Orbán in Budapest because of the strict Hungarian migration policy. Nevertheless, in the hours before his arrival at Heroes Square, the pope did meet the prime minister for an extended conversation, joined also by Hungarian President János Áder, and other prominent guests. At their meeting, Viktor Orbán asked the pope to "never let Christian Hungary perish."[9] The prime minister's official gift to the pope was a copy of a 1243 letter from King Bela IV of Hungary to Pope Innocent IV which informed the pope that Bela would strengthen fortifications along the Danube River in Hungary in preparation for a Mongol invasion—evidence of Hungary's long role in preserving Europe's Christian roots. According to the Vatican, the meeting was held in a "cordial atmosphere" and lasted longer than expected.

In his long-awaited speech to Zsuzsa Mézesné Makó and the rest of the crowd in Budapest, Pope Francis does not directly mention the clashing topic of migration. But he urges the Hungarians to be "grounded and open, rooted and considerate"—to remain steadfast in their religious roots, but not in a defensive way that closes them off from the rest of the world: "Religious sentiment has been the lifeblood of this nation, so attached to its roots. Yet the cross, planted in the ground, not only invites us to be well-rooted, it also raises and extends its arms toward everyone," says Ferenc pápa from his stage, suggesting that the cross can be a bridge between the past and the future of Hungarians.

Almost two hours later, Zsuzsa Mézesné Makó waves goodbye to the Holy Father. The historic mass in Budapest is over. She is clearly touched by what she witnessed today, and the moving experience adds a new, unforgettable chapter to her Catholic book of memories. While the crowds around her slowly leave the square, I ask Zsuzsa Mézesné Makó what moved her the most from the pope's speech? "He gave us guidance, encouragement, and lots and lots of love that is directed not only toward Catholics, but to all people. His guidance is essential in this chaotic, values-depreciating, confused world. His encouragement reminded me of the words of his holy predecessor: Fear not! Don't be afraid to swim face to face with the mainstream because that's the right direction," she says. We say goodbye and hope to see each other back in eastern Hungary. "My family and I feel so deeply blessed about today. Now I will take the pope's Christian messages with me back to Debrecen and share them with the children in the new kindergarten."

Chapter Seven
The Silenced Voices—
Should We Be Listening?

The Politically Incorrects
(and the Downfall of the West)

Not many Europeans took notice of a large-scale 2018 conference in Budapest titled "The Future of Europe." No mainstream media outlet outside of Hungary covered the event—except the Danish newspaper I represented—even though there were several notable international personalities among the speakers at the self-proclaimed "politically incorrect" conference, organized by the Visegrád Group and funded by people close to Viktor Orbán, including progovernment historian Mária Schmidt. To conclude the first day of the conference, the organizers had invited Steve Bannon, former advisor of President Trump who'd found a new pursuit coordinating European right-wing nationalist parties. Almost as an aesthetic counterpart to the sloppy-dressed, unkempt American, the final day of the conference was closed by Milo Yiannopoulos, a young British alt-right provocateur, who entered the stage wearing sunglasses, diamond earrings and self-deprecating gay jokes. Despite the divergent exterior of the two media personalities, there was no doubt about their common enemies: Muslim immigrants/immigration, mainstream media, and a "politically correct" left-wing refusing to face reality. Bannon's and

Milo's talk of such clear foes drew applause from the audience in the Hungarian capital.

Bannon, a former investment banker and chairman of Breitbart News, claimed that "Viktor Orbán was Trump before Trump, and that he is now a global political figure who is therefore under severe attack by the mainstream media, the real opposition." Nor did Milo Yiannopoulos shy away from praising Hungarians for their country's political leadership: "Hungary is a strong bastion between East and West, protecting the freedom of speech and the freedom for people to live as they please," he said, adding that he had even practiced correctly pronouncing the original first name of Orbán's political enemy number one, the Hungarian-born financier György (George) Soros. In a harsher tone, Yiannopoulos continued, to applause, "We must hate the politically correct, who make it difficult for ordinary people in Western Europe to celebrate the birth of Jesus Christ without fear or shame. We cannot stand the politically correct saying that it is offensive to say "Merry Christmas" and that we should say "Happy Holidays" instead. We must hate the social justice warriors, the progressive left and the broad network of globalists who preach diversity and tolerance, while in fact they are only provoking disharmony," he said, receiving applause from the audience.

If you disagree politically with Bannon and Milo, it will be easy to dismiss their arguments as "alt-right hate speech." That is, if it wasn't for a much wider recent trend dubbed the Intellectual Dark Web (IDW). The term symbolizes a much broader movement of popular intellectuals and media personalities, who through online channels such as YouTube and podcasts put forward similar arguments defending freedom of speech and speaking against identity politics and the politically correct "snowflake culture" on the left.

A third speaker at the conference in Budapest was Douglas Murray, a British journalist and the author of *The Strange Death of Europe*—one of Viktor Orbán's favorite books on Islam and immigration.[1] Douglas Murray appears at the top of the IDW movement's website, and in his conference speech, he summarized what he sees as the main problem with today's political correctness:

The idea that all opinions can only be placed on a Right-Left scale is perceived by many not only as unnecessarily divisive but also as an ignorance of the real polarization that exists in our society today. The real split does not take place between people who believe two different things on a given topic, but between those who are for *or* against even allowing an honest discussion on the subject. [...] We have to be able to ask the necessary, deep, and painful questions. With a more rational approach to Europe's challenges, one would not only realize what we are capable of, but also what we are not capable of.

The conservative Englishman believes that immigration from the Muslim world should be stopped if Europe wants to avoid "committing suicide."

That last statement on immigration is something that even many of Murray's fellow members of the IDW movement would disagree with, including more progressive thinkers such as Steven Pinker and Dave Rubin. Pinker is a Harvard professor in psychology and author of *Enlightenment Now*, a book on humanism and the continued progress of our globe.[2] Rubin hosts his own intellectual YouTube talk show, *The Rubin Report*, on which he discusses current topics with different guests.[3] Despite their different political standpoints, Milo, Murray, Pinker and the other IDW members share at least three common views, according to *New York Times* op-ed writer Bari Weiss, who has analyzed the movement: "First, they are willing to disagree ferociously, but talk civilly, about nearly every meaningful subject: religion, abortion, immigration, the nature of consciousness. Second, in an age in which popular feelings about the way things ought to be often override facts about the way things actually are, each is determined to resist parroting what's politically convenient. And third, some have paid for this commitment by being purged from institutions that have become increasingly hostile to unorthodox thought—and have found receptive audiences elsewhere."[4]

One of the most famous figures of the Intellectual Dark Web is Jordan B. Peterson—Canadian professor of psychology, best-selling author, and Internet phenomenon. Peterson has about a million viewers watching each of his online lectures on YouTube, and more than fifty million people have clicked on his videos. Most of his lectures focus on philosophical topics, but Peterson manages to communicate his knowledge with well-argued passion and with references to religion, science, and history. He even attempted to explain the IDW trend on a YouTube talk show with Russell Brand, a British comedian and leftist activist also said to be part of the movement: "What unites the people who are loosely connected to this forum is that they have serious conversations with an audience they respect. It is a consequence of the fact that the public conversation in mainstream media and in the political life has become unbearably superficial."[5]

Peterson experienced his worldwide viral breakthrough in January 2018 after an interview with him by Britain's Channel 4 journalist Cathy Newman appeared online. The main topic was a proposed new piece of Canadian legislation requiring citizens to use gender-neutral pronouns when referring to transgender people. Peterson insisted on his right to freedom of speech, and after many attempts to problematize his attitude, Cathy Newman eventually fell into the trap: "Why should your right to freedom of speech trump a transperson's right not to be offended?" she asked. And Peterson replied: "Because, in order to be able to think, you have to risk being offensive. Look at the conversation we are having right now: You are certainly willing to risk offending me in the pursuit of truth. Why should you have the right to do that? It has been rather uncomfortable." Subsequently, the clip went viral with millions of views on YouTube, and in the comment section below, thousands of viewers expressed appreciation that someone had struck back against the "politically correct" arguments.

In the wake of Peterson's success with his YouTube lectures and best-selling self-help book *12 Rules for Life*,[6] he went on a global lecture tour from the United States to Australia. On a few occasions, Peterson was joined on stage by other IDW members, including Sam Harris, an American critic of religion, and the aforementioned

Douglas Murray. The title of their joint lecture was "Winning the War of Ideas."

The debates on political correctness also reached Denmark, where historian Henrik Jensen is following the movement. He thinks that the criticism from IDW members and others is a justified one: "Identity politics and political correctness are basically an illustration of the polarization taking place in our democracy and society," Jensen observes. "Freedom of speech is at stake here, and when someone claims that you can only say something about a particular identity group if you are a part of that group yourself, then the necessary democratic conversation erodes."

He emphasizes that the criticism of identity politics does not exclusively belong to conservative circles—it can also be found among many center-left intellectuals, including political scientist Mark Lilla, who in his book *The Once and Future Liberal* argues how identity politics can damage the culture of democracy.[7] "These people strike a chord and lead a reasonable rebellion against some tendencies dating all the way back to 1968," Jensen states, addin:

> However, the problem with calling the Intellectual Dark Web a "movement" is that it is lock, stock, and barrel. For example, I view Steve Bannon and partly Milo Yiannopoulos as being on a political mission by using negative, hateful energy to change the political discourse. So, while some of these people criticize the political correctness of the Left, we should remember to be critical of the right-wing agenda as well.

Another debater following the IDW trend is Danish-Iranian Jaleh Tavakoli, a former local politician on the far left who broke with the Enhedslisten party in 2010 after disagreements on the issue of political Islam. Tavakoli puts herself on the same page as Ayaan Hirsi Ali, the Somali-born Islam critic, who is also part of the IDW network with her large following on social media. Tavakoli explains:

These intellectual voices are saying what ordinary people are thinking. They are being discarded by the mainstream media because they are talking about sensitive issues. But the problems do not go away just because you don't talk about them. Therefore, it is good to see that so many people follow the movement on the internet, where these issues are thoroughly discussed,

Like Bannon and Milo—the two keynote speakers at the conference in Budapest— Tavakoli supported Donald Trump during the 2016 US election campaign. Why? "Because he was a better choice than Hillary Clinton, who was the personification of the nice but false political correctness in the West. If we do not get a mainstream debate putting an end to this, then we end up with politicians like Donald Trump. "And"—so Jaleh Tavakoli concludes—"maybe that is what is needed for people to finally wake up."

Roma Minority Takes Control of Its Own Destiny

The outskirts of Vámospércs—where the town's paved road ends and turns into a dusty dirt road—is where the Roma live. There are many of them in very little space. Typically, families of eight to ten children and adults live in dilapidated houses along the dirt road. Their laundry hangs on wobbly wooden fences, plastic garbage has been dumped all over their front yards. Around 15 percent of the 5,000 inhabitants of Vámospércs are Roma. They speak the same language, but live differently and separately from white population generally thought of in Hungary as "ethnic Hungarians" (i.e., ethnic Magyars), people whose skin color, anyway, suggests the possibility that some of their ancectors had arrived in the region during the Magyar conquest of the Carpathian Basin in 896—never mind that in fact the ancestors of many "ethnic Hungarians" were ethnic Slavs or Germans in a past much more recent than the migration of the Roma into the region some 600 years ago.

The Roma go to separate schools, they have worse healthcare, they rarely share workplaces with their Hungarian compatriots, and many of them do not work at all. The Roma are living on the outskirts of town—on the outskirts of society.

In that way, Vámospércs resembles most other small towns in northeastern Hungary, one of the poorest regions in the European Union. Here I meet the political activist János Szűcs, who is currently driving around in his blue BMW to visit all the local Roma communities. He is himself a Hungarian-born Roma and comes from a poor family in the region. After graduating in England with internships in the European Parliament and at the US Embassy in Budapest, he has now returned to his home to make a difference: "The demographic development strengthens the Roma," he says, "because they account for a growing part of the population, but this is not reflected in the national policy. And thereby the minority stays poor, uneducated, and in bad health conditions."

According to a report from the University of Debrecen, there are almost one million Roma in Hungary.[1] In only three decades from now, the number is expected to double: Up to two million, or approximately one third of the Hungarian population at that time. Similar projections are seen in other Central and Eastern European countries with large Roma minorities. During communism, most Roma in Hungary had jobs, but since the fall of communism in 1989–1990, unemployment has multiplied and their living conditions have deteriorated year after year. Roma families account for an increasingly large part of the Hungarian population, simply because they have far more children than ethnic Hungarian families.

Neither changing Hungarian governments nor multiple EU projects have so far managed to improve conditions for the Roma. And for more than a decade, the so-called "Roma situation" has boiled over more than once in Hungary: First, around 2008 and 2009, when a group of Hungarian neo-Nazis committed a series of bestial murders on six innocent Roma, including one child. Then, during the past decade, as the ever-growing poverty among Roma people has combined with age-old racism by some members of the majority population, including politicians,, who are apt to call the Roma "wild animals" and "parasites." All these factors are not exactly helping in a time where human rights and solidarity for minorities are already under pressure all over Europe.

János Szűcs, the touring Roma activist, says it has gone too far:

> The social situation is getting worse and many of the Roma children are starving. And the prejudices and racism against Roma people are becoming more and more widespread. But political condescension is not the way to successful integration. We have been here in Hungary for six hundred years, but we can no longer wait for others to do something for us. For years, it has been discussed whether these problems are the Roma's own fault or whether it is society's fault. It's like discussing whether it's the mother's or the child's fault that the child is not doing well in school. We have to move on and take the matter on our own.

His political mentor is István Kamarás, a much-experienced and well-known politician in Hungary who is also Roma. A few years ago he founded the Opre Roma Party to come to the aid of the Hungarian Roma. Back in 2010, Kamarás was a member of the Christian Democratic People's Party (KDNP), which had come to power in Hungary through a coalition deal under which it supported Viktor Orbán's Fidesz in parliament. But after realizing that the prime minister's announced plans to lift the country's Roma community out of poverty turned out to be "empty promises," Kamarás moved to Canada in 2011 to get away from Hungarian politics and come up with an alternative strategy. When he returned to Hungary a few years later, he was ready with a solution. He explains to me, "The last resort to a decent life for the Roma is the establishment of an autonomous province in northeastern Hungary."

If the plan becomes reality, it will be the first time in world history that a Roma minority will get its own territory. Obviously that would be a critical moment, but how did it even come so far that the idea of independence is now being discussed as "the last resort" among Roma activists? Inspired by autonomous provinces in Europe, including Catalonia and South Tyrol, Kamarás gives a few reasons:

> Because Roma are being discriminated against in every aspect of society. Because Roma do not have a tiny chance of being politically represented on a national level. Because there is no possibility of proper higher education and better healthcare for the Roma. Because society's racism against the Roma has proved impossible to reduce. There is nothing else to do than to work for independence. In such a political and administrative situation, we would finally have the opportunity to shape our own lives.

The initiative of territorial independence for Hungary's Roma population is connected directly to the demographic change in the country's northeastern region. Here, the proportion of young people belonging to the minority is 40 percent, and the number is increasing. If this demographic development continues, the current minority will end up being a majority in the region. "It will take many decades to solve the problem," says Kamarás, "but if we do not start now, we may never be able to solve it."

However, the road to independence seems to be long and bumpy for the Hungarian Roma. First, István Kamarás and his supporters must collect at least 200,000 signatures to start a referendum. With almost a million Roma in Hungary, doing so is technically possible, but the minority's low level of civic engagement would make this another challenge. And before it even comes to that, a potential referendum must first be approved by the National Election Office, which seems unlikely to do so as long as Viktor Orbán is leading the country. Lastly, territorial discussions are historically a very delicate topic in Hungary. This is due not least to the massive territorial loss suffered by Hungary after the Trianon Treaty in 1920, in consequence of its defeat in World War I.

Kamarás is fully aware of the many obstacles on the road to independence, but he explains that the self-government initiative should be understood as a long-term plan:

> We know very well that the plan to implement an independent Roma province is currently far into the future. But we want to start a healthy debate, so this idea can be implemented as smoothly as possible at some point within the next twenty to twenty-five years. If we do not ultimately achieve independence, I think it will lead to some kind of civil war situation in this region.

Back in Vámospércs, János Szűcs asks the local Roma people what they think about the idea. A young woman, surrounded by some children playing along the dirt road, immediately backs up the proposal. She tells us that there are ten family members living in the house. Between them, they have less than €300 to live on each month. "I would definitely support the creation of a Roma province here in northeastern Hungary," the woman says. "It could improve both the material and the moral parts of our lives." On the other side of the dirt road, a middle-aged carpenter in blue overalls takes a short break from work renovating an old house. He is more skeptical about the autonomy plans:

> I fear that it would create even more suspicion and hostility between Roma and non-Roma. We are mutually dependent on each other. If we were not here, the Hungarians would not have anyone to build their houses, and conversely, we would not have any work. My wish is a form of peaceful coexistence, although it may be unrealistic.

However, to János Szűcs, it is just a matter of time before a consensus will develop among the Roma about autonomy. The envisioned autonomous province would welcome not only Hungarian Roma but all Roma wherever in Europe they are today. "We are one big family," says Szűcs, "sharing the same ethnicity, culture, and destiny. If we get independence here in Hungary, the door will be open to all Roma."

In the end, I ask János Szűcs what it would mean for him if Roma would ultimately get autonomy. "This would mean that we would get our own home," he replies. "Without a home, you just live in other people's yards and you never feel at home." Szűcs starts up his BMW and drives back on the dusty dirt road, on toward the next small Roma town on the map.

Welcoming Nationalists from all over Europe

In recent years, a significant number of opinion makers on Western Europe's Right have settled in Hungary, establishing ideological platforms free from the political correctness and liberal values in their homelands. They originate from countries like Sweden, Germany, France, and Great Britain, and they have moved to Budapest in order to turn the public conversation in Europe to the right and to spread the ideas of the Alternative Right to the rest of Europe. One of the most prominent such nationalists is Daniel Friberg. Some years ago, he moved to the Hungarian capital, and since then, the Swedish businessman has been the driving force behind the Arktos publishing house, the RightOn think tank, and the news site *AltRight.com*. Friberg has cofounded all of these platforms that, he says, all "present alternative ideals to the liberal modernity."

His ideas are in line with Viktor Orbán's nationalist conservative values, and that is exactly what appeals to the exiled Swede. He highlights other Central European countries as places with similar approaches, including Poland, where he also regularly resides. "There is way more freedom of speech in Hungary and in Poland," Friberg says. "Here, they do not have the phenomenon called political correctness like in Sweden, where you are forced to avoid discussing important issues like immigration. That situation does not exist here in Hungary, as far as I am concerned." He adds that throughout the former Eastern bloc there is low crime and minimal immigration:

All these countries have the same advantages. Partly, this is due to the dominating politics in the region. It is quite conservative. They do not accept migration and they reject the EU's refugee quotas. These are still white countries, they are still Europe. I feel more at home in these countries than I do in Sweden, or in Belgium or London, for that matter. The trend is caused by the horrible multicultural experiments in the West, which for many people have resulted in making their home countries inhabitable. I prefer to be around people who are similar to me, even those who speak a Slavic language or Hungarian.

Friberg is backed by his compatriot Kent Ekeroth, who moved to Hungary in early 2018. Ekeroth is a former member of the Swedish parliament for the far-right party Sweden Democrats and has close ties to the anti-immigration media network *Avpixlat*. "Hungarians have understood the problem with immigration," he says. "They stand firm on their principles and they do not back down to the left-liberals of the West." In a reference to Viktor Orbán's family policy, under which women with more than two children receive additional benefits, Ekeroth adds, "And not only that. The Hungarian government has also realized that [the nation's] demographic composition is essential for survival [...] and calls for the Hungarians to have more children."

According to many observers, the political messages of the governments in Hungary and elsewhere in Central Europe are increasingly attractive to right wingers in Western Europe. And the immigration skepticism in Hungary and Poland has indeed aroused resonance among many in the so-called Old Europe and in Scandinavia.

However, the political language seems more brutal in Hungary than in, say, Denmark, just as talk of "Christian values" is more pronounced. Countries in Western and Northern Europe are more used to immigration. Central and Eastern European countries are by contrast more used to emigration, and they see immigration as a threat. Furthermore, the fact that these countries are still struggling to integrate their own Roma minorities only makes their anti-immigration sentiments even stronger.

All this have helped bring forward Viktor Orbán as the spokesman for an alternative, illiberal Europe—especially when dealing with the migration problem. In Germany, among those people who defend Christian values and the nation state, Viktor Orbán is considered a hero. And many Germans have actually settled in Hungary, though not all of them for political reasons. An increasing number of Germans have settled in quiet countryside surrounding Lake Balaton—a recent development observed by Zoltán Kiszelly, political analyst at Kodolány János University. "This 'reverse migration' is not a mass phenomenon, and Germans are not arriving by the thousands as they are in Mallorca," Kiszelly explains in an interview with *Le Figaro*,[1] adding that Hungary is attractive for conservatives who care especially about church and family. "But it is a trend worth watching," he adds. "Since the migration crisis, Hungary's image has improved—not in the media, but among many European citizens. You feel like you were in Germany thirty years ago. And as long as Orbán is in power, you can rest assured that you will not come across too many migrants." The Lake Balaton area's growing German community even has its own newspaper, *Balaton Zeitung*. Restaurant menus are in German, and supermarkets like Aldi or Lidl stack shelves with those Germans' favorite products. "Things like these make Hungary a wonderland for some people," the political analyst points out. "If you already wanted to leave Germany, Hungary is a good choice."

In his annual State of the Nation address in 2017, Viktor Orbán highlighted migration as a subject that will remain on the Hungarian agenda for years to come. Orbán reasoned that the clear majority of Hungarians had made it clear in a nationwide referendum that Hungary will not bow to international pressure in setting its policy on this front, referring to the Hungary's rejection of the EU's refugee quotas. He added, "Of course we shall let in genuine refugees: Germans, Dutch, French, and Italians, terrified politicians and journalists who here in Hungary want to find the Europe they have lost in their homelands."[2]

That particular sentence did not go unnoticed in right-wing nationalist circles around Europe. "I saw the speech," says Kent Ekeroth, who agrees with Orbán. "The real refugees are fleeing multiculturalism, and they are doing the right thing before they can no longer live in peace in Western Europe. We have only seen the beginning of this kind of emigration among educated, ordinary Westerners who are moving to responsible countries like Hungary."

For his part, Daniel Friberg also supports the Hungarian prime minister's approach:

> Many of the those moving to Hungary are resourceful people with their own businesses and a certain flexibility. They can take care of themselves. From my point of view, that is quite beneficial for the eastern countries: To have people with good resources who bring with them capital into the country. This is the type of migration one would want, and I understand why Viktor Orbán brings it up. People just want to leave in peace.

A number of British nationalists have likewise made their mark in the debate, including the former leader of the British National Party, Nick Griffin, who resided in Hungary for several years. In March 2017, he co-organized the "Stop Operation Soros" conference focusing on the Hungarian-born financier George Soros, the liberalism-promoting scapegoat of the Hungarian government and other nationalist conservative circles. On that occasion, Griffin told the Hungarian news site *444.hu* that within six months he intended to move permanently to Hungary: "There is a small but quite rapidly growing Western European emigré community growing up here, so there are people from France, Britain, Sweden. I know there are several Germans who are probably moving here very shortly."[3] Griffin continued: "What I see is Hungary becoming a pole of attraction for a strand of thought within the whole of Europe, and further afield,

actually, of people who do not want to commit civilizational suicide."
He confirmed that Hungary's political scene, together with relatively
cheap living costs, is what draws nationalists from all over Europe.

"I am glad that Hungary is taking a leading role in saying that
Europe's sovereign nations have not only the right to live freely but
also to survive on the long run," said Griffin. "Hungary actually does
something about it over a wide spectrum—from building a border
fence to giving young Hungarian families support for large families.
It indicates a government that does not want to commit national
suicide and it is refreshing for people coming from the West,"

A member of the European Parliament until 2014, when he was
thrown out of the British National Party, Griffin went on to found
the likewise far-right British Unity Party.

In the early summer of 2017, Viktor Orbán's vow to grant
political asylum to "true refugees"—those from Western Europe—
was put to the test. The situation culminated in May that year, when
a German man named Horst Mahler arrived in Hungary. He was
eighty-one years old at the time, and his hope was to achieve political
asylum. In an online statement, Mahler wrote, "On May 12, 2017, I
asked the leader of the Hungarian nation, Viktor Orbán, to grant me
asylum in Hungary as a politically persecuted person."[4]

In his youth, Horst Mahler had cofounded the far-left militant
group Rote Armee Fraktion, but during a prison stay he made a
political shift and became a neo-Nazi. This ultimately led to a new
imprisonment in 2009, when he was sentenced to ten years for
encouraging racism and hatred against German immigrants and for
denying the Holocaust. Due to health problems, Mahler won early
release in 2016, but because he continued his propaganda against
Jews and immigrants, he was ordered to serve the rest of his sentence.
However, instead of returning to prison, Mahler fled to Hungary,
where he was arrested in the western city of Sopron and sent back to
the German authorities.

Before he disappeared behind the bars of a German prison cell,
the Holocaust denier explained his long-time disgust for Jewry.
"Sending me back to prison is part of the enemy's attack on our very

existence," he was quoted in the German media. "All I can say is that this is not about my own personal destiny, but concerns the fate of the German people, that of all Europeans and of Christianity, and the fate of the white race. They want to wipe us out to transform us into an unidentifiable biomass. That is their plan."[5]

Consequently, it seemed obvious that Orbán's "welcoming" statement had backlashed and that the Hungarian authorities had had enough of far-right extremists from other European countries entering Hungary's "safe space." Around the same time Horst Mahler was forced to return to Germany, Nick Griffin and his British companion Jim Dowson—another far-right politician based in Budapest—had both been expelled from Hungary. According to the official statement from the Ministry of the Interior, the expulsion was due to the fact that "for some time the government has been concerned about extremists from European countries moving to Hungary."[6] Furthermore, it was explained that the decision to expel Jim Dowson happened on the recommendation of the Anti-Terrorist Center, TEK, which stated that Dowson "poses a threat to the national security of Hungary."

Nevertheless, in November 2018, the Macedonian ex-Prime Minister Nikola Gruevski—an longtime political ally of Viktor Orbán—was suddenly granted asylum in Hungary, having fled a prison sentence in his home country. Orbán responded to the criticism of the decision in a radio interview, saying that the people who attack Hungary for granting asylum to Nikola Gruevski were "identical" to those people and organizations that support migration.[7] Despite all the controversy, people who concur with Hungary's views can be found all over Europe today.

Chasing Rainbows

The word "homosexual" originates from Hungary. But when the Hungarian journalist Karl-Maria Kertbeny died in Budapest in 1882, he had no idea of the impact his contribution to the dictionary would later have. He invented the term "homosexual," thereby laying the foundation for the understanding of sexuality and gender identity—issues that dominate the public debate more than ever today.

In the intellectual Central Europe of the nineteenth century, though, gender identity was not something that people talked about openly. Already back then it was a highly taboo subject, which was lacked a common name. Until Karl-Maria Kertbeny introduced the word *Homosexualität* in 1868, in a handwritten letter to the German queer activist Karl-Heinrich Ulrichs. The following year, Kertbeny repeated his description in a printed pamphlet, in which he also described heterosexuality for the first time—and two now forgotten terms to describe masturbation and bestiality: monosexual and heterogenit.

Karl-Maria Kertbeny himself lived a life as a closeted gay man with changing addresses in Vienna, Berlin, and Budapest. In his youth, he had a friend who kept his homosexuality a secret as well, and who felt suppressed by society because of his inclinations. The burden eventually led his friend to commit suicide, and the tragic event motivated Kertbeny to dedicate the rest of his life to fighting for the rights of sexual and gender minorities. He took the first small steps and provided the gender minorities with a common language so that they could begin to express and organize themselves. Today, Kertbeny's contribution is widely recognized by the LGBTQ community, and at the annual Pride in Budapest, many people visit his grave at the city's famous Kerepesi Cemetery.

Young Ákos Modolo knew nothing about this when he found out, in 2008, that he was gay. At the time, he was fourteen years old and lived with his Catholic family in the provincial town of Mezőberény, in the southeastern corner of Hungary. In this conservative town with just 10,000 inhabitants and few cultural activities, the church was the place where young people met, and he still has many childhood friends from his days in the Catholic Church. In his teenage years in Mezőberény, Ákos Modolo lived with a secret that he did not dare to share with either friends or family. "I didn't come out as a homosexual until I was nineteen, so for five years it was only people on the Internet that I talked to about it," he says when I meet him in Budapest, where he has lived ever since he moved away from home eight years ago.

In elementary and high school, Ákos Modolo didn't know anyone who openly identified as LGBTQ. "It held me back that I felt that the community around me knew little about it. My conservative family, those in church, even my friends. At the same time, I myself needed more information and more confidence. But as a homosexual, you see no role models—at least, I didn't see any role models in my small community." He elaborates: "One thing is to see, for example, that there are people in Budapest or abroad who openly live as gays. I did not experience that in my hometown. I knew that there were homosexuals in other places, but in my own community, things felt very different."

As a gay teenager in the Hungarian province, he felt alone, but his faith helped him feel less lonely. It was especially inspiring to read in the Bible about Jesus, who surrounded himself with people living on the edge—those who were not accepted by the rest of society. "In the Bible, I read that Jesus reaches out to those who are oppressed or disadvantaged," says Modolo. "In those moments, I came closer to God, closer to Jesus. It was a religious experience for me. Many Christian people may feel that it is sinful and shameful to be gay, but I have never felt that way. I have always felt that God loves me for who I am."

In June 2021, several years of anti-LGBTQ campaigns by Viktor Orbán's government culminated in a new controversial law. To begin with, the intention of the so-called "antipedophilia" law was to increase the punishment for child abuse, and in its original form, the bill was also supported by the opposition, including the progressive left-wing parties and the conservative Jobbik. But a week before the voting in June 2021, the government suddenly changed the text of the law to include paragraphs on homosexuality and gender identity, thereby, at least indirectly, linking pedophilia with homosexuality. The final text of the law states that the law must "protect young people under the age of 18 from pornography and content that promotes or portrays a gender identity at variance with gender at birth or promotes or portrays gender reassignment and homosexuality."[1] This means that in Hungary, for example, homosexuality must not be mentioned if minors potentially could be confronted with the information in, say, classrooms, children's literature, or TV commercials.

"After utility prices and the migrant issue, we will be right for the third time. We will protect our children. Hungary will be the first country in Europe in which we stop aggressive LGBTQ propaganda at the school gates," Orbán said in his October 23 speech on the 65th anniversary of the 1956 Hungarian uprising in 2021—referring to the main election topics that secured victory for his Fidesz party in the two previous elections.[2]

Since the 2018 parliamentary elections, the law was the fourth in which the Orbán government restricts the rights of LGBTQ people. In 2020, the country's constitution was amended to underline that in a family "the father is a man and the mother is a woman."[3] Earlier that year, the parliament first approved a ban on legal gender reassignment and then a ban on adoption for same-sex couples.

As usual, the people of Hungary are divided in their attitudes toward the subject. According to an IPSOS survey from 2021, 46 percent of Hungarians believe that marriage between two people of the same sex is okay, and 59 percent support the right to adoption for same-sex couples.[4] Among Fidesz voters, only 20 percent are "strongly accepting" of homosexuals, while 54 percent of Fidesz voters "reject" them, according to a 2021 analysis by Závecz Research.[5] When it comes to transgender rights, 41 percent of Hungarians do not believe that their country should do more to support or protect transgender people, as shown by an earlier survey by IPSOS from 2018.[6]

The first person Ákos Modolo shared his secret with was a female friend from his senior year at the high school back in Mezőberény. Shortly thereafter, he moved 200 kilometers west to Budapest in order to study language and education at ELTE University, without informing anyone from his hometown that he was gay. Neither friends nor family—and certainly not his grandparents, with whom he otherwise had a close relationship, but who were Fidesz voters to their bones and very backward-looking when it comes to sexual orientation and gender roles, as Ákos Modolo puts it. "In Budapest, I saw people talking about homosexuality in a natural way, whereas in my hometown it would have been like saying I came from another planet," he explains.

After getting used to life in the capital, Ákos Modolo started volunteering in the "Getting to know LGBTQ people" programme, which had been running in Hungary since the turn of the millennium. In his role as facilitator, he joined other LGBTQ volunteers and went to schools, universities, and companies to talk about life as a homosexual and the consequential challenges in Hungarian society. "It may sound like a paradox that I started each session by saying 'Hello, my name is Ákos and I'm gay,' while my parents were still unaware of this. But I needed to feel that I could talk about it openly, because for five years I did not talk to anyone about it. Just saying it out loud is a profound feeling," he says.

Since the summer of 2021, Ákos Modolo and the other volunteers have not gone to any Hungarian school anymore. Before the antipedophilia law was introduced, they met young people from the age of fourteen and shared with them what it means to be LGBTQ. The new law now prevents them from meeting with students under the age of eighteen. Moreover, even educational institutions with students older than eighteen refuse the invitation from the LGBTQ volunteers. "The law is very vague and it does not say exactly what the punishment is. We have talked with teachers, and many of them are afraid of the consequences if they allow our presence. They fear layoffs or criminal charges. It causes self-censorship," Ákos Modolo argues about the controversial law.

He explains that the "Getting to know LGBTQ people" sessions were always unique, depending on the questions posed by the young people. A typical activity was a kind of role-play, where half of the class had to identify as homosexual and the other half as heterosexual. "Then we gave both groups a scenario where they had to consider whether they wanted to talk to their parents about their love life or not. There were always some good discussions, and the students were brave in sharing their reflections. The most important thing was to have an open debate, without prejudice and taboos," explains Ákos Modolo.

I ask him if he can understand why some parents don't like their fourteen-year-old child to be introduced to that kind of thinking at school. "I think a lot of conservatives in Hungary think: 'It's fine if you're gay, but it's your private problem, so don't talk about it.' Many conservatives say they are tolerant, and argue that the progressives are the ones who are politicizing gender ideology. Therefore, the conservatives feel that they must respond to it, also politically. That's why we are seeing this polarization," says Ákos Modolo, who is currently also a board member of Szimpozion Egyesület, a Hungarian NGO working for LGBTQ rights.

Even in Western Europe and in the United States, one can easily find people who feel that gender ideology and rainbow flags are taking up too much space in politics and public life. According to Ákos Modolo, these attitudes are due to misconceptions and stereotypes: "A lot of people think that if we talk too much about being gay or transgender, then people become gay or transgender. Not because they were born that way, but because they heard about it in school, on Netflix, or on YouTube. This is absurd and based on a heteronormative perspective," says Ákos Modolo, referring to the Orbán government's image of the family as consisting of a man, a woman, and lots of children.

A year after moving to Budapest, he finally had the courage to tell his parents that he was gay. His mother especially had a hard time dealing with this. "She was not happy about it, but she wasn't against it, either. She told me that she already knew it to some degree because I had once written some homosexual poems that she had found without telling me. In the beginning, it was difficult for her because she did not want to tell anyone—and definitely not my grandparents."

In 2019, it created outrage in the LGBTQ community and other parts of Hungarian society that the speaker of Parliament, László

Kövér—a prominent member and cofounder of Fidesz—at a press conference compared homosexual adoption with sexual abuse of children: "Morally there is no difference between the behavior of pedophiles and the behavior of someone who demands the right of homosexual adoption," Kövér said.[7] "In both cases, the children are treated as objects, luxury goods, mere tools for gratification, for self-realization," the Fidesz politician stated. But Kövér added that he didn't want to make generalizations, because not all homosexuals are like that: "A normal homosexual is aware of the order of things in the world and knows that he was born this way, he became like this. He tries to fit into this world while he doesn't necessarily think he is equal."

Ákos Modolo remembers the statement as a political turning point in the Orbán government's view on LGBTQ people. "Until then, Fidesz had wanted to appear relatively moderate. But when one of the country's most important politicians says something like that, it means something. I think the government was looking for a new enemy to blame—a new topic to distract the Hungarian public. From that moment on, we knew we had become 'the new migrants,'" says Ákos Modolo about the role as a scapegoat in the Hungarian public.

Just as Fidesz was constructing a new political bogeyman out of the country's "dangerous gender ideologues," a flamboyant scandal hit Orbán and his party in the back, like a moral boomerang. By December 2020, most of Europe was in lockdown because of the Covid pandemic, but in Brussels, a group of men ignored the restrictions and partied in an apartment above a gay bar. Allegedly, the outlaws were also having group sex. In an attempt to escape a sudden police raid, one of them climbed down a drainpipe on the outside of the building, wearing nothing but a backpack containing ecstasy pills. The fleeing man turned out to be József Szájer, a longtime EU parliamentarian for Fidesz, and one of the main architects behind the government's own anti-LGBTQ policy. The story went viral around the world, and Fidesz was naturally accused of huge double standards.

Today, Ákos Modolo smiles when he thinks of the colorful scandal. The government has already gone too far, he argues; nothing can surprise him anymore. However, he is also aware that double standards—without comparison whatsoever—can be found in his own environment as well. For example, when it comes to the discussion about the Hungarian minorities in those regions that Hungary lost with the Trianon Treaty after World War I. "Since moving to Budapest, I have spent a lot of time in liberal circles. For me, national identity is very important, perhaps because I come from the border country. But when I talk to my liberal friends about Trianon, most of them say: 'Ah, come on, just forget about it, why are you still talking about that?'" Modolo's point is that progressives and liberals always say that they care about minority rights and that they will always stand up for the oppressed. "But we must remember that these people who live on the wrong side of the border, they have been oppressed through the past century, and in some places they still are. It's just as important to stand up for *their* rights as for everyone else's. So I say to my liberal friends: 'If you say that we must fight for the rights of the minorities, then why not the national minorities?' They can never really respond to that."

Ákos Modolo's grandparents have lived their entire lives in Mezőberény. At one time, his grandfather was a local city councilor for Fidesz. Everyone in their surroundings has a conservative worldview. "In a small conservative community, you see no LGBTQ people living an open and happy life. When I see it through the eyes of my grandparents, it seems obvious that you would rather try to be straight. Otherwise, the gossip stories start to wander, and it can be very hurtful for the person in question."

Nevertheless, a couple of years ago, his grandparents suddenly discovered what he had kept hidden from them for over a decade. On live television, they saw their grandson attend the Pride March in Budapest with a rainbow-colored umbrella over his shoulder and holding hands with another man. "It was a shock for them because it came out of nowhere. But their response was less aggressive than

I had feared, and they started asking me questions about it all. They still love me very much, but I know it's incredibly hard for them to accept. For instance, my grandmother asked me if I would participate in conversion therapy in order to become heterosexual. She didn't want to force me to do this—she did it with good intentions, as an offer to help me."

He adds that many conservative Hungarians still perceive homosexuality as a fetish or as an extravagant behavior. It requires persistent education and sharing of information to change that image. "With the rainbow colors, we are just trying to say that LGBTQ people also want a family. That we are as diverse as heterosexual people are. That there are also conservative LGBTQ people. We just want to spread the message that your sexual identity does not define who you are as a person."

With the Hungarian government's introduction of controversial anti-LGBTQ laws, the fight that Karl-Maria Kertbeny initiated in Budapest more than 150 years ago does not seem to be over just yet.

Chapter Eight

Under the Carpet

Corruption in the VIP Stands

In Hungary, there are hundreds of small villages of this size. A few thousand inhabitants, a dusty main street with a post office, a butcher and a vegetable market where older ladies are buying paprika for the evening meal, followed by an endless row of almost identical bungalow houses, also known as Kádár cubes because they were built during the era of communist leader János Kádár. But here in Felcsút—Viktor Orbán's childhood town, where he still resides—there also is a state-of-the-art football stadium. A gigantic cathedral in organic architecture with a capacity of twice the town's population. After the stadium was completed in 2014, it was hailed as one of the world's most beautiful football arenas.[1] "The idea of the architect, Imre Makovecz, was that it should feel like standing on an idyllic lawn in the middle of a forest," says Emese Tóth, a middle-aged woman employed by the club to show visitors around the stadium. The tour continues upstairs at the VIP lounge where trophies and medals won by legendary footballer Ferenc Puskás fill up several glass cabinets. Both the stadium and the club are named after Puskás, although he had no particular connection to this part of Hungary—in his career he played for the Budapest club Honvéd and later Real Madrid. But his name is familiar to many football fans, and it can attract valuable attention to the small village.

"You know, Viktor Orbán has only good intentions," the tour guide suddenly says about the football-obsessed son of Felcsút, defending Viktor Orbán preemptively, should the visitor group ask any critical questions. Moments later, we reach the stadium's exit, and right there, on the other side of the street, is Viktor Orbán's house. If you look over the brown wooden fence, you can see a Hungarian flag hanging by the front door. There is no more than 20 meters from the arena to his house. "My wife does not like the stadium," Orbán once told *The Guardian*. "She says it ruins the view from the kitchen window."[2]

Hungary hosted the pandemic-postponed EURO 2020 football championships, eventually held in the summer of 2021. The Hungarian team played two of its group matches at home in Budapest, an hour's drive from Felcsút. In the capital, the country's recently built national stadium—also named after Puskás—has space for more than 68,000 people. As the only country in the European tournament, Hungary played both of its home games in front of a fully packed stadium—all the ten other host nations had limited the capacity due to pandemic restrictions. Skeptics blamed the Orbán government for putting the prestige and grandiosity of being a EURO 2020 host above everything else—and that during a pandemic in which no other country in the world had had more corona-related deaths per capita than Hungary.

"Orbán and his people use football as political propaganda," argues Bence Bocsák, a sports journalist who in his spare time has played alongside the country's also quite football-obsessed foreign minister, Péter Szijjártó. "He was not very good, but he still appointed himself as the team captain. It was quite comical," says Bence Bocsák. He points to the fact that many of Hungary's hospitals are dilapidated and that they have been for a long time. Nonetheless, the Orbán government has spent public funds on building thirty-two new—but not very well-attended—football stadiums all across the country. Also, billions of forints were spent on getting the

Olympics to Budapest in 2024, until the government reluctantly had to withdraw its candidacy due to corruption allegations from the opposition. "Corruption has been present throughout society ever since the communist days. So it's only natural that it also hits football, but Orbán's party has taken corruption to a new level," claims Bence Bocsák, mentioning a handful of different club owners, all of whom have close ties to government politicians.

This brings us back to the football cathedral of Felcsút. While it can sometimes be complicated to explain to ordinary people why Hungary is highlighted as one of Europe's most corrupt countries, the stadium in Orbán's front yard can help illustrate that story. "Concepts such as the rule of law and democratic responsibility can make some people yawn. But if you go to Felcsút and watch football—or rather watch what happens in the VIP stands—then most people can see what's really going on," explains Miklós Ligeti, a lawyer working for the NGO Transparency International. In the report "Corruption in Sport,"[3] Ligeti has contributed to documenting the government's fraud with public funds spent on building brand new football stadiums like the one in Orbán's village.

Most of the 3,500 seats remain empty during home games in Felcsút, except in the VIP section. It is usually packed with people from near and far, including Orbán himself and his entourage, while expensive German car brands dominate the parking lot outside. Of the sports associations to which all Hungarian companies can anonymously donate an annual tax deduction, Orbán's local club is by far the one receiving the highest amount. These covert transfers have been criticized by the EU's antifraud unit and ruled illegal by Hungary's own Supreme Court.[4] The club owner is Orbán's childhood friend, Lőrinc Mészáros. A man who, over the course of just a decade, went from being an independent gas fitter in Felcsút to being Hungary's richest man. This happened primarily thanks to the award of a large number of EU-funded construction contracts worth billions of forints. In fact, companies belonging to Mészáros won public tenders worth €826 million in 2018 alone, 93 percent of which came from European Union funds.[5] Mészáros himself has said that three factors were crucial for his rapid rise to prosperity: "God, luck, and Viktor Orbán."[6]

Viktor Orbán's unconditional love for the sport comes from his own past as a semi-professional football player. In his first reign back in 1998-2002, Orbán still played on the local Felcsút team on the weekends. His first trip abroad as Prime Minister was to the World Cup final in Paris in 1998. And he enjoys telling an anecdote from the time when he was called out to the sideline during a training match in 1999 because Bill Clinton was on the phone. "Football," the prime minister has said, "is a strange combination of being free and being a soldier. You have to be in the squad, but it's also creative. Because this is the dilemma of all modern societies: to be organized and to be free. On the pitch I can find it, in politics it's more difficult."[7]

These days the game on the pitch has become serious for Hungary's powerful leader. Sport is now big business—whether the Hungarians want it or not. Since Orbán returned to power in 2010, state investment in sports has increased by 400 percent. The sports sector today accounts for more than half of the tax money spent on the entire social sector in the European Union's second poorest nation. Orbán has never responded directly to the allegations of corruption. However, when asked at a press conference in 2020 why the EU antifraud unit has found more irregularities in Hungary than in any other member states, the Prime Minister replied: "I simply do not accept the premise that Hungary should be more corrupt than, say, Austria or Germany or Denmark."[8]

Hungary's football heydays in the 1950s came to an abrupt end. In 1954, to everyone's surprise, Ferenc Puskás and the other "Mighty Magyars" lost the World Cup final to West Germany. Two years later, the Hungarian uprising was brutally crushed by the Soviet regime, forcing Puskás to leave his homeland in favor of Spain's national team.

Nowadays, politics is also mixed into Hungarian football, explains Bence Bocsák, the critical sports journalist. "For instance, the Orbán government used the case of Hungarian goalkeeping coach Zsolt Petry from Hertha Berlin to justify its own political agenda," he argues. Petry had been fired by the German club for his "homophobic and racist remarks." The Orbán government, on the other hand, claimed that the case was an example of the West's "dangerous political correctness."[9]

Another example can be found in the reaction to the recent trend of footballers kneeling before a match to show sympathy for the fight against racism. The football federations of Hungary and several other Central European countries believe that such political markings should be kept off the field. At a press conference in 2021, Orbán called the action a "serious moral burden": "As Hungarians, we do not feel this burden. We were not slave owners and we cannot help those who were. It is useless to take this burden onto the football field,"[10] he said.

The Hungarian goalkeeper Péter Gulácsi also ended up in a controversy of a similar nature because he publicly supported so-called rainbow families. According to Bence Bocsák, there is a lot of apathy in Hungary when it comes to political markings—whether you support Orbán's ideas or not. "Fortunately, football provides an opportunity to seek refuge, especially in difficult times like this. We Hungarians are patriotic because we have been oppressed for so long. We are proud of our historic endurance. Of course, there are mixed views on how to best restore the strength of the past on the football field, but in the end, it is the players down on the turf—not the politicians up in the lounge—who have to prove their worth," he concludes.

Surrounded by Dishonesty

When Sándor Léderer grew up in 1990s Budapest, he often saw his classmates cheat at school. They brought handwritten notes to the exam, even though it was forbidden. The cheating continued when he came to university, and the young Sándor found it wildly unfair. Many like him had to make a hard effort to get reasonably good grades in an honest way. While others could just cheat themselves into even better grades and jump the queue of good future jobs. When he was eighteen years old, Sándor bought his first car—an old, used Lada. At the auto workshop where his new car needed to be fixed, he wondered why the mechanics offered him a shorter waiting time for the repair if he paid them some extra money under the table. He had experienced something similar from a doctor when his grandfather was in the hospital. "I only really understood what corruption was when I became an adult, but in reality I have been surrounded by it all of my life," says Sándor Léderer, now an adult in his late thirties.

In the years after Hungary joined the EU in 2004, he discovered how local politicians in Budapest began selling old apartment buildings at low prices to foreign investors. These immediately tore them down or renovated them completely. Many of the residents could no longer pay the expensive rent of the new houses, so they were forced to leave. "I didn't think this was very nice of the local politicians to allow this to happen. But when I investigated the case, it turned out that the local politicians actually got something in return from the investors. Cash, luxury trips abroad and other secretive favors. I wanted everyone to know these stories. When people have to vote in an election, they should know which politicians are corrupt," says Sándor Léderer.

After discovering the injustices, he joined some other activists and founded K-Monitor in 2007—an organization fighting corruption. In the beginning, they collected all sorts of corruption stories from Hungary and put them in a database on K-Monitor's website. They categorized each of the cases and the persons involved in them, and thus made it easy for other people to search the entire database on their own. Up through the 2010s, technology developed at a rapid pace. This provided the activists with new opportunities for data analysis. With the help of hackers and computer geeks, Sándor Léderer and his colleagues have now developed various data-mining algorithms that automatically create an overview of the huge digital datasets. Their discoveries include everything from local politicians' shady construction plans to the government's misuse of the funding that Hungary receives from the EU.

K-Monitor has coded a number of "red flags," which are raised by the system if an EU-funded project has only had one tender. So instead of citizens or journalists having to manually search through all the databases themselves, they are now able to—thanks to K-Monitor's technology—find possible corruption cases without spending weeks of research hoping for a lucky strike. In other words, they can avoid wasting time and instead use their energy to investigate matters in depth and spread the story out to more people. "Technology makes it really, really easy to create transparency, which is the primary antidote to corruption. Transparency means that things cannot be hidden. This means that information on how public spending is done has to be available for the public to see it. It means that decisions must be presented openly so that you can keep an eye on what your government or politicians are doing," says Sándor Léderer.

Research shows that corruption increases the inequality within a society when rich and resourceful people with good connections benefit at the expense of the poor and powerless. Because by definition corruption takes place in secret, it is difficult to measure. According to the World Bank, the global cost of corruption is estimated to be at least $2.6 trillion, or 5 per cent of the global gross domestic product (GDP). In total, businesses and individuals pay more than $1 trillion in bribes every year.[1] However, there are huge differences in the extent of corruption between different countries. Every year, the organization Transparency International estimates how much corruption takes place in each country. There is relatively little corruption in New Zealand and in Nordic EU countries such as Denmark, Sweden and Finland—nations where people have great trust in each other and where the tradition of democracy is long—while most corruption occurs in poor developing countries such as Somalia, Yemen and Venezuela. In the EU, the most corrupt countries are located in the old Eastern bloc, with Bulgaria and Hungary topping the list.[2]

Over the past decade, Sándor Léderer has experienced that his homeland has become more and more corrupt. Hungary has slipped from a 46th place in 2010 to a current place as number 70 in the world on Transparency International's corruption index. K-Monitor and other organizations have uncovered hundreds of the corruption cases, many of them including people close to Viktor Orbán. The worst consequence for Orbán and his corrupt circle of friends has been a bad reputation in government-critical media and in parts the population. This has proven to be insufficient to stop the corruption. Transparency International's website states that corruption will continue as long as there is a perceived advantage in fraud or bribing. "One of the main reasons for ongoing corruption is that the risk of being discovered is considered to be less than the chances of a great reward."[3]

The question is: when Hungary just keeps slipping further down the corruption index, do K-Monitor's persistent attempts to expose corruption even matter? Do they even make any difference at all? From Sándor Léderer's perspective, it does seem a bit demotivating sometimes. But he thinks long-term. With time, technology will only improve the quality of the tools used for revealing fraud and bribery, he points out. "Technology also enables people to learn about public institutions. It helps them to get engaged and to make their opinion known. Do you want a park or a playground or a football stadium in your local area?" He elaborates: "As soon as you feel a sense of ownership in your local area, you will no longer ignore corruption. You will not let the politicians take your hard-earned tax money and spend it on corrupt projects. You want your money to be spent in a proper way instead of ending up in the pockets of certain politicians," says Sándor Léderer.

The biggest problem, he adds, might be that most people are not even aware of their own corrupt tendencies. This is why K-Monitor developed a digital personality test named K-Teszt.[4] Everyone— from young schoolchildren to experienced politicians—have the opportunity of answering some basic questions about their own behavior in some given everyday scenarios. At the end of the test, you will get a result that shows you how prone you are to being corrupt. "The test reveals some of the psychological mechanisms behind corruption, namely how selfish you are. Do you mostly care about yourself and your closest circle of friends, or do you also care for the wider society? Your country, your hometown, your school. Your behavior determines whether you want to accept corruption or whether you are ready to fight it," explains Sándor Léderer about the popular personality test. He hopes that K-Teszt and the other technological tools can at least contribute to a change in mindset, in order for young people to become active citizens who hold their politicians accountable. "Hopefully, it can help make it much harder to be a corrupt politician in this country in the long run," concludes Sándor Léderer.

Last Stop on the Silk Road

He had come a long way, Wen Jiabao, China's prime minister at the time. From Beijing to Budapest, the distance is 7,300 kilometers, and his arrival marked the first Chinese state visit to Hungary since the collapse of Communism. It was a hot summer day in June 2011. So hot that the limousine picking up the prominent guest at the airport probably had the air conditioning turned on at full throttle, all the way to the center of Budapest. In any case, the radio's volume was turned up to maximum, because during the 30-minute drive from the airport something strange happened. Something that listeners of *Klasszik Rádió*, a private-owned Hungarian radio station, would never forget. Suddenly—exactly during the time when Wen Jiabao sat in his limousine—the usual classical European string music was replaced by traditional Chinese chime bells, and an unknown host spoke mandarin between the tunes. "We were told by our superiors that we should insert this Chinese program in order to show the man in the limousine that even on Hungarian radio you can listen to broadcasts from China," explains Viktor Hankó, the editor of *Klasszik Rádió* at the time. The story of a Hungarian radio station that suddenly plays Chinese music may help to symbolize the growing influence of China that Hungary has experienced in the decade following Wen Jiabao's state visit.

The Chinese imprint culminated during the corona pandemic, when Viktor Orbán's government, among other things, imported overpriced respirators and Chinese vaccines of dubious quality, as well as initiating the construction of a controversial Chinese elite university in Budapest.

While the world economy lost 42 percent of global foreign investment during the 2020 corona crisis, Hungary increased its foreign investments by 140 percent.[1] And China was the key player, says analyst Julia Lakatos. She is the international head of the think tank Center for Fair Political Analysis in Budapest, and, according to her, the pandemic was an occasion for Prime Minister Orbán to connect even more closely with the powerful and wealthy Chinese investors. "Orbán is a pragmatic who does not believe as much in the future of the West as many in the West still do. He predicts a multipolar world where a country like Hungary will have to look both to the East and to the West if it wants to secure its future. The question is just when economic trade ends and when political influence begins," says Julia Lakatos.

In times of upheaval, during which the European Union regularly criticizes the Orbán government for violating the union's values and principles, and even threatens to cut support for Hungary, Orbán himself seems quite firm in his standpoint: "If the EU does not want to pay, then we will turn to China," the prime minister has said on several occasions.[2]

In New York resides the historian Mátyás Mervay. He was born and raised in Budapest, but he has researched Chinese history from a Western perspective for years. He has worked as a lecturer at Nankai University in the metropolis of Tianjin. He is currently writing a PhD in Asian-European history at the New York University, while regularly trying to nuance the perception of Hungary and China in both Hungarian and English-language media. "Orbán's so-called

'Eastern Opening' is something that the Hungarian government is criticized for, but often for the wrong reasons," argues Mátyás Mervay. What the real critique should consist of, we will get back to, but first and foremost, the historical context is important to understand. "You have to remember that when Eastern countries like Hungary want to open up to the lucrative Chinese market, it is something that Western countries have been doing since the 1980s," he says. After the fall of the Berlin Wall, nations like Hungary were busy with their Euro-Atlantic integration into NATO and the EU, and they didn't have an eye for the rising East-Asian giant until the 2000s. "Since then, the eastern countries in Europe have tried to prove themselves as good students by more or less copying the trade that the West had built up with China," the historian explains.

Another important point is the fact that Hungary's opening toward China was not initiated by Viktor Orbán, but rather by his political opponents on the center-left, who were in power throughout the 2000s. As early as 2003, Péter Medgyessy, socialist PM at the time, traveled to Beijing. "Actually Orbán was a fierce critic of both China and Russia before coming to power in 2010," Mátyás Mervay points out. In the years prior, Orbán had even had the Dalai Lama come visit and he gladly supported the Tibetan cause. Politically, Orbán was more interested in Singapore than in China in those years, but ahead of his election victory in 2010, he changed his mind completely. Launching his "Eastern Opening" in 2011, Orbán said, "We are sailing under a Western flag, though an Eastern wind is blowing in the world economy. Our sails must be turned accordingly."[2] At the same time, Hungarian politicians on both sides feared the consequences of the financial crisis on the European economy. This was another reason to strengthen Hungary's ties with China and thus reduce dependence on Western markets. "Across party lines, Hungary's political-economic elite has agreed to benefit from China's global economic success for almost two decades. Today, the right and left disagree on *how* to deal with the influence, but it is not exclusively Fidesz who wants Chinese money in Hungary," Mátyás Mervay points out.

Nevertheless, I have attempted to create a list of political and economic deals that Orbán's government made with China over the past few years. The first one that comes to mind is the Golden Visa Program. In 2012, Hungary launched a special visa program making it possible for non-EU foreigner to buy access to the country in different ways. Since then, approximately 20,000 foreigners were granted residence permits and Schengen visas in Hungary, including more than 16,000 Chinese citizens. The Hungarian National Security Service had only 30 days to clear the security of these individuals, and there are several examples of criminals and spies affiliated with Putin's Russia or al-Assad's Syria who have arrived in Hungary.[4]

The next example is the Hungarian real-estate market. Prior to the 2012 visa program, the share of Chinese buyers was just 10 percent. In 2019, a total of 3,000 properties were purchased by foreigners in Budapest—more than half of them Chinese. According to a source in Hungary's National Security Committee, "there is a traceable pattern: that real estate is often bought at unrealistically high prices in downtown Budapest."[5]

A third example is a much-debated railway project in the region. Chinese loans equivalent to $1.9 billion will finance a new railway between Budapest and Belgrade, the capital of the likewise China-friendly Serbia. The railway connection will be the last stop on China's Silk Road into the European Union. Furthermore, the Alibaba Group, China's largest e-commerce platform, chose Budapest Airport as its regional hub in Europe. The company ensures that at least 2.5 million goods will be transported from China to Hungary by plane every month. "This number will increase considerably in the future," said József Kossuth, head of Budapest Airport, in July 2021.[6] And then there is Huawei, the Chinese telecommunications giant, whose largest supply center outside of China is now situated in Budapest. Hungary also uses Huawei's technology for its super-fast 5G network, while other European countries and the US rejected such use for security reasons.

During the Covid-19 pandemic, Hungary-China relations became even closer. Early in the health crisis, the Orbán government bought 16,000 ventilators from China. Many other EU countries also bought Chinese ventilators, but according to *Direkt36*, Hungary paid "more than four times more per respirator than the other EU countries." By the spring of 2021, more than 30,000 Hungarians had died with coronavirus, making Hungary the country with the highest death rate in the world at the time. Finally, as a last example, Hungary was the only EU country to approve the Chinese Sinopharm vaccine against the coronavirus, and Viktor Orbán himself chose to get a jab of it. Hundreds of thousands elderly Hungarians did the same, but several studies have questioned its effectiveness, as many did not produce any antibodies from it.

What can the EU and the West truly criticize the Orbán government for with regard to its close relations with China? According to Mátyás Mervay, the main criticism should be that Orbán's "Eastern Opening" strategy has not really worked in practice. In fact, in several cases, the Chinese deals have resulted in setbacks for the Hungarian government, not least when it comes to the overpriced ventilators and the low-quality vaccines as mentioned above. He portrays the "opportunistic Orbán" as someone who is not afraid of reaching into the opponent's political toolbox whenever he finds it convenient, and this is not a new trick, according to the historian. In fact, this political balance dance between East and West has existed in Hungary since at least the 1940s and is now tradition in Hungary. "In 1942-44, Prime Minister Miklós Kállay balanced between the Allies and the Axis Powers, and through the 1970s and 1980s, General Secretary János Kádár balanced between the Cold War West on the one hand and the Soviet Union on the other," Mátyás Mervay explains.

But according to the historian, Orbán sometimes miscalculates this act of balance. This happens, for instance, when the EU issues moral condemnations of China, while still holding on to its economic interests in Beijing. "When the EU in joint declarations condemns China's handling of, say, Hong Kong, Orbán uses his veto power and singles out Hungary as the only country not supporting the statement," says Mátyás Mervay. Such declarations typically deal with soft issues that the EU has no real power to influence or change. In other words, these are moral statements, and even the Chinese know that they have no real-world consequences. "But in those cases, I think Orbán exaggerates the importance of showing his own unreserved support for Beijing. China has not asked for any veto sympathy from Hungary," Mervay says. On the contrary, Orbán's veto just increases the publicity of the criticism of China when one member state blocks it. "Paradoxically, shouting 'veto' backfires for Orbán, and he hardly needs more criticism in this aspect," says the historian.

If you take the metro southwards from central Budapest, you will reach the Ferencváros district. In one part of the district—in an overgrown industrial area that stood abandoned for years—the local roads were recently given new names. Usually, such an event lacks any broader news value, but these road signs and the story behind them ended up going around the world.

If you turn right along the area's construction fence, you will reach Dalai Lama Road, and if you continue around the corner, you can choose to go down Free Hong Kong Road or Uyghur Martyrs' Road. All the street names are a signal of protest and solidarity with the victims of human-rights abuses by China, and the man behind the idea is Gergely Karácsony, liberal Mayor of Budapest. In April 2021, leaked documents showed that Orbán's government was approving the construction site to turn into a giant campus with 6,000 students from a Chinese elite institution, Fudan University. The original plan, however, had been to build student housing for Hungarian students, but the leaked document—obtained by investigative journalists at *Direkt36*—showed that the government now rather planned on spending $1.8 billion to build a Chinese university. This is more than the overall amount Hungary spent on higher education in 2019.[7] The Hungarian state would finance around 20 percent of the project from its central budget, with the rest of the money provided by a loan from a Chinese bank. According to the documents, the construction would be carried out primarily by Chinese construction companies and made from Chinese raw materials.

Fudan University is sometimes called the "Yale of Shanghai," but it is also known for educating the future leaders of the Chinese Communist Party. Moreover, the university has launched a special spy-training program and in 2019 removed the term "freedom of thought" from its charter.[8] Gergely Karácsony did not like the idea of Fudan University in his city, and he said the following when he made the new street names official in June 2021: "Fidesz is selling out wholesale the housing of Hungarian students, and their future, just so it can bring the elite university of China's dictatorship into the country. The university is a tool for China to build its political influence, power and secret espionage in Hungary and in Europe."[9] Thousands of angry protesters hit the streets of Budapest that month, and a poll by the Republikon Institute showed that two out of three Hungarians were against the Chinese project. While the opposition, led by Karácsony, experienced political tailwinds in the polls, the Orbán government defended its decision by saying that Fudan is a leading university by global standards. Deputy Minister Tamás Schanda called the demonstrations "political hysteria," and China's Foreign Ministry said in a press release that the mayor's street name stunt was a "contemptible" act[10]. Eventually, though, the government's plans for the Chinese university were put on hold, and Orbán stated that no final decision would be taken until after the 2022 parliamentary elections. In Budapest, Mayor Karácsony crossed his fingers that the project was now off the table for good: "But if Fudan comes, it will be with these street signs," he said.

Chapter Nine

At the Crossroads

The Mother of Corona Vaccines

The year is 1985. We are in communist Hungary, and Katalin Karikó, a thirty-year-old biochemist, is considering her options. She has recently been fired from the University of Szeged because of austerity, and has been sending unsolicited job applications for months now to universities all across Europe, as well as one in the United States. Only a few of them even send her a reply: "Rejected." "No thanks." "Unfortunately, not at the moment."

Then one autumn day, a letter from Philadelphia lands in her mailbox. It's from the public Temple University and they would like to offer her a position. But it is a long way from Hungary to the United States—especially when you have a two-year-old daughter, a husband who doesn't speak English and a life behind the Iron Curtain's tight grip. Nevertheless, she accepts the offer. "I just realized that otherwise, I would most likely have ended up as some mediocre researcher at a university in Hungary," she says in March 2021 when I connect with her on a video link from her current home in Philadelphia.

Today, Katalin Karikó is widely saluted for her scientific research, which paved the way for the mRNA vaccines from Pfizer and Moderna. Without her efforts, these vaccines would never have existed, and the light at the end of the pandemic's tunnel would have been hard to glimpse. Karikó is now nicknamed "the mother of corona vaccines," and people have suggested her as a future Nobel Prize winner.[1]

For a Hungarian with wanderlust in the communist 1980s, it was not easy to leave the homeland, even though Hungary only had soft goulash communism and was the happiest barrack in the camp. For once, you were not allowed to possess any foreign currency, let alone bring cash out of Hungary. Katalin Karikó scratched her head. In order to raise enough money for the first month in America until she was paid a salary, she decided to sell the family's old Lada. She secretly exchanged the Hungarian forints into US dollars with the help of some Arab medical students in Szeged. Now she had $900, and she sewed the cash into her daughter's teddy bear so it wouldn't be discovered on the trip from Budapest to Philadelphia. Her mission was a success and the American dream was about to begin. Still, it would take another thirty-five years before Katalin Karikó gained both scientific and public recognition for her pioneering research.

Her life story is worthy of a bestseller. It's the story of eternal resistance, of countless rejections—having the will to never give up and the belief that you will succeed in the end. And not least, about the benefit of knowing that the most skilled scientists in the world are those who are able to collaborate and stand on the shoulders of each other's knowledge. Several book publishers have already approached Katalin Karikó, and today *she* is the one rejecting interviews when reporters are calling her. "The whole world wants to talk to me—from *The New York Times* to the Hungarian local newspapers—but I have to say no nine out of ten times," she says.

Katalin Karikó was born in 1955—the year before the Hungarian uprising—and she grew up in poor circumstances in the provincial town of Kisújszállás, out in the middle of the vast *puszta*. Her father was a butcher. "I loved watching him work and happily observed the viscera and the hearts of the animals—perhaps that's where my scientific vein came from," she says. In school, the science subjects came easy to the young Katalin, and by the age of 23, she had begun her career as a biology researcher at the University of Szeged. Coincidentally, she came across mRNA—the single-stranded molecule of RNA that corresponds to the genetic sequence of a gene. It had been discovered in 1961, but it had not received much attention since. In short, mRNA is a branch of RNA, which, together with DNA and proteins, form the three major biological macromolecules that are essential for all forms of life. Back then, most researchers failed to see much potential in further exploring mRNA. But not Katalin Karikó: "I couldn't let it go at all. I imagined all the diseases I would be able to treat in the future," she says. However, the faculty in Szeged did not share her vision at the time, and because the university's resources were scarce, Katalin Karikó was laid off.

After her arrival in Philadelphia in 1985, new problems occurred. In that decade, large sections of the scientific community were focusing on DNA, not RNA. Billions of dollars were invested in The Human Genome Project, whose goal was the complete mapping and understanding of all the genes of human beings. Sometimes when she had the chance to raise her opinion, Katalin Karikó tried to point out that most of the diseases we suffer from are actually due to pain and injury—and therefore not hereditary diseases. Nobody listened to her. "Most diseases don't require solutions that permanently change our genetics. For that reason, mRNA can be perfect for many kinds of treatment. But people were almost obsessed with gene therapy, and it forced mRNA to play second fiddle for many years," says Katalin Karikó. DNA had stolen the limelight, and the unfortunate timing became the start of an academic nightmare for the Hungarian emigrant in Pennsylvania.

For starters, both Katalin Karikó and her husband had problems with their visas. She then had to take a job at a military university further south, working long hours and spending the nights in a sleeping bag in the corner of the laboratory for nine whole months. When she returned to Philadelphia, she was lucky to get a job at UPenn, one of the most recognized universities in the United States. From her favorite position in front of the microscope, she did all she could to research her way past the obstacles, even though RNA therapy at the time—by the early 1990s—was criticized for being able to provoke strong inflammatory reactions.

In 1994, a group of investors from New York came to visit. They wanted to explore the possibilities of commercializing Karikó's research into mRNA and said they would finance and establish a new lab, which made her very hopeful. But then, for some reason, she never heard from these investors again. "Another time, pharmaceutical company Merck was offering six scholarships of $10,000 each. They received seven applications. You can probably guess who was at the bottom of the pile. It was always like that," explains Katalin Karikó about the many rejections. "I was probably a good scientist, but I was not a good salesman." Later she also experienced sexism at the workplace when colleagues repeatedly asked for her superior, even though she actually had her own lab at the time and was her own boss. At UPenn, she was soon to get a full professorship in 1995, but then instead she was demoted due to the lack of funding and interest in her field. It seemed to be the end of the road for Karikó's dreams to employ RNA to create new vaccines and drugs for many chronic illnesses. On top of all that, she was diagnosed with a malignant cancerous tumor in her throat, for which she had to be treated. "In situations like this, most people tend to say goodbye and thank you for everything. But I convinced myself that I just had to do better experiments. 'Go back to the lab,' I told myself. From the outside, it may have seemed crazy that I kept fighting for it, but I was always happy when I was in the lab," says Katalin Karikó.

One day in 1997, she met a man named Drew Weissman. They met over their department's copy machine at UPenn, and this was the start of something big. Weissman was an immunologist working on an HIV vaccine, he said. Katalin Karikó boasted that she could make RNA. "Before I met Drew, I had never given vaccines any thought," she says. They clicked immediately and started working together in the lab. But they were kind of an odd couple, Karikó remembers. She was among the lowest paid employees at the faculty, and she had so far not succeeded in getting mRNA to treat or protect against any diseases. Her lab rats died from inflammation. On the other hand, Drew Weissman was already a star in the academic world. For years, he had been working with Dr. Anthony Fauci, America's leading expert in infectious diseases. Nevertheless, the combination of Karikó's and Weissman's knowledge of the immune system would prove to be a gift for science—and for humanity. Just not right away. In 2005, the duo published a dissertation[2] in which they described a modified form of RNA that cannot be suppressed by the immune system. The lab rats now survived. Every strand of mRNA is made up of four molecular building blocks called nucleosides. But in its altered, synthetic form, one of those building blocks, like a misaligned wheel on a car, was throwing everything off by signaling the immune system. So Karikó and Weissman simply replaced it by a slightly tweaked version, creating a hybrid mRNA that could sneak its way into cells without alerting the body's defenses. In other words, they had paved the way for a future mRNA vaccine. "I knew it was big, and I expected all the science magazines and drug companies to look our way. But we heard nothing," says Katalin Karikó. "At that time, I began to fear that we would die before our idea would ever reach the world."

They continued working in the laboratory, and after five years of silence, something finally happened. In 2010, the famous stem cell biologist Derrick Rossi discovered the research in Karikó and Weissman's dissertation, and he began to dive into their findings. Rossi became extremely excited by what he saw. That same year, he founded a company called Moderna—its name is an acronym for "modified RNA," ModeRNA. Cleverly, Moderna acquired the rights to the research duo's patents. Neither Karikó nor Weissman would get rich from the deal, because as university employees, it was UPenn who owned the license and resold it for just $300,000. The whole process was a wakeup call for the then 55-year-old Hungarian. "Rossi has always been kind and referred to our research. Without him, nothing might have happened," she points out. "At the same time, I realized it was time to leave the university sector and take a job in the pharmaceutical industry," she says.

In 2013, Katalin Karikó decided to leave her family in Philadelphia and travel to Germany. She had come in contact with the then unknown biotech startup BioNTech, founded by a German couple with Turkish roots. At UPenn, the management thanked

Karikó for many years of good service, but at the same time mocked her decision, because this obscure German company did not even have a website. But BioNTech's director Ugur Şahin wanted to hire Karikó, and she immediately liked the people behind the start-up pharmaceutical business. "Ugur is an uncomplicated man. My father was a butcher, Ugur's father was a factory worker," she says of the now world-famous founder of BioNTech—the company that in January 2020 predicted the extent of the corona pandemic and initiated the work of developing a vaccine based on mRNA technology. "For a long time, we worked day and night to refine our methods. Later, I also came in charge of the presentation when the collaboration with Pfizer began," says Karikó. Meanwhile, she had traveled back to her home in the United States, from where she is today working for the German company as Senior Vice President.

On December 18, 2020, Katalin Karikó got a jab in her arm with the Pfizer-BioNTech vaccine that would not have existed without her work. It was a moving moment, but all the talk about a potential Nobel Prize is not exciting for her. Until her death three years ago, Katalin Karikó's mother was eagerly following who would win this year's Nobel Prizes. Every year—from the very first years at the Szeged University—her mother expected that now it would finally be her daughter's turn. "I always told her: 'But mom, I cannot even get a scholarship.' She would not believe me. 'But Kati, you work so hard,' she insisted."

Karikó's own daughter, Susan Francia, is today a two-time Olympic rowing winner, but for the world-famous Hungarian scientist, "victory" does not exist as a word in her dictionary. "Should I be completely honest? I'm not thinking about winning anything. For forty years, I have worked without any kind of support, and that makes you humble. I never thought about all the research funding I did not get. That philosophy has enabled me to persevere for so long and still be in a good mood," she says with a smile. "The most important award right now is to stop the pandemic with our vaccine," she concludes.

Before Katalin Karikó waves goodbye at the video connection, I ask her about her relationship to Hungary today. "Well, in Hungary, people love to blame someone else. The government, the opposition, the EU, the Chinese. Hungarians love to complain. The other day I was talking to an old friend in Szeged who was complaining that her neighbors had not knocked on her door to ask if they could help her with anything, now that she had been infected with the corona disease. I then asked her if at any point she herself had knocked on the door of her neighbors to ask about the same. 'No'. This is a typical situation in Hungary. Everyone is waiting for others to do something. And then nothing happens. Even the Hungarian journalist I spoke to yesterday was complaining on the phone because he had a deadline for another article the same day. In Hungary, the glass is always only half full."

On the topic of polarization, Katalin Karikó also has something to say. "These people on both sides who are the worst... I wish they were forced to become scientists. Because in the world of science, constructive criticism is the way we make progress. There is no way around the facts. I can sit and look at the same data as my colleagues—we see it with different eyes and may have different attitudes to it—but the facts don't lie. Then we have a constructive conversation about how we can move forward. We talk to each other, we listen, and we make things better."

Living on the Edge

From the town hall of Kübekháza, it takes only six minutes to drive to the border fence. Róbert Molnár, the mayor of this small south-Hungarian village, gets behind the wheel of his black Citroën Picasso to show me the place. As he drives toward the border, he makes gestures with both hands and turns his head to me at the back seat, in order to express how dramatic it is to be the next-door neighbor to one of Europe's most talked-about and most controversial border conflicts of a generation.

During the chaotic refugee and migrant crisis in the summer of 2015, more than 10,000 people came here every day to cross Hungary's southern border. Many of them had heard Chancellor Angela Merkel's welcoming words *"Wir Schaffen Das,"* but on the doorstep to Viktor Orbán's Hungary they were instead greeted by barbed-wire, brutal officers and a traveling world press. Europe suddenly spoke with two tongues, but it was Orbán who licked his mouth in the end, and ever since mid-September that year, Hungary's 175-kilometer-long border fence has protected the European Union's external border.

Everyday life around Kübekháza is no longer dramatic because of an influx of migrants, states Róbert Molnár, who was appointed Minister in Orbán's first government. Nowadays, the fence on the border with Serbia gives rise to a different and much more disturbing development, he says: the growing enthusiasm of both Hungary and most of the EU countries for technological tools that can be used to stop migration to Europe.

The mayor parks his Picasso on a dirt road. On foot, we cross a freshly harvested cornfield and in front of us, we see the four-meter tall, double iron lattice with barbed-wire on top. Less than 30 seconds from the moment we enter the border, a police car shows up. The officers quickly recognize the mayor and greet him dutifully. Our footsteps have automatically been detected by the ultra-sensitive heat sensors on the ground, even here on the Hungarian side of the border. Immediately, the locally patrolling border guards were warned. So was the National Police Headquarters up in Budapest, 200 kilometers further north. From there, the police chief and his colleagues can watch us via the hundreds of video cameras observing the border fence.

A soft tingling sound comes from the nearest camera, as it turns its lens toward the spot where Róbert Molnár stands. He looks away and walks over to read from a sign: "Electric Fence," it says. "Actually, I haven't tried if the fence really gives you an electric shock when you touch it," the mayor says with a smile. He immediately switches to a more serious tone. "I can accept the fence itself. But all the technology that comes with it makes me really uncomfortable. Now they have started testing drones in the air—we can hear them buzzing at night." Even more gloomy is the anonymous loudspeaker voice that occasionally roars robotic words in Arabic and English over the empty cornfields, even when an innocent fox shows up: "Attention, attention, I am warning you. Go away," the voice says. Molnár finds it creepy. "Where is the limit of technology?" he wants to know. But no one in Kübekháza's tech-dominated no-man's land is able to answer the mayor's question.

The Hungarians did get a small glimpse of an answer when the Orbán government presented a report on the country's future surveillance technology: By the end of 2022, Hungary and several other European countries will send swarms of autonomous drones in the air, patrolling both Europe's internal and external borders from a bird's eye perspective.[1] The report also states that unmanned vehicles on the ground must "optimize the protection of our borders" at a time when there is a shortage of border guards of flesh and blood. The government will also launch a new command center in Budapest with access to infrared and radar surveillance of the entire Hungarian border area. From the command center, operators can also program the drones to perform specific tasks in addition to the automated routine work. "None of these drones will be armed," the report assures.

The plans are part of the so-called Roborder project, funded by the EU's research and development fund, Horizon 2020. Altogether, in recent years the EU has spent more than €100 million on at least 14 research projects related to security and surveillance technology. This is documented by the NGO Privacy International.[2] "The projects testify that the EU has chosen an approach that criminalizes migration and focuses on security," says Antonella Napolitano from Italy, head of the organization's migration and surveillance department. "Private companies are helping to incite the story of migration as a security threat, where the solution, according to these companies, is more security in the form of military and technological tools that only they can provide." She believes that the EU has a "Security-Industrial Complex" in the same way that America has a "Military-Industrial Complex"—an often-criticized commercial alliance between the US military and the American weapon industry.

Lawyer Petra Molnár has a similar view. She works at the University of Toronto in her native Canada, but is currently staying in Greece where she is investigating how the corona pandemic is affecting border and migration conflicts. "We are experiencing a large increase in technologies monitoring and controlling migration worldwide, especially in Europe," says Petra Molnár, who has Hungarian roots but no relationship with the mayor of Kübekháza despite the same surname. "In the hunt for new border technologies, a number of dubious projects have emerged that are based on bias and discrimination against strangers," she adds. Petra Molnár mentions a pilot project called iBorderCtrl, which is funded with €4 million from the Horizon 2020 fund. The project is based on artificial intelligence and is, in short, a kind of "automated lie detector." Hungary is one of the pilot countries. The concept is to put a digital officer at the border, who from a screen with a camera analyzes facial features, eye movements and voice data of the visitor in order to determine whether the visitor is telling the truth or not. If the system detects suspected untruthfulness, real border guards will step in and take over the interrogation. "But what happens if an asylum seeker engages in such an interaction? Can the system take into account trauma and the effect of trauma on memory? Can it take into account the cultural differences in communication? Many new problems arise, as soon as you try to solve a complex problem with artificial intelligence," says Petra Molnár.

The pilot project has now been completed, but no conclusions are available. I therefore contacted the co-founder of iBorderCtrl, a British tech entrepreneur named James O'Shea. He rejected the criticism of the project. "I would rather turn it around and say that iBorderCtrl has actually to some extent contributed to the public awareness of ethical and legal issues regarding artificial intelligence," James O'Shea argued.

In the United Kingdom—one of the most surveilled societies in Europe—university researchers have for years analyzed the ethical issues surrounding surveillance technology. One of them is sociologist Andrew Balmer from the University of Manchester. He believes that artificial intelligence for border protection is a dangerous slippery slope. "Lie detectors can never work, neither the old polygraphs nor the new robots. For there is no valid connection between lies and bodily reactions. The body is no more truthful than the mind," he points out. "The problem with lie detectors and algorithms is that we treat technology as if it is objective, but of course it isn't. Technology is built by human beings and it is used by human beings. And human beings make mistakes," explains Andrew Balmer, adding that such technology often lead to racist, sexist or even age-discriminatory feedback. "What we need at the border is less automation and more humanity. We need to challenge the political narrative that automation can speed up migration and transport processes," says Andrew Balmer.

The drones buzzing above Hungary's southern border have also come to stay. The aforementioned Roborder project is just the beginning, says Noel Sharkey, author and tech professor at the University of Sheffield. "Drones and robots provide many more eyes in the sky to catch illegal border crossings, but it is extremely difficult to make them work autonomously," he explains. "Governments are often seduced by the hype and the promise of technological innovation. The cameras on drones can find migrants crossing the border, but what can they do about it other than let the border guards know so they can try to catch them?" Sharkey asks. According to the professor, it is not inconceivable that armed robots will eventually be used to apprehend or shoot people who are illegally trying to cross a border. "It is very tempting to automate the borders along Europe to prevent people from entering. But technology can take many forms that would ultimately lead to cruel injustice," he warns.

Petra Molnár, the Canadian lawyer, is not optimistic about future border surveillance. "Technologies such as drones and artificial intelligence completely ignore the reasons why people migrate in the first place. Technology reduces the solution to a nonhuman algorithm, and that development can lead to profound violations of human rights," she argues. "If the past is any indication, then more and more technologies will be used all along the continuum of a person's migration journey in the future—before the border, at the border, and beyond the border," says Petra Molnár.

Back at the border in Kübekháza, Mayor Róbert Molnár tells me how Viktor Orbán's Fidesz party turned its back on him in 2015 because he publicly criticized all the fuss surrounding the famous fence. "There comes a time in a man's life when he has to stand up for his principles. So that is what I did, but it has had huge costs for me," says the mayor. Before we go back to the village, Róbert Molnár would like to show a paradox at the Hungarian border that few have noticed. We walk a few hundred meters further east and now stand right where the Hungarian border with Serbia stops, and where the border with Romania begins. Oddly enough, the border fence also stops right here. "So in theory, these 'dangerous migrants' could just have walked a little bit further east and crossed the border from Romania into Hungary, because here there is no physical barrier," explains Róbert Molnár. To him this proves that the border fence is in fact pure symbolism. "Orbán didn't have to build it one meter longer, because he had already managed to scare the whole of Europe into believing that this was what was needed," says the mayor. Soon enough, though, European leaders may not even need to build any more physical fences at all, he believes. "Drones, heat sensors, robots and other invisible technologies can soon do the job instead," concludes Róbert Molnár and gets back into his Picasso.

Cold War Comeback

Every morning Gyula Csák walks into an office building a little south of the Hungarian parliament. On his way to work, he tends to walk past Szabadság tér—Liberty Square—to remind himself of his daily mission: to bring free and independent journalism out to the

Hungarian citizens. As editor-in-chief of the Hungarian-language online media *Szabad Európa*—part of the American organization *Radio Free Europe*—it is up to Gyula Csák and his staff to deliver neutral and sober news in a country where media, politics and population are more divided than anywhere else in the EU. "*Szabad Európa* is a public service news media company and we represent a neutral position in the highly polarized Hungarian media," Gyula Csák explains. As a nonprofit organization, according to the editor-in-chief, *Szabad Európa* is completely free from economic and political pressure. "It helps us to be independent, objective and middle-ground. We cover stories we believe affect the lives of Hungarians the most," he says.

Originally, *Radio Free Europe* emerged as an anticommunist media outlet launched by the US Congress, and the mission of the radio station was "to promote democratic values and institutions by spreading factually correct information and ideas."[1] From its headquarters in Munich in West Germany, the radio station broadcasts since July 4, 1950— the American Independence Day. The first signals reached Czechoslovakia, as the Soviet Union and other socialist countries tried to block the radio waves with noise transmitters. Before long *Radio Free Europe*—directly funded by the CIA—had become part of the American information war against the authorities of socialist countries in Eastern Europe.

The 1956 riots in the Polish city of Poznań were covered in depth, and according to the book *Cold War Radio*—written by former radio editor Richard Cummings—this inspired the Hungarians to revolt against the Soviet regime later that year. In the 1970s, *Radio Free Europe* was merged with another Western freedom radio, *Radio Liberty*. While the former continued to broadcast to satellite states such as Hungary and Czechoslovakia, *Radio Liberty* focused on getting radio signals and journalism into the Soviet Union. Today these efforts are widely considered to have had an enormous impact on the eventual collapse of Communism. "It turned out that the best propaganda is the truth," said Pavel Pecháček, then editor of the Prague office.[2]

After the fall of the Berlin Wall, *Radio Free Europe* said thank you and goodbye. Its mission was fulfilled and the last signals left their stations in the mid-1990s. But now—three decades after the end of the Cold War—the US-funded media outlet has returned to the other side of the old Iron Curtain with a similar mission: once again supply Eastern Europeans with thorough and independent journalism. And they are far from being the only ones. The German *Deutsche Welle* and several EU-supported online media projects, as well as a $700,000 grant by the US State Department entitled "Supporting Objective Media in Hungary," have also found its way to countries like Bulgaria, Romania and Hungary. *Radio Free Europe* launched in Bucharest and Sofia in early 2019, and the Budapest office opened in September 2020. The so-called "Iron Curtain" no longer exists in reality, but seen from the West, freedom in the old East Bloc is once again under pressure, and their citizens need help from the outside: "We play a key role in these countries because we tackle stories that journalists in the independent private media are not willing to go after because of threats to their safety or government pressure," said *Radio Free Europe*'s president Jamie Fly.[3]

But what is really at stake? What interests does the West—and not just the EU, but also the United States—have in interfering in the media coverage in the eastern European countries? To find the answer to this question, I reach out to the Danish-Czech journalist Ota Tiefenböck. He grew up in communist Czechoslovakia and today is editor-in-chief and founder of the Copenhagen-based media company *Mr. East*, writing news, travels pieces and books on Central and Eastern Europe. "The situation in Hungary today—and for that matter also in Poland—is unacceptable and problematic in terms of the governing parties' control of the media, including the state radio and television stations," Ota Tiefenböck says.

According to several NGOs—including Freedom House and Reporters Without Borders—press freedom in Hungary and Poland has decreased dramatically in recent years. The low rating of press freedom in both countries is due to, among other things, the point that their governments are instituting policies that "hamper the operations of opposition groups, journalists, universities, and nongovernmental organizations (NGOs) who criticize it or whose perspectives it otherwise finds unfavorable" as Freedom House wrote in its 2021 report.[4] "But this is not the same as saying there is no government-critical media in those countries at all," argues Ota Tiefenböck. "There is indeed a critical media presence, and that kind of thing was completely unthinkable under communism. So the importance of *Radio Free Europe* today can in no way be compared to the time leading up to the collapse of Communism," he points out.

From Tiefenböck's perspective, the polarization of our time—and the intensified, pan-European fight for certain narratives—is rather due to the fact that there is often just a one-sided coverage. For instance, he argues, Hungary is often seen only through the glasses of the West in large-audience media outlets such as *The Guardian* or *Washington Post*. He notices this trend every day when trying to get an overview of the media coverage in the east and west, respectively. "In my opinion, Western media more or less run on autopilot without having the will—or rather without the ability—to see the nuances and uncover the real extent of the problems," he says, mentioning the debate on the Orbán government's so-called anti-LGBT law in Hungary, which was condemned by large parts of Western Europe. The government said the law is meant to protect children, but critics of the law say it links homosexuality with pedophilia. "How many Western journalists and politicians have actually read the law? I have my doubts. Criticism of the media landscape in Hungary is alright, but Western politicians and the media should, in my humble opinion, concentrate on real problems in Hungary, such as the power of the state media, rather than blindly criticizing everything that goes on in the country," argues Ota Tiefenböck.

To counteract the trend, a number of Hungarian-funded, nationalist conservative media outlets based in Western Europe have been launched in recent years, including *Remix* and the *V4NA* news agency, both of which have links to the Orbán government. In the summer of 2021, Viktor Orbán even published an advertisement for his politics in some Western newspapers, including the Danish daily *Jyllands-Posten.* "All these political attempts to 'balance' the news only leads to disastrous polarization, and in reality, it only makes the situation in Hungary even worse," says the founder of *Mr. East.*

Every year the *Radio Free Europe* organization is provided with a budget of $124 million from the US Agency for Global Media. In total, it now has newsrooms in over 20 countries and produces journalism for approximately 40 million weekly media users. The question is just whether financial support for a media site like *Szabad Európa* in Hungary will make any difference for the Hungarian citizens. "It doesn't change anything," argues Ota Tiefenböck. "Media platforms like these only cater to the same small segment—namely, the progressive and liberal Hungarians in Budapest, who already feel well-informed and have a certain view of the state of affairs," he claims. According to Ota Tiefenböck, the funding of the project has probably more to do with the people behind *Radio Free Europe* who, in his view, want to "behave like the real progressive forces, rather than having a genuine desire to do something good for Hungary," as he argues. "They should rather be sending some of their dollar grants to someone like *Klubrádió*," Tiefenböck suggests, referring to the government-critical Hungarian radio station, which is in great financial difficulties due to political pressure.

The same view has media professor Gábor Polyák from the University of Pécs. According to him, the biggest problem for independent media in Hungary is that they are underfinanced. "The United States should have given direct support to existing Hungarian media outlets, which have readers even in the rural areas, instead of launching a whole new Budapest-based media," Polyák says about *Szabad Európa*'s US-financed comeback in Hungary.

Back at the office building in Budapest, editor-in-chief Gyula Csák does not agree with the criticism. "Of course it makes a difference," he emphasizes. "Even though we are a small team, we have the will and the resources to dive deep into stories that would otherwise not have been published." He highlights a series published by *Szabad*

Európa, documenting how Hungarian state media journalists faced pressure leading up to the European Parliament elections in 2019, including orders to push an antimigrant narrative—a key issue of the government of Viktor Orbán. The investigative story went viral in Hungary and was cited in the national Parliament. It even reached the European Parliament and became a point of reference when talking about state media in Hungary. "Obviously, working in a polarized media landscape is not easy. But we do everything to reach out to the community and uncover the Hungarians' everyday lives and problems. Hopefully we can ultimately help to slow down the polarization," Gyula Csák concludes.

Part III
Conversations

"When people talk, listen completely.
Don't be thinking what you're going to say."

—Ernest Hemingway

Chapter Ten

On Politics

Zoltán Kovács: Viktor Orbán's Right-Hand Man

The first thing I notice is the bracelet on his right wrist, featuring the red, white, and green stripes of the Hungarian flag. As he shakes my hand to say hello, the wristband appears from underneath his jacket sleeve, and his bearded face turns into a friendly smile, elevating his distinct, dark-brown eyebrows a few centimeters above his rimless glasses. Zoltán Kovács is in Copenhagen to give a lecture to dozens of curious Danes as a part of his European tour to various Western capitals in order to "clear up the misunderstandings of Orbán's political vision."

Shortly after the event, we meet in an upstairs office for the interview, but we are not alone. Although I have long had a clear understanding with Zoltán Kovács that this was to be a one-on-one conversation with him, there are three other persons around the table. One of them is none other than Hungary's ambassador to Denmark at the time, László Hellebrandt—the two others are his and Kovács's political advisers, respectively. I politely greet the trio and ask them: "Excuse me, but why are you here for my interview with Mr Kovács?" The ambassador's advisor responds as the others nod, "We just want to make sure that we stick to the agreed topic." The topic we agreed on in advance is quite a broad one, though: "Hungary's view on freedom of speech, migration, and the future of Europe." Furthermore, with years of experience as the Orbán government's most competent communications guy, Zoltán Kovács does not come across as someone who is exactly in need of moral support or external guidance on how to handle the press.

The situation reminds me of an episode that happened many years ago when I visited a school in Manchester, England, to report on video surveillance in English classrooms. My colleague and I wanted to interview two young pupils to hear their candid opinions on the matter, but it was not easy to ask critical questions with their headmaster sitting right next to them at the table. Now Hungary's ambassador is sitting next to me at the interview table, albeit the circumstances admittedly are different than that time in Manchester when it was children and not adults who needed "protection." Eventually, I come to the conclusion that the ambassador and the two advisors are probably just curious to listen in on our conversation.

"Are we ready?" Kovács asks, interrupting my stream of thought, and we can finally begin the interview, which is neither censored nor disrupted in any way by the unexpected presence of the three officials. Through several months, I have tried to get a personal interview with Viktor Orbán, but with no luck. To put a plaster on the wound, I get to talk with the second best alternative. Kovács's visit to Denmark is an obvious occasion for him to talk with a Danish journalist, and I am the lucky one, hence, I have taken the flight from Budapest to Copenhagen on this rainy Monday in October. The article was later published in *Berlingske*.[1]

In introductory remarks at Kovács's lecture, the Danish organizer, from the Free Press Society made clear that Kovács is a key figure in Hungarian politics: "It is not Viktor Orbán we shall hear today, but it is as close as we can get to that,"

In other words, Zoltán Kovács is the closest possible access to Viktor Orbán's otherwise hermetically sealed political powerhouse. The Hungarian prime minister is usually surrounded by only a handful of advisors, and among them, Kovács is said to be his right-hand man. He is the one explaining to Hungarian and international media why Hungary is doing what it is doing these days. For Viktor Orbán, there is a need for someone who is skilled at cutting through the noise and misunderstandings, someone who can spin the perspective of the Hungarian government. Zoltán Kovács meets these needs. Like Orbán, Kovács came of age as Hungary transitioned from communist rule to democracy in the late 1980s and, like Orbán, Kovács hails from the countryside. With British-accented English, he speaks in terms of "we" and "our" to make clear that his views and Orbán's are one and the same.

*   *   *   *

Soon it will be fifteen years since Hungary finally joined the European family as a member of the European Union. One could argue that today's global challenges must be solved jointly by the member states working together, but this does not seem to be the case when you look at the EU. So let me ask: What are the global challenges of Europe as seen from Hungary?

If we talk about the challenges that the European Union is facing, migration is just one of them. It is probably the litmus test of European integration, of the European borders and of Europe's ability to act. But we all know that there are more challenges than this one. The economic efficiency issues, decision-making procedures that also relate to efficiency, and, not least, digitalization. Name one challenge that the United States and China are facing, and it will obviously also be a challenge for Europe. We strongly believe that if Europe is able to come back to consensus—back to a proper decision-making and a proper cooperation effort—then it is in a European framework that we are able to face these challenges. One by one, it is most definitely going to be more difficult. That is why we believe in the EU. Because the nature of the global challenges is so immense, it necessitates something like the EU. However, it *does* matter what kind of European Union we build. Our lesson from years past is that a member state such as Hungary has a political mandate and it can execute what it decides. This approach can contribute to the EU in a different way than is being suggested by Brussels, in all respects.

Is it constructive to go against the EU and make decisions on your own, instead of coming to agreements with the other member states?

Having arguments with Brussels is not the same as going against Europe. We are trying to demonstrate that it is possible to make change in alternative ways, but with the very same effect.

Do you mean that for Europe to progress, it is more efficient to be pragmatic on your own, rather than having a fight of different beliefs before agreeing on a common decision?

Well, our suggestion is that we believe in a stronger and more effective Europe through stronger and more effective member states. It is coming back to down-to-earth, common sense issues. If a member state is able to face, react to, and act on a challenge in a rapid manner, while the EU is not able to do so, why don't we follow the example of the given state? Why don't we let the member states give answers to elements of the challenges on their own?

I believe you are referring to Hungary's decision in 2015 to stop the migration flow by building a border fence?

Yes. At the end of the day, it comes up as a European effort. As more people are now finally realizing, we believe that there are limits for integration. Natural limits. We are against integration or against the European process of integration, but we are what you could call a "common sense integrator," suggesting that if you use your common sense, you are going to recognize that the member states can be more effective in some instances than the EU itself.

In September 2017, two years after Hungary built the fence, the European Court of Justice dismissed Hungary's and Slovakia's complaints over the refugee quotas. On the same occasion, Jean-Claude Juncker, President of the European Commission, wrote a letter to Viktor Orbán, stating that "solidarity is not an á la carte dish."[2] What is solidarity from your point of view?

Well, we see a new type of solidarity appearing. The true sign of solidarity is to follow the rules that you initially agreed on in the European Union. We need a long-lasting solution, but instead, the Brussels bureaucrats just create new rules in the middle of this fight between different values. We stand out because we have acted on our own. If you are waiting for consensus to be reached, it will be too late. To be honest, we really don't like the border fence. It is ugly. But it is the best available solution we have for protecting the outer border of the European Union. We don't want to sound silly, but it would actually be nice if Hungary didn't have to pay for it all alone.

You have argued that Hungary's confidence, pragmatism, and decisiveness are all too often misunderstood, especially by Western journalists and opinion-leaders. How are you trying to handle the struggles that you face from people misunderstanding Hungary and its politics?

It all comes back to context. You need to take a look at the whole picture. If you have a picture of how Hungary sees the world and the challenges ahead of us, and if you just talk about one pixel or one element of that picture, it is fully possible to paint a bad image of what is happening. Even if you take a look at more pixels, it is possible, so you have to be aware of the complete picture to have the contextual knowledge. Also, you have to be very careful if it is about guided opinion. Then you will be biased. In many situations, journalists and politicians come to Hungary with a guided opinion or a prejudice instead of looking at the whole picture. It is like the question: Why are we building an "illiberal democracy"? What does that even mean? The term "liberal" has a very limited meaning—it is just one element of political life—and we reject that someone is monopolizing the entire picture as liberal.

Can you explain what you mean by that?

What I am emphasizing is the existence of alternatives to the liberal democracy. There are many alternatives. For instance, there is social democracy, there is Christian democracy, there is communism, and so on. In Hungary, we just want to live in a Christian democracy. The point is this: There is not just one way. There is not just one interpretation of the future of Europe. And we would like to lead the way in this respect.

How are you trying to create support for this viewpoint?

At home, for example, we have done something in the past couple of years. Something new. I am talking about the much-criticized national consultation that we run.

You mean the questionnaires that the government regularly sends out to all Hungarians in order to receive the public's opinion on certain political issues, such as migration, family policy, and the European Union?

Yes. You might not like it. Many are calling it "populist" and "manipulative," but the fact is that no other European government is using it. We believe they should. The world is changing so rapidly that even within the four years of an electoral cycle, you need feedback as a government. You need to talk to the people. Even if it is a guided discussion—and obviously, when politicians talk to their audiences, doing so will always be biased, because we talk about issues in a manner that we believe is proper. However, if you receive feedback from the public, and if you *don't* recognize that the feedback has relevance, and if you *don't* recognize the direction of the reflection, *then* you are in trouble. If you are not following the wishes of public opinion, you will not lead the polls for more than ten years like Fidesz has done. You can call it "populist," but populism is about reaching out to the people to try to get a sense of what they want to achieve. We try to get a sense of how people think about politics.

As international spokesman for the government, you are also very active in blogging about politics, in English, on AboutHungary.com. For instance, you have criticized some foreign newspapers and their coverage of Hungary, including the New York Times, *saying "it's easy to be charmed by the human rights nonsense when you're penning editorials from an office in Midtown Manhattan.*[3] *What is your relationship with the critical media?*

We are facing huge problems when it comes to the media. They have lost their original role. I can accept criticism, but I have never seen so many lies as now, and many media outlets and journalists are not living up to their responsibility of political independence. Do they want to be journalists or political activists? The liberal narrative overrides everything else.

Can you give an example of what you believe to be media lies?

One of the lies that has been repeated over and over in the liberal mainstream media is that George Soros does not mingle in European politics, and that there exists no such thing as a "Soros plan" about migration into Europe. That is not only a misleading truth; that is an outright lie. The Soros plan exists, plain and simple. In a public article, which Mr Soros wrote himself, you can read his suggestion that the European Union should take up to one million refugees in the coming years.[4] Everyone is allowed to have his own opinion, but our problem is this: Unlike the Hungarian government, and all other elected governments in Europe, George Soros has no political mandate. Nobody ever voted for him—not in Hungary, and not in the European Union. Therefore, his plan is pure manipulation.

The debate about what the European Union is and should be is very intense these years. Often it seems like Hungary is on the forefront on this debate in Europe. Are we in the middle of a transition period? What role is Hungary playing in this discussion?

First of all: Yes, we are indeed in a transitional period. Everybody sees that. Still, we are fully aware of the size and difference of Hungary. Many would like to put us into the forefront of the debate, but we are aware of our limits. Hungary does not want to lead the discussion of the future of Europe, because our size is actually quite moderate. We are not the smallest state, but we are a middle-sized EU state. What we would like is that the leaders of the bigger countries and the leaders of Brussels would listen to us. But it is impossible and because we are not big enough, nobody really listens to what we have to say. In a negative way, so far we have been put onto the forefront of this debate. As a negative example, we are portrayed as the black sheep of Europe. It is not a comfortable situation, but, at the same time, it is also a good political position from which we can talk and draw the contrasts.

Do you think you will be able to change the mainstream opinions in Europe also outside the Central European region?

What we already see is that reality eventually is going to override dogmatism and unreal thinking. We have already contributed to changing the conversation in Europe, especially when it comes to illegal migration. And since we talk about reality, it is unavoidable that we will be on the winning side of the argument. As the prime minister always says, we do not like to be vindicated, because it is not very good in politics. We will win the argument not because we are particularly smart, but because we talk about reality.

If you simplify the opinions, it seems like an argument between promigration and antimigration politicians. Do you see think there is enough space for such contrasting opinions within the European Union?

It is really up to European democracy. You can enforce neither promigration nor antimigration opinions on the people of Europe. They have to decide for themselves. We don't tell the Western European countries what they should do, and I don't think it is helpful if they tell us what to do. If dogmatism is going to rule, then we are in trouble. Our view is that, unfortunately, there is a chance for this if the Western press and politicians don't change.

Since we here in Denmark talking about Hungary—and since we have the Hungarian ambassador to Denmark present in the room—I want to ask whether you see similarities or differences between our two countries?

Well, Denmark is in a different situation because you have an opt-out option regarding migration and other issues. We don't. In that respect, you are not supposed to compare Denmark to Hungary. Regarding migration, what you see coming to Denmark is just fragments of what is coming to us in Hungary and the southern part of Europe today. Because you live in the wealthiest part of Europe, this dynamic is unavoidable. It is just a natural process that those who are targeting Europe are trying to come here to Scandinavia. So, when we defend the borders in Hungary, we are, as a matter of fact, trying to defend you. That recognition is still missing from Western Europe. There are philosophical differences around Europe, and some might not like to hear and talk about it, but this is the reality: There are countries—I don't believe Denmark belongs to them—that have a migration past. Especially some Western European countries, those which had larger empires, are used to migration, so they take it as a natural process. In many respects, among policy makers, they believe that it is an option for them. For us it is not an option. We never had a colony. We have not been through this for centuries, and we don't want that to be the case in the future.

If there is a rift between East and West, then how do you compromise within the European Union?

That is the problem. How do you compromise? The only compromise is that you do not let other countries enforce something on you that you do not like. We are not trying to enforce anything on them. That is the difference. In Denmark, I hear from some people that there are claims that what is happening here with migration is "unnatural," whatever that means. When your people have a sense of something unnatural, you'd better listen. Because the people are going to sense when something is organic and natural, and when something is not. That is the lesson we have learned.

What is the most important factor for Hungary to achieve its goals? Do you want to make the rest of Europe follow your political path?

We would like to demonstrate that it is possible to stop migration, both for our own sake and for the sake of Europe. Having said that, our perspective is not to force anyone else to follow Hungary or Central Europe. Instead, we suggest that the European Union does not set up criteria and rules that cannot be followed in real life. We think that if you let us do it, as we do it the best, it will be for the benefit of the entire European Union. Why would you like to enforce something on the Poles, the Slovaks, and us that is not going to have the same result as when we do it on our own? Let the European member states perform as best as they can, instead of enforcing something you believe would be the best for everyone. Migration relates to very fundamental issues such as sovereignty. That is something we have never given up on, something that we never will give up on. Hungary has always been the heart of Europe, but we were cut off for nearly fifty years during communism. Nevertheless, we still managed to preserve the traditions that make us proud to be Hungarians.

Ferenc Gyurcsány: Should I Stay or Should I Go?

"Do you want a cigarette?" the gangly gentleman asks me as he welcomes me into his rooftop office near the Nyugati train station in central Budapest. I don't smoke but decide to stand next to him by the open window where he lights a cigarette for himself. Actually he is not allowed to smoke inside, he tells me, but if no one finds out it, it won't do any harm—an approach that has caused him huge trouble earlier in his political life.

That Ferenc Gyurcsány has a likeable, informal personality is not the only thing I notice before our interview this April morning in 2017—exactly one year ahead of the 2018 general elections. At the entrance to his office, I also notice three electric guitars. They are yellow, blue, and purple, just like the logo of Gyurcsány's self-established political party, the Democratic Coalition (DK). Once, at the party's annual convention, he danced onto the stage with an unplugged guitar around his neck, playing air guitar to The Clash's punk classic *Should I Stay or Should I Go*. I saw the video clip of his performance. A sore sight. Charming and awkwardly forced at the same time. Many Hungarians think that he should have gone away long time ago, others are glad that he stayed.

I have come to Ferenc Gyurcsány's office to find out who this former prime minister of Hungary really is. What I know is that he is a man whom most Hungarians have an opinion on. Not least because he was the subject of an enormous political scandal back in 2006, which according to many observers paved the way for Viktor Orbán's landslide victory in 2010. During that period, support for Gyurcsány's then-governing party, the Hungarian Socialist Party (MSZP), was halved from 40 to 20 percent, while Orbán's Fidesz and the newly founded radical right-wing party Jobbik experienced a solid breakthrough.

The main reason for this change in support was a speech Prime Minister Gyurcsány held during an MSZP party convention at Lake Balaton shortly after the 2006 election victory. The content of the speech was strictly confidential. However, later that year, it was leaked and broadcast by *Magyar Rádió*. Said Gyurcsány in the speech, "We have f**ked up. Not a little, but a lot. No European country has done something as boneheaded as we have." He was referring to the fact that his socialist-liberal government had misled the electorate over Hungary's actual budget deficit—the largest in Europe at the time—during its election campaign, in order to win re-election. Which it did. Gyurcsány concluded, "We have done nothing for four years. Nothing. We have lied morning, night, and evening."[1]

Not surprisingly, the leak scandal resulted in massive public protests in front of the parliament building, some of them leading to riots and police violence. But Ferenc Gyurcsány refused to leave and instead tried to defend what he had said. Until 2009, almost three years later, when he finally resigned as prime minister , the global financial crisis having hit the Hungarian economy hard. In Paul Lendvai's 2017 biography *Orbán*, Ferenc Gyurcsány is described as "the most capable, controversial, and unpredictable (and certainly the richest) politician of the Left; he has gone down in history as one of the very few prime ministers in Europe who has publicly and completely unnecessarily committed political suicide."[2] Orbán's 2010 victory plummeted the Left into a deep crisis, and Gyurscány saw it necessary to break with the MSZP and instead create a more modern, center-left party, the Democratic Coalition. For the party leader himself, the story of DK is a success—a kind of "personal political comeback." Despite widespread public skepticism surrounding his persona, his party has in fact witnessed a growing voter base ever since its founding in 2011. At the parliamentary elections in April 2018, DK received nine mandates, thereby doubling its previous election resul, from 2014. Nevertheless, the party's real political influence is hard indeed to see, and many Hungarians point out that Gyurcsány's insistence on staying in national politics has only helped to fragment the Left even more.

After a few minutes of small talk about his actual guitar-playing skills, Gyurcsány puts out the cigarette butt, sips his coffee, and we start the interview.

*   *   *   *

With Jobbik in opposition on the Right and a handful of fragmented, small parties in opposition on the Left, it seems difficult to challenge the power of the Orbán government. How do you see today's Hungary from a personal point of view?

Political life in Hungary is turbulent right now. But I am optimistic about the long-term future, to be honest. In Europe, Hungarians are some of the most supportive members of the European Union and the values of the European idea. However, Viktor Orbán's permanent attack on Brussels will backlash, and I hope that people will realize this before it is too late. Hungarians now have to actively show that we would like to belong to the Western or European world, otherwise we will move closer to Putin's Russian model, the illiberal model. Eventually, my prediction is that Orbán will lose this political rivalry because most Hungarians actually say: "No, we are European.

We don't want to support someone who jeopardizes our European position."

At the DK party congress, you walked on stage to the song "Should I Stay or Should I Go." So far you have decided to stay. However, many voices on the Left have been criticizing you for still being on Hungary's political stage. Why do think that is? Why do you think you still have a role to play in Hungarian politics?

Listen, we set up our new party not so many years ago. We are still supported by 500,000 people, more or less. I am responsible for these people. I can understand that a couple of my rivals would like me to exit this rivalry, but I am much more interested in my voters' opinions than in what the leaders of other parties have to say. I think that a democratic rivalry is a democratic rivalry. My fate will be decided by the voters, not by other political leaders. Moreover, it is unfair to identify DK only with me. We are a political-spiritual gathering place of left-wing, liberal, and conservative people. As for me, there have been several attempts at my political life. They were unsuccessful, and the growth of DK refutes the success of the character assassination. I wasn't worth a dime a few years ago, but since then, our party has been constantly growing.

There is an obvious fragmentation on the Left in Hungary. Aren't you contributing to this fragmentation by creating your own party and by still being around? Several new, smaller parties have emerged on the Left. In order to beat the government, you have to cooperate, but for a long time you seem instead to have been kind of slowly killing each other.

I hope we will be wise enough to avoid any kind of political suicide. You have to understand that without my followers, Mr. Orbán cannot be defeated. We are the most united party, according to research. If I am closed down, my voters will stay home. They will not vote for anybody. We have to respect these people, and you know, there is only one way ahead: Sitting down and reaching an agreement. I am ready for this kind of compromise.

From a right-wing point of view, these fragmentations on the Left had a positive outcome on Viktor Orbán and his government. Meanwhile, the Hungarian Left seems to be in ruins.

I do not believe that the political Left is in ruins. There are 1.5 million left-wing voters in Hungary today. Sooner or later, we will be all right. In 2006, there were 2.3 million left-wing voters. Why not find most of them again? That is what we are trying to do.

You talk about numbers and supporter potentials, but not so much about actual political solutions or compromises. What is the main challenge for the center-left that you are representing?

In a historical sense, a period full of disillusionment does not favor moderate parties. We have such a situation right now. It favors radical or antielitist parties. Instead, we are trying to rationally appeal to the disillusioned people who are looking for something to cling to, even though our moderate voices and the complete rejection of radicalism might seem less attractive. I can understand this. But look at Greece's Syriza party. Radicalism may win elections but it cannot govern a country.

Addressing people is part of politics and the political Right seems to be more successful in this area. Especially when it comes to a topic like immigration, which is leading the European agenda these years.

For me, this is a question of principle. Deciding when to give up one's own views because they do not represent those of the majority is always a dilemma. In this case, we decided on a simple, humanistic approach after many internal consultations. I am responsible for others, too, and I can argue on the grounds of both Christianity and simple humanism. Immigration is a tremendous challenge to Europe as a whole, but in reality it is less of a direct challenge for Hungary. Nevertheless, it allows Viktor Orbán to strengthen xenophobic feelings in a country already saturated with tension, and thus reap communication and political success. But I don't think0 we should compete with him. We need the European Union to solve this challenge, and I don't consider it functional and fair to hold out our hands when we want something from Europe, but then when we have to participate in solving common European challenges, such as the refugee quota case, we choose to stay out of it. That is not solidarity.

However, regarding Hungary's own challenges with regards to democracy, I never had the expectation or hope that Europe would overthrow Orbán. This is *our* job. We in the opposition are responsible for cleaning up the country. I still believe that there is morality in this world. National selfishness is not right. It can be successful for a while but it still isn't right.

In 2015, while the Hungarian government was responding to the migration crisis by building a border fence, you and your family helped some of the new arrivals. You made room for migrant families to stay in your house here in Budapest, you offered them food and shelter. But by inviting the press to cover your welcoming gestures, was it as much a political response as a human one?

First of all, I must admit that helping those families gave me an incomparable emotional lift. More than anything else I have done in the past years, to be honest. It cost me a couple of hours from my life, but what's that compared to the fate of these people? It's nothing. From a political angle, the government's cracking down on migrants and those who assist them made us consider the whole situation. My wife and I held a family meeting to discuss whether we would continue bringing migrants into our home in this worsening political climate. We came to this conclusion: There is a rule of life, and there is a rule of government of Hungary. And if these two rules are in conflict, we must choose the rule of life. However, since the migration flow decreased over the course of 2015 and into early 2016, we haven't hosted any migrants or refugees. Building a fence is a spectacular and attitude-forming solution to the problem, but in my view it will solve nothing.

Still, even after all this turmoil, I can look at our nation with a sense of pride knowing that, essentially, we are good people. It's just that we have been taken hostage by a political propaganda machine. A friend of mine recently moved to a German village. The village was about to receive a family from Syria for integration, and the locals had been working for months to ensure that they would have a place to stay and work, even teaching local children Arabic words to help them welcome the newcomers. I found this very impressive. I would prefer a Hungary like this, but if a country of ten million people cannot integrate a few thousand people, then that country is in deep trouble.

Until the fence was erected in September 2015, more than 150,000 migrants walked over the Hungarian border that year. Many would argue that this was an unprecedented situation that needed an immediate response. Was it?

These were not illegal but irregular entrants, and the Western world had to learn after the World War II that they have a responsibility not just to themselves but also to others. The United States has very strict immigration policies but. at the same time, very humane programs, such as assigning many thousands of green cards annually based on well-established principles. There can be a strict immigration policy only when balanced by a generous humanitarian measures. I do not see this in our government. I see the lack of mercy in their eyes.

Bernadett Szél: Women are Different

"Women cannot endure the style of Hungarian politics, because it's built on continual character assassination." The harsh words came from Viktor Orbán in 2015, after he was asked why his government had no female members.[1] "I don't deal with women's issues," the prime minister responded two years later when a reporter asked him about the unexpected withdrawal of Hungary's ambassador to the United States, Réka Szemerkényi.[2]

The lack of women in Hungarian politics is quite noticeable. Initially, before I did any research on the subject, I expected this to be a general postcommunist phenomenon, but it turns out that Hungary is actually well behind the other countries in the region when it comes to the proportion of seats held by women in national parliaments. The EU average is 30 percent female MPs. In Poland, the rate is 28 percent, in Romania it is 21 percent. However, as of 2019, only 12 percent of Hungarian MPs are women, ranking Hungary as number 150 in the world.[3] Nevertheless, at the Women in Politics conference in Budapest in 2017, the organizers revealed a representative opinion poll showing that four out of five Hungarians oppose the statement that "women are not competent enough to be politicians."[4] Later that year, former prime minister Péter Medgyessy—an independent politician who led the socialist-liberal government from 2002 to 2004—shared his personal view on the importance of women in politics:

> A woman sees the world differently, and Hungary could definitely use a female leader. This manly, macho warmongering gets boring after a while and people eventually become disinterested in politics. More than half of the population is female. Gender equality and the fight against sexual harassment is more credible when it comes from a female's mouth. A mother better understands the importance of family, the need to improve opportunities for a child, how to improve the conditions of those raising a child, and the strong desire for living a peaceful life.[5]

Medgyessy specifically mentioned Bernadett Szél as a woman who could play an important role in the future of Hungarian politics.

In recent years, I have met and talked with Bernadett Szél on several occasions. She is an energetic sort unafraid of disrupting the interviewer or finishing other people's sentences. She is also a happy mother of two children who are in the habit of posting family selfies on her Instagram page. She wears sneakers and a backpack when attending antigovernment demonstrations. Just a few days prior to our interview, Bernadett Szél was involved in the most action-packed protests in Hungary since the historically violent riots back in 2006. The December 2018 protests were sparked by the so-called "slave law," which allows employers to demand more overtime from their workers. The law was passed by the Hungarian parliament the week before, which led Szél and other female opposition MPs to block the speaker's podium and blow whistles in protest at the law. The peculiar happening was followed by large street demonstrations and public speeches in central Budapest. That evening, several thousand protesters marched to Hungarian state television headquarters, where Szél and a handful of other MPs entered the building in an unsuccessful attempt to get a list of demands read on air. Instead, the MPs were roughed up by security guards and tossed back on the street. "I had a feeling they wouldn't touch a woman," said Szél. "They did."

Hungarian politics are tough, indeed, just as Viktor Orbán pointed out. Bernadett Szél has experienced this first-hand several times since she first became a member of the parliament in 2012. For instance, when she criticized Orbán's environmental politics during a parliamentary debate with Fidesz MP Zoltán Illés in 2013. With little hesitation, Illés responded to Szél's criticism: "Just because you're pretty, that doesn't also mean you're smart."[6] He later apologized for his sexist remarks.

Bernadett Szél's political story also symbolizes the fight of the fragmented opposition in Hungary. For many years, the opposition was unable to cooperate, something that is necessary if it wants to beat Viktor Orbán. Szél was the cochair and leader of the green party LMP's parliamentary delegation for several years, but after the opposition's defeat in the 2018 national elections, she was partly blamed for the political failure, humiliated by her fellow party colleagues, and eventually stripped of her voting rights. She finally left the party in October 2018 and remains an independent member of parliament. I meet her outside a pressroom in the National Office Building by the Danube River.

* * * *

In the EU, the average proportion of seats held by women in national parliaments is 30 percent. In Hungary, the number is 12 percent, which puts Hungary close to the bottom of the list when it comes to gender equality in politics all over the world. How do you look at these statistics?

Well, first of all, we definitely want more women in politics. The name of my former party is Politics Can Be Different (LMP), and women really are different. We are pragmatic. But the political life in Hungary, with its hate campaigns and negative atmosphere, keeps women away. They don't want to get into this. The old politicians are putting people off, not only women—but also men. I mean, people say, "Argh, I don't want to watch the news anymore, I am not interested in Soros, I don't care." If we do not get a different political culture in this country, people will not engage at all. They will say that they are better off doing something else. I understand these people. I said this before, but I understand that if we do not invest in changing it, politics will stay like this. And, to be honest, it is very complicated to work in such an environment, being a politician.

Is there a way to change the trend?

Yes. We are already working to increase the number of women getting into politics. I know that my former party, LMP, uses gender quotas and also other mechanisms and forces that can help, and we are advising women to get into politics. Not only to get into politics, but to be able to perform well in political life. Those of us who work with this, we use traditional methods and we learn from the northern and western part of Europe. Before the 2018 national elections, LMP were quite successful in changing the trend. Half of LMP's faction are women, and a lot of women are in leading positions. For example, the campaign manager was female, the top policy planner was also female, and we had a female prime minister candidate—myself. There is a quota system in the party, saying that if you have two males in a meeting, then a female also has to be there. And if it's a meeting with two females, a man has to attend as well.

During the demonstrations in December 2018, the political opposition was being voiced in a united and distinctly female front. What was the reason for that?

Well, after the 2014 elections, the number of female MPs in Hungary was less than 10 percent. Today it is 12 percent, so that is already an improvement. From the stage, we wanted to send a message that female parliamentarians, and women in Hungary, should be heard. And I sense that this approach is actually helping us unite the fragmented opposition. We are now finally communicating, and you are going to feel this "women power" a lot in the future, too.

In 2018, the Orbán government effectively banned the teaching of gender studies in Hungary. The government's standpoint is that "people are born either male or female" and they do not consider it acceptable to talk about "socially constructed genders, rather than biological sexes."[7] What is your response to this development?

There are many misunderstandings regarding gender studies. Sooner or later, everyone will have to realize that we are living in the twenty-first century. Everything has changed, and the government should rather consider how we can create the most viable relationships between men and women instead of trying to turn back time. I know that gender is a controversial subject for some, but we cannot ignore it and we need scientists who are also familiar with the area from a Hungarian perspective. Viktor Orbán is often talking about his family policy; he wants Hungarians to have more children, but I am not sure he is aware that, according to gender studies research, more children are born when the inequality between the two sexes is decreased.

As an opposition MP, you have now lost to Viktor Orbán twice since you came into Parliament in 2013. Many people actually partly blame you for the lack of cooperation among the opposition parties, which resulted in a new two-thirds majority for the Orbán government in 2018. Since then, you left your party, LMP. Will you also leave Hungarian politics?

I know that many people are using me as the scapegoat to blame for the defeat, but neither I nor LMP produced the two-thirds Orbán victory on our own. This naming and shaming is a ruthless old politician reaction, and it shows a terrible responsibility. I know what my role in this story is, and I was ready to take responsibility for the results. The real change will not come from this shouting, but only from persistent, stable, and coordinated work. That is what motivates me to continue.

According to the opposition, Viktor Orbán has crossed the red line several times, but the reaction does not seem to escalate. Why not?

It will come eventually. Orbán will go on until he sees resistance, and this is true not only for Hungary but also for Europe more broadly. Even during the darkest times, you have to keep the lines; we have to show that you cannot do everything to us. This is our common cause in the opposition.

But what if Hungarians are essentially just relatively happy with what Orbán does?

If that was the case, then Hungary would be full of satisfied people. I can assure you that this is definitely not the case.

Márton Gyöngyösi: Political Theft on the Right

"It was a bad sentence, it was a not-well-thought-through sentence, it was a disastrous sentence." Without a doubt, Márton Gyöngyösi has learned to be very careful with his words after he drew international attention back in 2012 when he called for a list of all Jews in Hungary, particularly lawmakers, arguing that they could pose a "national security risk."[1] He quickly apologized to the Jewish communities, but it was already too late: Gyöngyösi's controversial comment aligned perfectly with the general perception people had of his party, Jobbik, and its unsophisticated right-wing rhetoric. Reversing this picture still to this day seems like an almost impossible challenge.

We are meeting in an upstairs conference room in the National Office Building overlooking the Danube River, and Márton Gyöngyösi carefully adjusts his red silk tie and his glasses before he sits down at the end of the table. The polite and polished son of a diplomat spent the most of his childhood in Egypt, Iraq, Afghanistan, and India, and graduated from Trinity College in Dublin. So, despite the controversy, Márton Gyöngyösi is not your stereotypical far-right politician. That may be exactly the reason why he is now a leading figure in Jobbik; because he is thoughtful and intellectual, and personifies the radical change of tone that the party has promoted in recent years.

Before Viktor Orbán rose to fame on the European political stage as Hungary's strongman, Jobbik was usually the one attracting international press when Hungarian far-right politics was on the agenda. The party was founded in 2003, and its name is in fact a play on words. In Hungarian, the word *jobb* has two meanings: The adjective for "better" and the direction "right," both similar to the English phrase "right choice," which could mean "a choice on the right side of the political spectrum" as well as "the better choice." Starting out as a radical nationalist student movement in the early 2000s, Jobbik won its first seats in Parliament in 2010.

The first ten years of the party's existence were dominated by extreme rhetoric on race and religion, most frequently directed at Jews and members of Hungary's large Roma minority. In 2007, leaders of the party established a paramilitary group called Magyar Gárda, the "Hungarian Guard," whose stated goals were to strengthen national self-defense and to maintain public order. On several occasions, the Gárda marched through Roma communities with slogans such as "Hungary for Hungarians," creating fear and panic among Hungary's poorest minority group. Magyar Gárda was later sued and, indeed, banned by the country's chief prosecutor, but during the economic and political crisis of 2008 and 2009, hatred toward minorities culminated when six Roma people in the northeastern part of Hungary, including one child, were murdered by neo-Nazis related to Magyar Gárda and Jobbik.

However, since around 2013—after Márton Gyöngyösi moved up the party ranks—Jobbik has undertaken an explicit and concerted shift to the center, toning down its rhetoric and bolstering its policy program to focus on economic inequality and stopping the flow of workers leaving Hungary for other European countries. For instance, Márton Gyöngyösi has proposed a so-called Wage Union between Hungary and its neighbors. The initiative aims to eliminate the economic and wage inequalities between the EU's western and eastern member states. In the same period, Fidesz has seemingly moved the other way, passing on much of the rhetoric and policies initiated by Jobbik.

The party's former party leader, Gábor Vona, who resigned after the 2018 parliamentary elections, has explained Jobbik's transition toward becoming a conservative people's party: "We are growing out of our teenage years. So many times teenagers realize, 'Wow, I was so wrong....' Jobbik may be a teenager who collided with brick walls a few times before realizing life is not black and white."[2]

I am curious to ask Márton Gyöngyösi why Jobbik made this transition, why it did not ensure them a better election result in 2018 than the 20 percent they also got in 2014, and how they will convince the Hungarian people to believe that Jobbik is now truly a moderate conservative people's party. There is a political joke in Hungary about the difference between a rat and a squirrel. The joke addresses the differences—or lack thereof—between the right-wing Fidesz and Jobbik parties. What is the punch line? A squirrel is just a rat with much better PR skills.

Jokes aside, Márton Gyöngyösi adjusts his tie once again and tells me that he is ready to answer my questions.

* * * *

Jobbik is not the first far-right party in Europe to consider rebranding. From Marine Le Pen's National Rally in France to the Austrian Freedom Party's announcement of a commission to examine its history of Nazi ties, several far-right movements across the continent have worked to

*shed their most unsavory elements and broaden their appeal. What is the
reason behind Jobbik's shift toward the center?*

This is a natural progression for a young and radical party. We have
left our teenage years and have now become more responsible adults,
if you like. When I saw what Orbán's government was capable of
once he took power, we began to recognize that we want to stand for
something different. Viktor Orbán and Fidesz have basically become
what we would have become had we not started to change. This
was a lesson for the party, and it contributed to our development, it
helped us to exit from our teenage years.

Some might say that Fidesz just adopted the same policies as Jobbik.

Well, it was Jobbik that first proposed a foreign policy opening
toward the East because of the importance of having good relations
with countries like China, Russia, and Turkey. That idea was stolen
by Viktor Orbán, but simultaneously he slammed the door n the
EU and created a diplomatic crisis between Hungary and Brussels.
It was also us who as early as 2012 suggested building a fence on
the southern border in order to strengthen the Schengen zone's
external border. That idea was copied by Viktor Orbán in 2015, but
he implemented it in such a hysterical way that many of our friends
in Europe are shaking their heads at us today.

*Ironically, it sounds like Jobbik actually achieved these proposals, just
with Viktor Orbán in the forefront. Why don't you then support the
Fidesz government instead of opposing it?*

Because Orbán's corrupt elite of politicians and oligarchs are only
thinking about themselves and not about Hungarians. We have
entered the most critical period in our nation's history since 1989,
and the near future will determine whether Hungary will remain a
democracy in the long run or whether it will transform into a banana
republic where all the skilled citizens will leave Hungary in favor of
better salaries in Western Europe.

After the parliamentary elections in April 2018, Jobbik and other opposition parties faced large financial penalties from the State Audit Office, whose independence is being questioned because the institution is led by a former Fidesz member. Someone from Jobbik said about the situation: "First they steal our ideas, then they take our money." What is your view?

The whole situation with the State Audit Office is quite gloomy, and it appears now that they are going to collect the money and the penalty straightaway. This will basically lead to the party to financial dire straits and collapse, because our account is dry after the election campaign. We will just see what happens. It is quite clear to us that this is a political decision. We are not negotiating here with independent authorities, we are negotiating with authorities that are basically executing political orders. They are following political guidelines. I don't know what will happen. This might be our last occasion to meet like this, but we will try to concentrate on the political tasks ahead of us.

The reason for the penalty is that Jobbik allegedly bought advertising space from Orbán's friend-turned-foe, oligarch and businessman Lajos Simicska. Is there a factual basis for the State Audit Office's statement that you got these advertisements for a price below market value?

Hungary's media and advertising market is imperfect indeed, with much of it connected to Fidesz oligarchs, which is why we had to contact Mr Simicska for our campaign ads. He had something we wanted and something he could not sell anywhere else—ad space. I am an economist, so I know that market denand basically determines the price. Simicska was willing to negotiate a deal, and we were ready to make this deal. I worked for ten years in multinational companies as a tax consultant, so I know from professional experience that determining the market price in an industry like advertising is a difficult task. Of course, a billboard right by the Danube River in central Budapest will cost more than a billboard on a rural, village road.

I also happen to know that the State Audit Office does not have the expertise to determine such market value. This is something that experienced companies like KPMG and Ernst & Young have the capacity to do. But these people in the State Audit Office, they don't even have the capacity to name the market price for a bottle of milk, let alone advertising prices in the Hungarian market. Therefore, the penalty is completely absurd. Clearly, there is no factual basis for this penalty. There is no reasoning, no calculation behind it. It's a joke and it cannot be taken seriously, but unfortunately, we have to take it seriously, because we now live in a dictatorship. That is the bottom line.

When Jobbik became popular, the party had a very distinct brand. We can argue if it was a good or a bad phase, but Jobbik at that time had a very recognizable voice in Hungarian society. This seems to some extent to have been lost as Jobbik shifted to become a moderate conservative people's party. Are you afraid that your party will be less and less important in future politics? In other words, what will become of Jobbik?

Jobbik did have a very distinct brand and rhetoric up until the end of 2013. Since then, we have put a lot of energy into rebranding ourselves and changing this rhetoric. I know that this is a credibility issue that takes time. Is it not something you attain by simply declaring that you have changed. You can achieve this credibility only if you declare your new standpoint over and over again while proving it with certain political actions. Many observers might say that this strategy looks like a trick, and many are still not convinced that Jobbik will hold this line and not move back to the previous brand and rhetoric.

After the previous elections, Jobbik was criticized—both inside and outside the party—for not laying a great enough emphasis on migration. Will Jobbik's policy change in this matter?

We cannot be criticized for not focusing enough on the migration issue. We were the first to suggest the border fence, in spite of all contrary allegations.

But what about Jobbik's current stance on the migration topic? It used to be your primary domain.

We want to discuss migration on the basis of common sense. It is an important issue, it is a global challenge, but there is no such thing as single-minded strategies to global challenges. You cannot have a single-minded strategy to global warming, and you cannot have a single-minded strategy to migration. It is just impossible. We still want to protect our country, and conserving our national identity is an important point, but we have to find some kind of common solution together with our European partners. We have to respect international law, in particular the Geneva Convention. We cannot lead a campaign against world religions, the United Nations, and all our European partners. This is crazy. It might be effective for winning one or two elections, but it isolates our country for the rest of human history. Therefore, it is a bad direction.

You still have not come up with a response to Fidesz's harsh take on especially Muslim migration?

Although we reject the redistribution of migrants in Europe on the basis of quotas determined by Brussels, like Fidesz does, we also warned the government of making statements that basically spark Islamophobia. We cannot go against a world religion. Moderate Islam is our ally in fighting extremism.

You seem to be constantly evaluating your previous strategies. What are your reflections on Hungarian politics these days?

One conclusion is that the political discourse has changed over the past couple of years. This is not a Hungarian speciality. If I look overseas to the United States or even to Germany or Italy, I can see that the political debate has narrowed down there as well. Politics has transformed itself to consist of oversimplified political messages. Today, a political campaign is not an intellectual activity anymore, it is a PR and communication activity.

What did Jobbik do wrong in this respect?

In Jobbik, we were completely wrong when we thought that we could focus on things like the Wage Union campaign, even though both socially and economically it is a question of life and death for a country not to lose all its talent. Hundreds of thousands of Hungarians are leaving the country for social or economic reasons, and we have to deal with this. There is a demographic decline in this country, and in every country in this region. Our best people are leaving. Economic difficulties are ensuing from these problems: we have an enormous shortage of labor in the construction industry, in the service industry, and in tourism, which has been booming. In the healthcare sector as well. This will cause Hungary huge headaches. We thought that with such an important topic, we would do well in the elections, but we were not able to break it down into simple communication. We want to see intellectual discussions about topics like this one, with voters, with experts, with civil society, with our political opponents.

Politics should be like the Agora in ancient Greece, where we get together and talk about these significant issues. It's a painful realization that it is not the case. You need one topic: Migration, for example. A very simple message, which everything else is built around. It should be burned into the voter's head. You just have to push that message through at whatever cost. Orbán and Fidesz did that very effectively. So when you simplify complex matters, the people will come along, and this also goes for positive topics. You do not have to find a scandalous topic to move people, but you have to simplify it and narrow it down completely. The lesson we have learned is that we have to simplify our political messages, break them down and find the means of communication to disseminate them and thus mobilize people. We will have to find some kind of counter-instrument to fight Fidesz in the same simple way.

It sounds to me as if Jobbik then would have to return to the simple rhetorical messages from its past?

I don't believe so. We have a complex topic like the Wage Union that is already being discussed intellectually among academics and EU bureaucrats, but we are well aware that that is not how we can win elections. We have to go down to the streets, which we do, and explain the idea on a different level as well. You have to find the right topics and mobilize on that basis. Previously we found simple topics, but we realized that they were not leading Jobbik in the right direction. Instead, I say that, for instance, the integration of Roma communities into our society is something we have to start dealing with urgently. But how to deal with this topic is a complex matter we need to specify; we did not address such matters very well previously. Nevertheless, I think that we in Jobbik have shown that you can change and approach topics from new angles, now as a people's party, which will benefit a broader sector of society in the long-term.

András Fekete-Győr: My Generation

There is a park in Budapest, located near the parliament building, called Olimpia Park. The small park is used mostly by people walking their dogs and by children there to play, but its iconic memorial monument—the Olympic rings painted in the Hungarian colors, red, white, and green—tells a bigger story: Hungary is a proud Olympic nation.

Few people know that Hungary is actually among the most successful Olympic nations in history, having the most gold medals per capita, and winning more than 500 medals at the Olympic Games since its beginning back in 1896. The country's most symbolic victory was the infamous "Blood in the Water" match in December 1956, during the Summer Olympics in Melbourne, when Hungary's water polo team beat the Soviet Union 4-0, just a few weeks after the Hungarian uprising had been brutally suppressed by the Soviet forces. The brave water polo stars from Hungary's "Golden Team" saw the Olympic Games as an opportunity to restore some of the country's pride. "We felt we were playing not just for ourselves but for our whole country," said Ervin Zádor, the Hungarian hero who at the end of the match had blood pouring from his eye and into the water after being violently punched in the face by a Soviet player.[1]

In Hungary, the "Blood in the Water" match became a national memory of Olympic dimensions. For Viktor Orbán, the country's Olympic traditions and national pride would be elevated to an even higher level if Budapest were to host the Games. Therefore, when he first became prime minister in 1998, Orbán was already plotting to hold the 2012 Olympics in Budapest, but after he lost the election in 2002, the new, left-wing government withdrew the bid. After Orbán returned to office eight years later, his Olympic plan was once again on the agenda. A new bid was now finally being prepared for the 2024 Olympics. "Budapest is the right city, because the developments associated with hosting the Olympic Games in Hungary—such as construction of new roads, railway lines, green spaces, cultural and sports facilities—will mean that audiences would find truly twenty-first century conditions," Viktor Orbán said in August 2016.[2] By that time, more than €20 million had been spent on preparing Hungary's bid to host the 2024 Olympics,[3] but despite the large spending, everything seemed to go according to plan. However, just a few months before the International Olympic Committee was to decide whether Budapest should be the chosen candidate for 2024—thereby fulfilling Viktor Orbán's longstanding dream—something came in the way.

That something was an unforeseen campaign led by a young activist named András Fekete-Győr. In 2016, he had created a new political formation called Momentum Movement, after returning home from his studies abroad. A year later, in the dead of winter, András Fekete-Győr and other activists supporting Momentum went out on the streets to collect signatures among locals in support of a referendum about not holding the Olympic Games in Budapest, citing prohibitively high costs. They dubbed the campaign "NOlimpia." The campaign quickly gained widespread attention on social media, and by being very present in Budapest's many metro stations, squares, and other central locations, the Momentum activists managed to amass more than twice the number of signatures necessary for a referendum. In total, more than 266,000 signatures were collected during the thirty-day NOlimpia campaign. The consequences were quite tangible: The overwhelming support for the campaign eventually made the Orbán government withdraw the bid. "They killed the Olympic dream," a defeated Viktor Orbán said about András Fekete-Győr and the other activists, shortly after the campaign ended in February 2017.[4]

The first time I met András Fekete-Győr was in an office building in central Budapest, not far from Olimpia Park. A few days after he submitted all the signatures, I came to ask him how it felt to challenge Hungary's most powerful man—and win. Also, I wanted to know what his future plans for Momentum were. For someone who'd basically just forced Viktor Orbán to trash his Olympic plans, András Fekete-Győr seemed quite shy and even a bit nervous. He was obviously not used to the huge attention he was now receiving here in the Hungarian capital. He was well-dressed; his dark brown beard followed a sharp, precise line on each of his cheekbones; and his light blue shirt was tucked in. He told me that he lives in a downtown flat owned by his parents. "I live with my French girlfriend. We speak German together, but we watch television in English."

András Fekete-Győr was born into an upper-class family in 1989, He was raised in Budapest, where his father worked as the director of the National Deposit Insurance Fund for many years. His conservative father taught him from a young age that Fidesz was the only hope for Hungary, and even though András Fekete-Győr had a more privileged and urban-cosmopolitan upbringing than did Prime Minister Viktor Orbán—with his relatively poor, rural roots—the two politicians have some things in common. For instance, Fekete-Győr and Orbán both studied law at and graduated from Bibó István College at Budapest's Eötvös Loránd University. Fekete-Győr even voted for Fidesz in 2010—before his disillusionment apparently set in—and he described Orbán as a "helluva talented politician who can speak the language of the common man with his coherent worldview."[5]

To this day, Fekete-Győr still supports Orbán in his efforts to keep immigrants out, but says that this should be done "not so aggressively."

Both Fekete-Győr and Orbán entered the political stage in their twenties, practically from out of nowhere, both out to change the system by forming a party comprising liberal youth.

Finally, they also share a passion for soccer. "But Orbán is a striker and I am a midfielder. This says a lot about our thinking about politics," András Fekete-Győr pointed out.

* * * *

Why did you start Momentum?

We started Momentum because we felt a need for a change of the system. We felt that the Hungarian political elite didn't really change. We have huge systemic problems in Hungary within education, healthcare, and corruption. We believe that we should find mutual solutions, and that we don't have to divide our society on a left-wing/ right-wing basis. So this is what we would like to get beyond. We are the new political generation of Hungary basically. We were born around 1989, while the nation's political system was undergoing a huge change, and we don't want to emigrate from Hungary. We want to stay here.

So what are Momentum's political goals?

The goal is to complete the change of system, so Hungary can become a real democracy. In order to do that, we need to build a Hungary that is stable and secure, and where you can plan your family life in a decent, European way.

What do you mean by a "decent, European way"?

This means that Hungary will be a nation of solidarity, democracy, and freedom. And future-oriented, meaning that we will constantly developing our country and looking for new, innovative solutions to do so. We would like the Hungarian people to think like that as well. This is the Hungary we believe in. Overall, three changes are vital as Momentum sees it. One is to restore a sense of national solidarity, which is missing among the right-wing parties. Hungary has almost four million people living on the edge of poverty, for example. And right-wing politicians like Viktor Orbán don't really care about them. We have to change this. The other challenge we must overcome is this: loyalty is the basis of everything in this country. If you want to get a job or start a business, you have to kiss the hand of politics. And it is going to stay like this, which is why so many people are leaving the country. There is no competition, and your performance is not really evaluated. We would like to change that. Third, we need a national sentiment connecting all sides, some connection that can bring us together to fight for our national causes. Just like with the "NOlimpia" campaign.

Can you elaborate on that campaign? You challenged Hungary's most powerful man and won. Why did you see this approach as a way for people to connect to politics and to society?

It was a very catchy topic, because we could touch on every theme of public interest having to do with politics: corruption, the future of Hungary, national pride, sport, youth, and the nation's political culture. We believe we must solve problems of education, healthcare, housing, rural infrastructure, and poverty. So through the Olympics you really find everything that you can talk about on these issues. To be honest, I think there was a chance that Hungary could have gone bankrupt. Not just like Greece after they hosted the Athens Olympics in 2004, but because our politicians aren't capable of doing business well. Their approach is neither economical nor cost-effective. Therefore, the Olympics in Budapest would have been a project where a few people and businesses would have profited a lot, but not the people. Economically and socially, it could have been a disaster, and to those who say that hosting the Olympics could have improved the Hungarian national pride, I would like to say:

We don't have to build stadiums or organize an Olympic Games to feel this pride. We have to invest in good governance, in human resources, and in long-term prosperity.

Momentum was started by young people like yourself who have been living abroad, and this has been an important issue for you. Why is it essential to mobilize Hungarians living abroad? Do you want to get them to move back, and how are you going to do that?

First of all, they want to come back. A lot of Hungarians don't really find their homes abroad. They love this country, they have their own language. They want to do something for Hungarian society. What Momentum can do for them is to provide them with a perspective. Provide them with a challenge that they can be part of this building process. They all know that they have a lot of knowledge and experience, and, fortunately, money from abroad that they could invest back here in Hungary. That would really bring us to the next level as a society, an economy, and a culture—as all three together. This is really important. This could revolutionize Hungary. Many of our members have university degrees, but they didn't want to join the multinational companies or law firms. They wanted to change something in their environment, and in this historic moment we are experiencing right now, my generation has to stand up and do something.

* * * *

A year after our first conversation, I met András Fekete-Győr again for a short second talk. It was on May 1, 2018, and he was waving a large EU flag over his head, marching in front of hundreds of people who were all marking May Day in central Budapest. In the general election a month prior, Prime Minister Viktor Orbán and his Fidesz party had won their third consecutive win, securing a new two-thirds majority in Parliament. Momentum received 3 percent of the vote—not enough to get any seats in Parliament.

* * * *

Last time we talked, you said you would like to get beyond the left-wing/ right-wing division in Hungarian society. However, many people don't seem to be convinced of what Momentum's political project actually is. Can you elaborate on this? Who is your political inspiration?

As for the party's general political orientation, we are not far from Emmanuel Macron's *En Marche!* movement. We are still communicating that Momentum is neither on the Right nor on the Left, and it takes time to explain this to people, because it is a relatively new approach in politics. When it comes to immigration, we insist that every nation has its right to protect borders and say no to migrants. We are pro-EU, we support gay marriage, and we would like to restore constitutional checks and balances. All in all, we are neither Right nor Left. Our policies are based on issues, not ideology.

How is Momentum going to defeat the Orbán government?

With the enthusiasm that we have right now. We have some really enthusiastic volunteers, and we have all kinds of policy experts, young policy experts, who really put an emphasis on the fields they are working in. We are very mobile and very active. We call the people to action instead of calling on the old political culture. So we are fresh, we are new, and we know our jobs.

It seems like the Right still has a very strong hold on the Hungarian population, and that their views are spreading in Europe. How can you change that?

Time is never-ending; it works in cycles. At the moment, I'll admit, the Right and the populists are having golden days. But after this wave, a new one will appear. And we will be the driving forces behind that wave.

Chapter Eleven
On Activism

Márton Gulyás: The Unorthodox Protester

For the first and only time in my career as a journalist, a dog is sitting at the interview table. In fact, the dog does not really sit for very long at a time, because it runs around in the room and keeps rolling on the floor, but for the most part, it remains relatively quiet under the table. The dog's owner is Márton Gulyás, and he is the one I am about to interview in this meeting room on the Buda side of the Hungarian capital. "It's a Hungarian breed called a Pumi, known for its intelligence and active personality," Gulyás explains. I cannot help but respond: "Well, like owner, like dog." He smiles.

Márton Gulyás is a young civil rights activist, today a household name in Budapest, where most of the public intellectuals are well stricken in age, such as Gáspár Miklós Tamás and academics from the Budapest School. To his mostly young, left-wing followers, Márton Gulyás is a twenty-first century icon of resistance. He is wearing a black leather jacket, and his brushed-back hair and stylish beard make him look more like a Hungarian hipster than a political activist. Márton Gulyás is not just an activist, he is also an influencer, and his YouTube channel—which initially made him famous— has more than 200,000 subscribers. On the crowdfunding page Patreon, monthly fan donations of almost $35,000 help fund his weekly Internet show *Partizán* (previously called *Slejm*), in which he conducts live interviews with primarily left-wing voices, organizes civic happenings, and publishes short documentaries critical of the Orbán regime.

To his detractors, Márton Gulyás is a hooligan. For instance, after a meeting in Parliament's national security committee, a Fidesz MP said Gulyás was a "threat to national security."[1] And when he was caught trying to throw a bottle of orange paint—orange being the Fidesz party color—at the presidential palace during the large anti-Orbán protests in 2017, he was held in police custody for three days and later sentenced to three hundred hours of community service. Known to his supporters as "Marci" (pronounced *Muhr*-tsee), the arrest sparked a demonstration for his release, with hundreds chanting "Marci out, Orbán in" outside a building where he was believed to be held.

For some years now, Márton Gulyás has been under the skin of the Hungarian authorities because of his unorthodox methods of protesting. Another time, he had a scrape with the law when, screwdriver in hand, he arrived at the National Election Commission and removed the plate bearing its name. He received a one-year suspended sentence for this act.

So why would I interview a young hipster-looking dog-owner who constantly gets into trouble with the authorities and hosts his own YouTube show? Because of what he did when he came out of jail in 2017. After his release, he launched the Közös Ország Mozgalom, the Country for All Movement, with the aim of drawing up a new electoral law. The reason: At the national elections in 2014, Viktor Orbán's Fidesz-KMDP alliance received 45 percent of the votes but got 67 percent of the seats in Parliament, a two-third majority. By contrast, Jobbik, the second biggest party, received 20 percent of the votes but got only 12 percent of the seats. The same dynamic was seen at the 2018 national elections. According to Márton Gulyás, this is due mainly to controversial amendments to the electoral law passed in 2011, when the Orbán government—single-handedly, without consulting any other party—decided to make it easier for the biggest party to become even stronger in Parliament.

By creating a new national movement, Márton Gulyás sought to raise awareness about Hungary's nonproportional electoral system, and eventually to make the politicians redress this. If politicians will not meet this demand, says Gulyás, the movement will initiate civil disobedience, strikes, and more.

* * * *

Can you elaborate on your plans for the Country for All Movement? Why is this the way to go?

While I was sitting in jail, I started thinking about my actions. I thought thoroughly about the current situation in Hungary, and I felt that this was the right political moment to give a vision to the people who want change.

And why did you define changing the electoral system as the movement's only goal?

Because the unjust electoral law is the very foundation of the current Hungarian regime. Its purpose is not to reflect the will of the voters, but to keep Fidesz in power. Of course, there are major issues in Hungary, like corruption and poverty, but the root of every problem is that the government cannot be held accountable. The electoral law—which was passed with a two-thirds majority in the National Assembly in December 2011, but without any consensus among the parties—ensures that a strong minority can and will keep Fidesz in power, at least as long as the opposition remains as fragmented as it is now. Without electoral reform, it's nearly impossible to maintain a fair democracy in Hungary.

But if you're right, and the electoral system is so important, Fidesz would never agree to change it. And they still have a majority in Parliament. Why do you see your plan as a realistic way to convince the politicians, who are already in the system, to change the system?

Of course, if Viktor Orbán were sitting here right now, I would ask him to please change the system, and he would not do it. Of course not. Because inaction is not costly enough for him. Besides, this system is vital to maintain his power; it is a fundamental pillar of power for Fidesz. But if there were hundreds of thousands people on the streets ... and if there were nonviolent but very effective civil disobedience, movements— not just one particular action, but a chain of constant actions—then it would be more costly for him to keep this system alive.

And then what?

Then he would have to make a decision. It would be kind of a trade-off for Orbán: "Either I keep the system alive and there will be more people on the streets, more actions, more strikes, and I have to take people to the curb, and I have to sentence them to go to jail." Stuff like that gives your country a very, very bad image—even Hungary, which is a member of the European Union. The other option for Orbán would be: "Or I make the system fairer, and the pressure will be off." The result of the latter decision would be fewer seats in Parliament, but somehow Orbán has to realize that the power he has right now is absolutely not equal to his support among the people. So if he doesn't want to keep this system alive, then he will have to make a decision. We will not be afraid to launch a civil disobedience campaign and use all the necessary tools to put pressure on the government to change their minds.

For a long time, the two most popular parties in Hungary could be categorised as far-right. Fidesz and Jobbik. Actually, for three consecutive elections, two out of three Hungarians voted for these two parties. Could that mean that the Hungarian people maybe do not want to live in a liberal democracy, but prefer a strong, right-wing political leadership instead?

I do not think so. When I travel around the country and talk to people with varied backgrounds, what I see is that everybody wants change, and everybody says they are willing to act. However, in the end, almost no one acts, because they think nothing they do will have an impact, and thus they think there is no point in even trying. The Hungarian people were taught by their governments before and after 1989 to be silent and not to act at all. An environment like this is very favorable to our protofascist regime. But once there's a system that encourages and listens to them, a lot of creative energy will be released.

In recent years, Viktor Orbán has only retreated when confronted with a force more powerful than his or that could jeopardise the system he built.

All I am saying is that there is no other option than a nonviolent civil disobedience movement. If we cannot achieve viable results with this, society will completely lose faith in the possibility of change. In that case, the result will not be apathy, but frustration and aggression. And we have to avoid this scenario at all costs.

* * * *

A year later, I meet Márton Gulyás again, this time without the company of his dog. Since we first met, in 2017, he played an active role in the 2018 national elections by helping the Country for All Movement conduct opinion polls in many of Hungary's electoral districts in an effort to discern which candidates had the best chance of defeating Fidesz. The operation was a success, but the patient died, as we say in Denmark: Viktor Orbán won a new two-thirds majority in Parliament, and the opposition remained fragmented.

This time around, I want to ask Márton Gulyás what his plans as a political activist are in the long term.

* * * *

Your Internet platform used to be called Slejm but is now called Partizán. What is the reason for the name change?

We want to build a left-wing platform critical of capitalism and to do so by way of nonviolent, irregular warfare, just like the Orbán regime has done with its System of National Cooperation. This is what the name *Partizán* expresses. Hungary's left-wing traditions have a weak social memory, and parties that swear to the Left are somehow always betraying their own values. We are committed to a characteristic political position that promotes public discourse on the Left. If there is no such turn-around, the Orbán regime's destruction cannot be stopped.

Doesn't the battle against capitalism contradict the need for a broad social consensus? Your position might seem quite radical for most Hungarians.

Because I cannot imagine how the Orbán regime could be overthrown in the short term, now is the time to expand the radical left-wing position in order to convince society in the long term. Why shouldn't this left-wing platform have much more support in the future than it does now? Fidesz also built a systematic approach over many years. If it succeeded in shifting society in toward the far right, then society can also move back toward more egalitarian, community-oriented policies. This is not impossible, although it is a difficult mission. I would love to spend decades of my life making this happen.

Would you take part in the founding of a new left-wing movement or party, or just add the platform to it?

What I am doing now is political work that can grow into a movement and then into a party. But as long as there is no ideological community—no unified worldview or way of speaking—it is not worth organizing a new movement yet, let alone a political party.

Daniel Friberg: A Western Refugee

Trump winning the US elections. The Brits leaving the EU. Marine Le Pen almost taking power in France. Viktor Orbán ruling Hungary. For Daniel Friberg, these events—and many more in recent years— all prove that the people have had enough of "liberal modernity."

"Now it is time to consolidate," he says when I meet him in a downtown Budapest hotel lobby where he is sipping a drink. The Swedish alt-right activist is only in Budapest for a few hours before he flies northward to Warsaw.

Originally, he moved to Hungary back in 2014, but over the past year, he has been spending more and more time in Poland, now regularly commuting between the two countries, both of which are very appealing to the self-proclaimed Western refugee. Which is lucky, because he simply had enough of his home country Sweden. Why?

"Because we live in a world, at least in Western Europe and the US, that is completely dominated by liberal values," he says, and I ask him why that is a problem. Friberg sighs. He does not even know where to begin, but then he does:

> The list is endless. Liberal values are antitraditional. They have an integrated interest in destroying traditions and old hierarchies and structures and instead establishing this liberal utopia where all individuals are equal. Therefore, we have feminism and the general atomization of society, as well as the destruction of national identities.

Daniel Friberg is a controversial person to many. His voice is rarely listened to in mainstream media; his books are not on the shelves in regular bookstores. Nevertheless, I have decided to talk with him, to listen. I am curious to learn what he thinks. Friberg is one of the leading figures in the global Alt-Right movement that became famous during the 2016 US election campaign. Think Steve Bannon, *Breitbart News*, Richard Spencer, and the like. The movement stood out, not least because of its alternative, postmodern approach, combining a brutal—in some cases racist—online vocabulary with a confident intellectual appearance. Daniel Friberg himself is wearing a suit and tie. He argues that after Trump and Brexit, after the radical Right and its fight for white people's identity, the approach finally found a way into the public debate. He believes that the time has come to make the trend permanent. Period. Therefore, the current task is to give the intellectuals a framework, to provide white people with a common language, one that can accommodate their feelings of alienation and atomization that exists here "at the end of individualization."

As Viktor Orbán said after his 2018 victory in the national elections, "The era of liberal democracy is over."[1]

Daniel Friberg could not agree more.

Friberg's childhood in Gothenburg was happy and secure. He grew up around left-wing, politically correct, middle-class citizens and he saw himself as one of them. However, slowly but surely, he began to realize that the idea of a multicultural society was letting him down, time and time again, and he started his long journey toward the Right. He read alternative books, he researched Swedish crime statistics on his own, and he later he joined the far-right Sweden Democrats. Meanwhile, he studied economics at Gothenburg Business School, held business lectures at universities, and became a nomadic businessman—until he eventually started to miss his "own civilization." He couldn't find it in Sweden anymore. That's when he moved to Hungary, in 2014. Since then he has written several books on the far-right movement—and published many others through his independent publishing company, Arktos. He also cofounded the online platform *AltRight.com*, one of the world's most popular far-right news sites until it was taken off the Internet by the host in 2018, stating that it crossed a line in encouraging and promoting violence.[2] Overall, there is enough to talk about, and we don't have much time before Friberg has to leave for the airport. He takes one more sip of his drink, and we begin the interview.

* * * *

Why did you choose to move to Budapest in 2014, and why are you still staying here in Hungary on a regular basis?

It was not really for political reasons, to be honest. Hungary is a very nice place, Budapest is a beautiful city, there is a very low crime rate, and there is a minimal immigration. This goes for the whole former Eastern Bloc; all these countries have the same advantages. Partly this is due to the dominating politics in the region, which are quite conservative. The region does not accept migration; it rejects the refugee quotas. I do not believe in multiculturalism. A terrible concept, it is the largest catastrophe we have been facing, and mass immigration leads to huge problems. If you look at statistics from Sweden, a very large portion of the population is non-European, and in five years, this will be even more the case. The same tendencies are seen in Great Britain, Belgium, the Netherlands, and Germany. I do not like that trend. I prefer to be around people who are similar to me, even if they speak a Slavic language or Hungarian. That holds more value to me, and the old Eastern Bloc is in better shape in this respect than Sweden, where, in many areas, you will only see non-Europeans.

What is it about Hungary that appeals to you and to many others on the European Right? Is the political environment different than that of Scandinavia?

I am no expert in Hungarian or Central and Eastern European politics, but I am very interested. The most important reason for liking these countries is their approach to migration. They do not want multiculturalism. That is why more and more people are moving from Western Europe to Hungary, for example. Not because they want to engage in the political life of these countries. No, what they care about is coming to a country with security and low crime rates, somewhere they can feel safe in their own neighborhood. Even though I am interested in political developments in Hungary and Poland, I am no expert in their policies. I care more about politics in Sweden, my home country, where the politicians are doing a horrible job and are destroying the country's future. I do not think one should come to a new country and interfere in its politics. Hungarians are very good at dealing with Hungarian politics without external help.

What else appeals to you in countries like Hungary?

There is way more freedom of speech in Hungary and Poland. Here, the pressure to be politically correct is absent, unlike in Sweden, where it forces you to not discuss important issues like immigration. That situation does not exist here in Hungary as far as I am concerned. In Sweden, my views are probably seen as extremist, but here, my conservative perspective is mainstream. The books I publish through Arktos are sold in bookstores everywhere in Hungary. Nationalism is quite natural for these countries. And I am quite sure that communism— though I oppose that ideology—was less destructive than is liberalism. That is why we see certain differences between Western and Eastern countries in Europe. Central and Eastern Europe would never accept immigration. "Why on earth should we?" its people would ask. They have seen how it turned out on the other side of the old Iron Curtain, in Western Europe.

Is the continual division between East and West caused only by their different political and cultural approaches? Or is the economic situation also an explaining factor?

I do not think that the difference between East and West is caused by an economical factor. Relatively speaking, people here are poorer than those in the West, but when you talk about living standards, people are not as unequal here. Because of the low costs in Central and Eastern Europe, Polish people are richer in their own country than Swedish people are in Sweden. In Sweden it is almost impossible for young people to buy a house, and the situation is easier for people in the Visegrád countries, in my opinion. The financial factor is not why people here are rejecting migration. They look at Western Europe and they see what is going on. They do not want their fellow countrymen to be replaced by Africans or people from the Middle East, they do not want mixed races. Western countries have seen "white flight," with citizens of the native ethnicity moving away from certain areas that have large immigrant populations. In Sweden, it has become a luxury to be able to move away from the problems, and many ignore them.

In February 2017, Viktor Orbán gave a speech in which he invited Western Europeans who have become "victims of liberalism" to get political asylum in Hungary. He said:"Of course we can give shelter to the real refugees: Germans, Dutch, French, Italians; scared politicians and journalists; Christians who had to flee their own country; those people who want to find here the Europe that they lost at their home."[3] Does this perfectly align with your own approach, as it seems?

That could not be more true. I totally agree. People are moving from West to East because they do not want to live among migrants. This goes for both liberals and conservatives. These are still white countries, they are still Europe. I feel more at home in these countries than I do in Sweden, or Belgium or London, for that matter. The trend is caused by the horrible multicultural experiments in the West, which for many people have resulted in making their home countries uninhabitable. Many of the those moving to Hungary are resourceful people with their own businesses and a certain flexibility. They can take care of themselves. From my point of view, that is quite beneficial for the Eastern countries—to have people with good resources who bring capital with them into the country. This is the type of migration one would want, and I understand why Viktor Orbán brings it up. People just want to live in peace.

In your 2016 book The Real Right Returns, *which was translated into fourteen languages, you argue that the left-wing is dying and that the "authentic right-wing is about to flourish." What do you mean by that?*

We have been seeing an enormous influx of people to the Alternative Right, and that has created a need for an introduction to our rich world of ideas. The book communicates alternative ideals to the liberal modernity. That is a perspective needed more than ever in a time where liberal modernity is on its deathbed, and when left-wing intellectuals are unable or unwilling to face up to reality. I see myself and my books as a mirror of liberal democracy. To bring forward the perspective that there used to be something to hold on to in this world. Or something that you were fixed to. Like a gender. A family. A religion. A people. A nation. A hierarchy. Maybe you could not leave these identities or move up through this hierarchy, and maybe you were not free to move anywhere at all. But at least you were something, and you knew *what* you were. Today, we are all alone with ourselves in a world we don't know how to navigate.

That sounds almost poetic. Who was your inspiration to unify all these reflections in your so-called "handbook for true opposition"?

In my eagerness to understand the problems with immigration that I experienced in my home country, I began to read books written by the French philosophers Alain de Benoist and Guillaume Faye. They are two of the main thinkers behind the Nouvelle Droite movement—the French "New Right." They emerged in the 1970s and later laid the ground for the political breakthrough of National Front (Marine Le Pen's party, today called National Rally). Their intellectual approach was a true revelation for me. I couldn't find anything that I disagreed with.

Besides writing your own books, you also publish other authors through your publishing company, Arktos, and you cofounded the AltRight.com news site. Why is there a need to promote far-right political views on these platforms?

That is like asking why we need newspapers that can reflect readers' opinions. We feel that there is a need to create a media platform that in the long term can communicate and spread these views that we have. The readership is growing, and we are on the right track. We have a staff of forty writers and editors with various backgrounds. Most of them are from the US and Europe, but some are from countries like Japan. Arktos is publishing books that are exploring the alternatives to the liberal modernity. The authors' focus is mostly outside of the mainstream.

How do you think Hungary can contribute to the understanding and dissemination of your thoughts and ideas? Are you not afraid of ending up like an echo chamber on the Right?

I do not think that what I do can be equated with an echo chamber. We are selling more books, we are attracting a broader audience. We have been reaching a lot of people, and this has been happening almost automatically as people face up to reality. We are experiencing a turn toward the Right. We still have a lot of political correctness to deal with, and the road ahead is long. But the fact that more and more journalists, politicians, and other opinion makers are talking about the migration problem shows that we are moving in the right direction. I just wish we could move even faster.

János Szűcs: Roma, Fight for Your Rights

On a cold Saturday afternoon, in front of Debrecen's busy outdoor mall, I am waiting for János Szűcs. We have planned to go on a small road trip today, on an unspecified route around northeastern Hungary. A few minutes later, he picks me up in his dark blue BMW. The driver's seat is on the right-hand side of the car and the license plates are not Hungarian. He tells me that he purchased the car in England while he was working and studying there, before bringing it with him to Hungary a couple of years ago. "So, where do you want to go?" he asks. "Let's head east." He speeds up, takes a sharp right turn, and soon we are on the roads outside of Debrecen.

János Szűcs is a young activist who grew up in a poor Roma family in the region. After having internships in the European Parliament and at the US Embassy in Budapest, he has now returned to his birthplace to try to make a difference. "Nobody else is doing anything for the deprived Roma population, so we might as well do it ourselves," he says. Hungary's Roma minority has doubled in size over twenty-five years, according to a 2018 study conducted by researchers at the University of Debrecen.[1] Today there are close to one million Roma people in Hungary, and in large parts of northeastern Hungary—where we are driving today—the Roma community comprise 20-25 percent of the total population. Moreover, all demographic projections estimate that the minority will continue to grow in the coming decades. Yet, according to János Szűcs, none of these demographic trends are reflected in the country's Roma policies, which, he points out, means that this minority will remain poor, uneducated, and in unfavorable health circumstances.

On our road trip, we make stops in villages such as Vámospércs and Újléta to talk to people from the large Roma communities living on the edge of civil society. Later in the afternoon, we drive further north where the situation among the Roma people is even worse. If you did not know better, you would not believe that we are in an EU country. Along the train tracks, a boy of five or six is walking alone, barefoot, seemingly with no sense of direction. In one small village, the houses are so dilapidated that I cannot help thinking about the henhouse from the Danish film *Little Virgil & Orla Frogsnapper*. Down the bumpy gravel road, a middle-aged man lets us in his 100-square-foot, almost roofless hut, where he has lived his whole life without running water or electricity. "It makes me sad to see that the situation here is not only not better than when I grew up, but that it is actually worse," says János Szűcs. We get back into the car. He sighs, but says that he is ready to share his reflections on the whole situation.

* * * *

How would you describe the Roma situation in Hungary today?

The Roma situation in Hungary, overall, is the worst situation in the country. There are other countries where the Roma people are living under even worse conditions, including Romania and Bulgaria. But here it is not good, either. Many people live in terrible conditions in very poor houses, under very bad circumstances, with little money. Thousands of homes in northern and eastern Hungary have ten people or more together in one house. They have maybe €300-

400 to share between them for the month, and surviving on this is impossible. Many Roma people don't have work. I know that the situation for [non-Roma] Hungarians is not the best, either. For the Roma population, it is horrible. One reason is a lack of jobs. Another reason is intense discrimination and racism.

Why do you think the Roma people experience this discrimination, this hatred and prejudice, from non-Roma Hungarians?

The main reason has to do with money. The Roma people don't have money, but they have to live. Because there is no money and there are no jobs, they have to do something. They are forced to steal, to commit crimes; there is no other way. Often they are stealing trees that they can burn to heat their houses, or they steal from other people. If they don't steal, they will die. Somehow they have to survive this very bad situation.

Do you understand the perspective of those [non-Roma] Hungarians who see this crime and turn it into mistrust and hatred toward the Roma people?

Yes. But very often, Hungarian people do not think about the reason behind this crime. Why do the Roma people steal? They only see the Roma crime, and they see that they live in very bad conditions and that they have poor or no education. Non-Roma Hungarians only see these things, but rarely do they think about why the situation is like this. Why are these people not studying? Why do they not go to school? Hungarians have to ask themselves these questions as well. They focus on what is visible, not on the deeper reason behind all this.

One of the prejudices non-Romas have about Roma people is that Romas have a lot of children. Why do most Roma people have so many children?

Mainly because they don't have jobs. They stay at home, they just live for the kids. If a mother gives birth to one child, the family wants more. They really love this part of life. And if they are at home and don't have jobs, why not have some children? Family is very important for Roma people. Hungarians work and don't have the time or desire to have more than one, maybe two children.

Some argue that Roma people have many children in order to get more support from the state.

I think this is kind of ridiculous. For one child, a family gets €70 a month. For this amount of money, you would barely be able to buy diapers for the child.

Human rights and solidarity for minorities seem to be under pressure in Hungary—and in Europe and in the world in general. What is your experience of this?

From the Roma perspective, I would say that, logically, political condescension is not the basis for a successful integration. Since the fall of communism, in 1990, the situation of the Roma has been deteriorating continuously. Roma people are excluded from workplaces, we get a worse education, and our children are often forced into segregated schools. The social situation is getting worse; many of the kids are hungry. Prejudice and racism are getting stronger. Furthermore, politics excluded us. The nation's electoral law has been transformed so that Roma people cannot really have parliamentary representatives on their own. Social policies, such as the CSOK family program, have been transformed so that the Roma are left out.

What needs to be done to help the Roma people?

Well, they need political support. They need a political party that really wants to help. This is what I am working on. The European Union sends a huge amount of money to improve Roma integration, but unfortunately, more than 70-80 percent of this support just disappears,[2] and the result is that the "Roma problem" continues to exist. There needs to be a real, Roma minority party that can represent these people, because they cannot really make any sustainable change without help from others.

Are the Roma people doing something wrong? Is there something they could do themselves in order to help their own situation?

The Roma people themselves have to change, too. They have to adapt to the norms of Hungarian society, the majority population. Indeed, many of them want to do so if they see that they are being treated nicely and accepted by others. This won't work if only one side wants to adapt to the other side, no, it needs to go both ways for this minority and the majority to be able to live together in Hungary.

What norms must the Roma people adapt to?

Many of the norms are the same; the differences between Hungarians and Roma are not as big as many people think. Maybe the clothes they wear are different. Everybody knows that the Roma people love their families more than anything else, that they will do anything to protect their children. It's the only thing that matters. This is the same for non-Roma Hungarians. Also, the language is the same. Most Roma people don't even speak the Romani language, they only speak Hungarian, like everyone else.

How have you experienced this yourself?

I am a Hungarian Gypsy, a real *cigány*. I grew up around Hungarian people as well as Roma people. I went to the same school as non-Roma Hungarians, who were among my friends; we share the same culture. The Roma culture goes back a long time. It goes back many centuries. For more than six hundred years, the Roma people have been here in Hungary. We speak the same language, we are Hungarian citizens, and we have Hungarian passports.

So what is it that still divides those who deem themselves ethnic Hungarians and Roma people in Hungary? What are the main differences?

Honestly, there is no difference other than the color of our skin. That is the only real difference.

How is that playing a role in the division?

Let's say that a white Hungarian meets a person who is a little bit browner than he is. Immediately there is discrimination. The Roma people have been here for six hundred years, and they behave like Hungarians. But still, there is this discrimination.

How does it feel for Roma people to be Hungarian, to speak Hungarian, to have lived in Hungary for many centuries, and then still experience this discrimination?

If you have a conversation with a Hungarian, you can feel it in how they answer you. In how they look at you, in their tone of voice. If you go to a job interview you experience it as well. I have three degrees, a good CV that details jobs I've had with the European Parliament and the US Embassy in Budapest. But, still, when I have gone to job interviews, I experience discrimination. Not really face to face, but between the lines. Hungarians don't explicitly say "fucking Gypsy" or something like that. But their tones of voice say a lot. If you talk with someone, you can feel that they are not sympathetic toward you. You don't hear it, you *feel* it.

How was the Roma situation before the fall of communism in 1990?

I am too young to have experience`d it myself, but I have studied this and many people have told me that the situation was better then. The [country's socioeconomic] structure back then aimed to ensure that all people would have the same opportunities—something akin to a broad middle class. After the fall of communism, this middle class disappeared. Since then, there has been a very long distance between the top and bottom rungs of society. Back then, the system demanded that everybody had a job. Not being employed was a crime. So everybody was officially employed and getting almost the same salaries. But then the multinational companies arrived in Hungary and everything changed.

What did the fall of communism mean for the Roma people?

It meant that many people lost their jobs. After that, they were segregated from the rest of society, living on the outskirts of the villages, isolated from the lives of other Hungarians, with no jobs, and every year since then the situation has become worse and worse. I don't know how it will be in ten years or so, but if we don't do anything to solve this problem, it will be a huge catastrophe.

How so?

The demographic figures show that the nation's Roma population is growing. Today it is 15 percent, that will become 20 or 25 percent, and so on. Nowadays, in northeastern Hungary there are areas with only Roma people; there is a village with an all-Roma school. We are a minority, but 20 percent of a country's population is not really a small minority, so we—and by "we," I mean our political organization and other activists—argue that Roma people should have their voices heard. Solving the problem will take many decades, not just five or ten years, but if we don't start now we will never solve it.

In Western societies, similar problems have emerged after decades of immigration, especially of Muslim people from the Middle East. In some places, this has led to segregated areas and ghettos with poor immigrants and high crime rates. Are there parallels to the integration problems with the Roma people in Hungary?

In some ways, yes; in other ways, no. The Muslims in Western countries have their own original countries and their own languages. The Roma people have lived in Hungary for centuries; they are Hungarian and speak Hungarian. We are a part of Hungary. Therefore, the situations are a bit different. We are not foreign people in Hungary. Actually, many Hungarian people do not discriminate against the *cigány*, because they know we are also Hungarians. We have a common culture, a common language. The immigration from the Muslim world is different; their religion is very different, and their cultures are very different. Muslims have their own, original countries, at least most of them do. Roma people don't.

Your party, the Opre Roma party, has presented the idea of establishing an independent Roma province in northeast Hungary. What is the point?

Our first idea was to suggest that all Hungarian citizens, not just Roma people, but everyone, would get 100,000 forints, or €300, a month. As a basic income. All over Hungary there are many poor people, and our aim is not to just help the Roma people but to help all poor people. We want to eradicate poverty in Hungary. We want to reach a situation where everyone feels comfortable and live under normal circumstances. We proposed it to Parliament, which rejected it completely. After that, we realized that if Parliament and the government don't want to do anything to help the Roma people and the poor people, then we have to do something. If the government is not listening, we will try to do something ourselves and solve the problem. That is why we suggest a Roma province, because within this framework we could have some authority, some law of our own, and be able to manage our issues. If we would get funding from EU projects or from somewhere else, we would be able make sure that the money would reach this province and come directly to the Roma people living there, not into the pockets of Hungarian politicians. We think it is unacceptable that some Roma families of ten people live on €300 a month. That is why we suggested this idea. We think this could be the first step toward creating our own country.

How would this Roma province work in practice?

We don't want to break away from Hungary, because we are Hungarians. So this province would be a part of Hungary consisting mostly of Roma people who we would make sure could have an acceptable life through the autonomous authority. We would establish our own police force, our own hospitals, and so on. We want more power and authority, but we don't want to segregate ourselves from the rest of the Hungarian society. It would still operate under Hungarian law.

What are some challenges of bringing this idea to fruition?

Well, there are many. We are a young party, and the political establishment regards us as a bit silly, to be honest. We want to learn, we want to develop. Our ears are open to all kinds of advice, not least from other countries.

Would Roma people from other countries be welcome as well?

Yes, of course. We make no distinctions between the Roma citizens of different countries. We share the same ethnicity and culture; we are one big family. We are all *cigány*. If we are successful in establishing this province, the doors will be open to all Roma people.

One could argue that if you create your own, autonomous province, you might be discriminated even more by the majority of ethnic Hungarians. How do you see this?

The majority population would probably view autonomy as separation from Hungary. This is a big challenge. If Roma people from this autonomous province would go to, say, western Hungary, the discrimination awaiting them there would be even harsher: "Why don't you stay in your own province?" they might then be asked. And yet we have asked many Roma people what they think, and 70 percent of them support the idea of an autonomous Roma province. They support it because they live in very bad conditions and because they think that things could only get better.

Is that why the idea came up in the first place? Like a loud cry for help, the last possible solution to the problem?

For the Roma people, this idea seems to be the lesser of two evils. No one has been willing to really help us in our plight, so we're ready to handle our issues ourselves. Optimally, we hope, the Hungarian government will do something, or we will be able to solve the problem jointly with them. If we push this idea for an autonomous province, the government eventually might realize that it needs to help us, because otherwise it will lose us. Hungarian history has seen many great losses—like the post–World War I Treaty of Trianon, under which Hungary lost most of its territory—and, we think, most Hungarians don't want to lose more people or territories. The same goes for us, actually, which is why this is a last resort. We'd prefer to solve the problem jointly with Hungarians.

What do you think would be the ultimate consequences if Hungary does not solve its Roma problem?

Like I said earlier, the Roma population is growing, and we will be a bigger part of Hungary in the future. More than 25 percent, and in the long term, even more. If all these people continue to live under such poor circumstances, this will lead to civil war. I think this is common sense. I hope people won't kill each other, but this is the future we face, and I don't really know where it will end.

What would it mean for you to have your own country?

It would mean having our own house. Without a house, you just live in other people's garden. You don't feel comfortable there. Maybe a country is just a name, but it matters a lot to have your own place. But unfortunately, we don't have a house. If we don't do anything—and by "we" I mean well-educated Roma people—then who will? Nobody will.

Chapter Twelve
On Culture

Éva S. Balogh: Hunting for Historical Justice

I always find it quite amusing to tell my friends and family that a fair portion of my knowledge about Hungary originated from a US-based blogger in her eighties. Yes, that's right. Éva S. Balogh was her name, and she was the woman behind the daily political news blog *Hungarian Spectrum*. Until her sudden death, in 2021, every single day of the year—just around midnight, Budapest time—she published a well-written news digest in English summarizing the latest political affairs in Hungary, full of source references and often including her own take on developments. Especially in my first years as a correspondent, the blog helped deepen my understanding of Hungary, and I know that *Hungarian Spectrum* was widely acknowledged by ambassadors, expats, journalists, academics, and many others with an interest in current affairs related to Hungary.

Raised in Pécs and educated in Budapest, Éva S. Balogh left Hungary in 1956 as a twenty-year-old university student, after the Soviets crushed Hungary's popular anti-Soviet uprising. She became a landed immigrant in Canada, studied history there, and completed an MA and PhD at Yale University in New Haven, Connecticut, not far from where she settled down. Throughout the second part of the twentieth century, she pursued an illustrious academic career as a professor of history at Yale University, writing numerous studies on Hungarian foreign policy and party politics, mostly focusing on the period between the two World Wars, in which she was born herself.

However, in 1993, when Éva S. Balogh first visited Hungary after the fall of communism, she realized that, despite her background as a historian, she was "totally ignorant" about the real state of the country that she had left almost forty years prior. In a video interview from 2014, Balogh recalled that she had expected everyone in Hungary to be overjoyed after the political transition and was dismayed to find that this was not the case:

> You know, there was democracy, and we were free, there were no more Russians, everything was just splendid. It was a terrible surprise to find that everybody hated the government, everybody was outraged, everybody hated each other, and they announced that this was the end of the world. So, I thought it was time to learn something."[1]

In order to better understand what was really going on in Hungary, she began to dig deep, using her research skills to find the best sources of information. Over the years, Balogh shared her findings, and her opinions, on various online forums, and in 2007, she finally decided to launch the *Hungarian Spectrum* blog. Slowly but surely, her daily posts gathered more and more attention, and as of 2021, the site had more than 7,000 active subscribers.

Unfortunately, I never got the chance to meet Éva S. Balogh in person. From the video interviews and pictures that I have seen of her, she looked very much like a typical Hungarian grandmother. Short gray hair, glasses, and often wearing a wool sweater. But make no mistake: Her analytical pen was as sharp as a razor, and she might have been the world's most insightful, up-to-date mediator of Hungarian politics. From reading *Hungarian Spectrum* for almost a decade, I was well aware that Éva S. Balogh was not impartial when it came to political life in Hungary. She was a stern center-left critic of the Orbán government and its actions, and even though her coverage was in-depth, it was also quite subjective.

One of the subjects Éva S. Balogh often returned to was the continuous political fight over Hungarian history. Hungary has many historical wounds that never really healed, including the one that made her flee the country in 1956. I was curious to ask the practised historian what she made of all this, so I sent her an email she replied to. The following interview, then, is the full email correspondance between an old Hungarian history teacher in Bethany, Connecticut, and a young Danish journalist in Debrecen, Hungary.

* * * *

In the years following the fall of communism in 1990, Hungary was considered one of the most prodemocratic countries in the former Soviet Bloc. What are the historical reasons that Hungary has taken a new direction since Viktor Orbán came into office in 2010? What is his motivation?

In the last 10–15 years of the Kádár regime (János Kádár having been Hungary's communist leader from 1956 to 1988), few people felt that they lived in a dictatorship. The regime carefully avoided intrusion into people's private lives. There were about 800,000 communist party members, but membership entailed little actual involvemenensured that this was added to the nation's constitution: t in politics. At the same time, living standards improved steadily, at the cost of serious foreign debt. By the late 1980s, Hungarians equated democracy with much higher living standards, which many experienced first-hand during their visits to Austria and Germany. After 1990, living standards dropped, unemployment rose—and disillusionment followed. Unfortunately, between 1990 and 2010, the successive government could not solve the country's economic problems. The 2008 economic crisis gave the final push for a government with immense power that would solve the problems without all the endless give and take typical of democracies. Even some liberals thought Fidesz would use its power wisely. More disappointment was to follow.

In 1956, Hungarians protested against the Soviet Union and fought for freedom also from the oppressive nature of the communis regime. In recent years, the Fidesz government has protested against the EU and is fighting for independence and self-determination from Brussels bureaucrats. On several occasions, Viktor Orbán has even compared Soviet rule in Moscow with EU rule in Brussels. Do you see any similarities between the two historic events? What are the obvious contrasts?

Such a comparison has no basis in reality, and even Fidesz makes it only sparingly. Yes, Orbán here and there has talked about Hungarians' devotion to freedom, but the fact is that Hungarians are usually quite satisfied with being obedient and loyal subjects. What happened in 1956 was unique. Both the political and economic situation was close to being unbearable for all segments of society.

From politicians to everyday citizens, Hungarians ascribe a lot of meaning into certain events in Hungarian history. Often they interpret the same events very differently. It can take years, even decades, to obtain historical consensus. Are Hungarians getting closer to some kind of agreement about what happened in 1956, for example?

I still don't think that there is consensus about the events of 1956. Not at all. Fidesz over the years has tried to rewrite the history of the revolution several times. First, in their "bourgeois" phase, Orbán announced on one of the annual commemorations of the October 23 anniversary that 1956 had been a bourgeois revolution. In the last 10-15 years, the new script is that the real heroes of the revolution were those 12-16-year-old boys who fought on the streets with guns in hand. So the revolution was in fact a massively anticommunist uprising. The truth, of course, is much more complicated. The revolution began as an anti-Stalinist movement in the hope of "reforming" the socialist system, and only in its final days did parties re-emerge. As for the "people," the majority wanted to keep the factories in the hands of the workers' councils.

You are a historian with a long academic career at a prestigious institution, Yale University. In recent years in Hungary, many have argued that academic freedom is under pressure. Looking back, how would you describe the conditions of scientific research behind the Iron Curtain before 1989?

One must distinguish between different time periods between 1948 and 1989. Prior to 1956, suppression was complete. As a result, practically all historical texts that emerged during that period in Hungary and addressed events jn the relatively recent past, such as the nineteenth and twentieth centuries, were of extremely low quality. Literary history was no better. Sociology was banned. The immediate post-1956 period was better, but it took a fairly long time before serious historical debate could take place again. By the mid-1970s, some very good historians, publishing excellent monographs, came to the fore. Their books are useful even today. By that time, sociology appeared again as a legitimate subject and researchers working in the institutions of the Hungarian Academy of Sciences did a lot of good sociological work on poverty, public opinion, and other so-called "sensitive" subjects. Nevertheless, there remained taboo subjects, including the 1919 Hungarian Soviet Republic; that era's communist leader, Béla Kun; the Soviet Union's role in Hungary after 1945; and the influence of the illegal communist party in the interwar period. Otherwise, the situation was infinitely better than in other socialist countries.

What happened to science and research in the years after 1989 in the new Central and Eastern European democracies? Was everything set free, or was there still some kind of control during the first years after 1989?

According to people who lived through those first few years, there was a real flowering then of scholarship, as well as of journalism. There were no more taboos. Also, because of easy communication and the opening of some Soviet archives, a great deal of more information became available. At the same time, it became easy for Hungarian researchers to visit French, German, British, and American archives.

The arrival of capitalism brought one drawback, however. During the Kádár regime, book publishing was heavily subsidized and therefore books were inexpensive. Thus, it could easily happen that 2,000-3,000 copies of a serious historical text sold out in days. Nowadays, it is difficult to find a publisher—books are expensive and few people can afford them. The only restriction I can think of is that all Hungarian governments have been reluctant to completely open the files of the network of informants during the 1945–1989 period. All have worried that skeletons might fall out from the ranks of their own politicians.

In the early 1990s, George Soros cofounded the Central European University, and after starting out in Prague, it was eventually headquartered in Budapest. The university soon became a symbol of free academic research in Central Europe, but in 2017, the Orbán government got Parliament to change Hungary's higher education law, thus pressuring CEU to close down. Can you explain what is at stake here?

Everything has radically changed since 2010, when Fidesz won the elections with a two-thirds majority. Clearly, Orbán considers the current set of researchers in the social sciences and the humanities hopeless liberals who distort the past. So he began setting up "alternative" institutions, financed by the government, which are supposed to rewrite history according to the wishes of the current government. I call it falsification of history.

The old elite's "monopoly" on knowledge and the media seems to have been broken in this new era marked by populism, fake news, and social media. Where does that leave Hungary's academic researchers? How have they been responding?

In Hungary, the response has been mostly silence. Or, rather, academics are still publishing critical articles, but their work reaches relatively few people. Moreover, the Orbán government completely ignores them. None of their suggestions are ever accepted. The government has made snap decisions about key issues, like education, decisions that experts often saw as ill-advised, but the government has gone ahead anyway. So no wonder academics have been giving up.

How do you think the academic situation in Hungary will develop in the next few years?

I am afraid that the situation is becoming increasingly worse. As is, Hungary is no longer a real democracy, and tightening control can be seen in every facet of life, including research. One must not forget that the best researchers have already left the country.

In broader terms, how do you think Hungarian society will develop— politically, economically, socially—over the next decade or so if things continue as they are?

Given the system that Orbán has devised, changing direction can be done only by Fidesz, which is unlikely. And there is no one on the other side, on the center-left, who seems capable of getting the support of the majority of the population. But I am almost certain that the country and its people cannot possibly survive another ten years of this regime. Something eventually will have to give.

Mária Schmidt: A New Era has Arrived

History ended more than thirty years ago. At least that has been the dominating narrative throughout the Western world ever since 1989, when political scientist Francis Fukuyama published his epoch-making essay "The End of History?," which went on to become the 1993 book *The End of History and the Last Man*.[1] Fukuyama's argument was that, with the collapse of the Soviet Union, the last ideological alternative to liberalism had been eliminated. However, in postcommunist countries like Hungary, the fall of communism didn't mean that all the pieces of the jigsaw suddenly fell in place. Rather the opposite. The country's newfound freedom meant that old historical events could be debated again by the Hungarians, after they had been more or less silenced or tabooed during four decades of one-party rule. These historical events included the Treaty of Trianon, the Holocaust, and the 1956 Revolution, but, as it turned out, there was little consensus on any of them.

In the mid-1990s, the Hungarian historian Mária Schmidt started working as a professor at a Catholic university in Budapest. However, she bitterly discovered that her conservative interpretation of Hungary's history clashed with the mainstream narratives, which often align with the West's liberal perspective. A couple of years later, in 1998, she was appointed chief advisor to the young Prime Minister Viktor Orbán, and since then, Mária Schmidt has worked very closely with Orbán, with whom she shares many of her conservative views on history and political ideology.

It is only my second boat tour on the Danube River. The first time was years ago, shortly after I first arrived in Budapest, when I drank red wine and observed the beautiful city from the rooftop of a tourist ferry. This time it is more serious. A government-friendly organization, the Friends of Hungary Foundation, has invited me and a dozen other foreign journalists on a boat tour where Mária Schmidt, among others, will be available for interviews. Of course I take the invitation. For almost a year, I have tried to get a personal interview with the government-appointed historian, and now finally the chance has come to get a better understanding of her views on Hungarian history.

Mária Schmidt is a divisive figure in Hungary. Her government-funded museum, the House of Terror—which she opened on Budapest's Andrássy Boulevard in 2002—focuses on the communist and fascist regimes in Hungary and regularly has tourists lining up around the block. However, critics say that the popular museum does not adequately address Hungary's role in the Holocaust. Furthermore, over the past few years, the Orbán government's plan to open the House of Fates—a Holocaust museum in Budapest, directed by Mária Schmidt—sparked additional controversy. The historian has repeatedly equated and lumped together the Holocaust and the Soviet domination of Hungary, stating that Nazism was no worse than Soviet communism. Her standpoint caused Jewish groups and the Yad Vashem, Israel's state museum on the Holocaust, to boycott the House of Fates, fearing that the museum will "ignore anti-Jewish laws passed by the Hungarian government in 1938, the deaths of tens of thousands of Hungarian Jews during World War II in forced labor imposed by the government, and the participation of Hungarian authorities in the deportation of Hungarian Jewry to Auschwitz."[2]

Without a doubt, history still is a delicate topic in Hungary. But Mária Schmidt has not given up the fight for her readings of the truth. That is what stirred my initial interest in her work, and that is why I am now on this boat, cruising up and down the Danube River while Mária Schmidt is explaining her points. I notice the cross hanging from her necklace as we sail pass the Hungarian parliament building. When she realizes that I am Danish, she casts a smile. "Oh, your government is doing exactly the right thing, limiting migration into your country." The historian certainly is a politician, too, and perhaps history and politics are more intertwined than some of us might think. In Hungary, indeed, Fukuyama's end of history has been postponed indefinitely.

* * * *

What is important to understand about Hungary's history?

One perspective that comes to mind is the difference between Europe's East and West, and their different understanding of history, culture, and values. Hungary has always been somewhere in the middle, but of course the time behind the Iron Curtain meant that we were bound to the East for forty-five years. For us Hungarians, independence and national sovereignty was an unexpected gift at the end of the twentieth century. We fought for it, many of us, through centuries, and we want to preserve it. National sovereignty is the most important thing for us. We think that a nation state based on Christian conservative values has a future in the twenty-first century. We believe in our Christian roots, in our national independence. We think that freedom is very important, and so is courage.

Coming from a historian, that sounds like a political statement. Is your portrayal of Hungary's past more about how you see the future of the country?

Not only that, but they are connected. For example, because the protecting power of families was crucial during the communist dictatorship, today we consider the family and the raising of kids particularly important. That comes from our past. We think that our past and our history are important in order to preserve our national sovereignty in the future. Nations are formed by what their people have in common—stories, pasts, failures, and successes. We don't want to give up all this, which is why we deem the teaching of history very, very important, for instance.

On several occasions, you have called for a history curriculum in schools that can help increase the national pride of young Hungarians.

Yes, I suggest that history education should be used to strengthen national identity. Hungarian history offers an abundant basis for reinforcing a positive identity. Young Hungarians should study more Hungarian history and abandon the linear, Marxist approach and the underlying idea that Hungary has historically lagged behind the progress of more developed, Western nations. I believe that new history course books must be written, and slowly but surely we will have to deal with things. Time will take care of it.

You have criticized Western countries for not fully understanding Hungary's current actions and history's influence on them. What is the West misunderstanding about Hungary?

A large part, the majority, in fact, of Hungarian society believes in those values I mentioned before. National sovereignty, independence, freedom. We feel that those in the West wants to force their own values upon us. They want to civilize us the same way they used to do in their colonies. The West's historic colonization of faraway countries is shameful already, but apparently they do not feel that it is more shameful with us. This is what we are fighting in this culture war of our time. Historically, the West never paid attention to us, they never did. The West always looked down on us. Just consider the "peace monument" of World War I, the Treaty of Trianon, where they decided on our fate. They never even considered what kinds of people inhabited those Hungarian territories [annexed to neighboring countries], just whom they were deciding on.

There seems to be an existing conflict between Hungary and the EU, which also has to do with history. Do you think that Hungary can influence it positively, so the EU can come to care more about the historical heritage of its member states?

I believe that Hungary is part of Europe—it has always been and will always be like this. We Hungarians consider ourselves a big part of Europe and that we belong here. It is not by accident that our founding king, Saint Stephen decided to convert to Western Christianity and not to Eastern Christianity, which would have been an otherwise convenient option. We think of Europe as a group of interests within which every member has the right to be on its own track and maintain its own interests. And yet we Hungaerians have been expected to subdue ourselves, to distance ourselves from such thinking. We already had our share of this as part of the Soviet Empire, with which we subdued ourselves, carrying the torch of a distant administration. We would not like to commit the same mistake again. The EU must fight to maintain the sovereignty of its member states, which can then agree on shared issues.

Is migration a shared issue?

Migration is not a shared problem. Migration occurred first because some Western European countries had been colonizing other countries in the past. They believe—at least the intelligentsia and opinion makers in these countries do—that all of Europe has a burden of guilt because of this and therefore must help migration. But this has nothing to do with us. Maria Theresa, the Queen of

Hungary between 1740 and 1780, decided not to participate in colonization, and so we never colonized any lands. Hungary never went to distant lands to demand what should be done, and how, and how people should live there. We do not even consider ourselves as having any debts toward these people. On the contrary, Hungary has historical experiences when it comes to being occupied ourselves, such as the Turkish occupation, which saw us almost perish. For 300 years we fought against the Turks, and we were under Turkish occupation for 150 years. And then of course the Soviet occupation. On the other hand, Western European nations are ashamed of their actions during the colonialist era. the suffering they caused, and want to compensate for that. But because Central Europeans never went to other countries with the aim of dictating how their people should live and think, we do not owe Western Europe a thing.

So a lot of the conflict has to do with the West's "hypocritical" attitude toward the East?

Yes, Western European powers should not force us to adopt their attitudes and policies. French President Emmanuel Macron talks about migration and refers to solidarity, for example, but I would ask: Did anyone from Western European countries ever come here and ask if *we* wanted compensation for *our* historical losses? No, nobody. So what kind of solidarity are they talking about? When did they ever show solidarity toward *us*? When the Soviet Empire collapsed, no Marshall Plan was sent here. It was just Western companies that came here and bought up our markets. I would ask these countries to be slightly less holier than thou and slightly more modest, and less colonialistic in their approach.

You have caused controversy because of your views on Nazism and communism. The new Holocaust museum in Budapest has been criticized and delayed, and when in 2014 the government put up the German Occupation Memorial on the Liberty Square, criticism followed. What do you make of all this?

There is huge pressure on us to face our Nazi past in Hungary. I have been arguing that for some countries, the sins of communism were equally bad. There are similarities, however. The Nazi system lasted "only," let's say, ten years, while the communist system persisted for almost half a century here. This perspective is one of the main challenges that have hindered the successful preservation of Hungary's history since the transition of 1989–90. The socialists presented a one-sided interpretation of Hungarian history for forty-five years, and the postcommunist era preserved that historical narrative. The first freely elected postcommunist Hungarian government faced tremendous resistance because media outlets remained under the same management they'd been under during communism. Left-leaning intellectuals from Western Europe had good relationships with Hungarian socialists, even during the Soviet era. When looking for information on Hungarian issues, they always relied on the same old sources, and this tendency continues to this day.

According to some sources, press freedom in Hungary has declined since Viktor Orbán took power in 2010, and a large percentage of Hungary's media outlets are in the hands of pro-Orbán businessmen.

Well, when the Left used to own everything, back then, interestingly enough, freedom of the press was not an issue. It's only interesting now that the Right is in control.

Where does this lead us? I sense more polarization in Europe between the Left and the Right, and also between the East and the West.

I believe that leading Western European politicians would like to go back to the times when Eastern Europe was a second-rate region. Instead, I invite them to meet the new challenges, those of the modern era. A new era opened in world politics with the Trump presidency, and it marked a shift from President Wilson's old idea of transforming the globe to America's image to a situation today where countries and alliances must shape their own strategies. That is what Viktor Orbán did when he put forward his idea of illiberal democracy, by which he meant that his government would stick to Christian democracy and the social market economy. That idea can be freely debated while others are free to propose alternatives.

Who is proposing alternatives?

The only Western European leader who is trying to do so is President Macron of France, though I find his approach inconsistent; for sometimes he advocates a two-speed Europe, and every so often a completely federalized European Union. As for other notable Western leaders, they don't even try to formulate a vision. They are daydreaming of an old world order in which, tucked under the American nuclear umbrella, they felt superior to the Eastern European nations languishing under Soviet rule.

What significance does history have for the Orbán government's vision for Hungary?

Hungary is a sovereign state. We don't need outsiders telling us how to think about our own history. We couldn't talk freely about Miklós Horthy (Hungary's leader from 1920 to 1944) for forty-five years because of Soviets didn't allow us, and now we shouldn't because the Americans won't let us? This is our decision; this is our history.

Vilmos Kondor: The Burden on Budapest

Have you ever daydreamed about travelling back in time with a time machine to change the course of certain events? Me too. Especially since I came to know Budapest and its both fascinating and fear-provoking past. Budapest carries on her shoulders an enigmatic history that sometimes makes you wonder how on earth this place is still alive and well. When you walk the streets of District VIII today, or go around Kossuth Square, you can literally see the city's wounds on the walls of the buildings. Bullet holes. The distant sounds of war and revolution. The hopes and dreams of freedom being crushed, repeatedly throughout history. In fact, you don't even need that time machine to imagine what Budapest life was like in the past. You just need Vilmos Kondor and his books.

Vilmos Kondor is the author of a popular series of Hungarian crime novels, all of them set in Budapest, dealing with historical events such as World War II and the 1956 uprising. The first of these, the bestselling, prize-winning *Budapest Noir*, takes place in 1936 as the determined crime reporter Zsigmond Gordon sets out to solve a murder that everyone else in his soon-to-be fascist country wants to leave buried.[1] Gordon is the story's main protagonist, but throughout the series, he vies for attention with the city of Budapest, something of a protagonist in its own right.

Even more shrouded in mystery than Budapest is the life of Vilmos Kondor, the author of these books. He never makes public appearances and only does written interviews, by email. This has led to speculations about his real identity, and that his name is merely a pseudonym. Every time he releases a new book, the press material repeats the same information about him: "Vilmos Kondor was born in 1954. He began his studies in Szeged and completed them in Paris, earning a degree in chemical engineering. He currently resides in Western Hungary in a village near Sopron, where he works as a high school mathematics and physics teacher." In 2017, nine years after the first book was published, *Budapest Noir* was adapted into a movie. Apparently, Vilmos Kondor was asked several times if he would contribute to the screenplay, but he declined, and, indeed, he even stayed away from the premiere, at least as a person recognizable as Vilmos Kondor. It's almost a cliché: The celebrated writer who gets his bestselling book adapted to a movie but doesn't want to have anything to do with it.

Naturally, I was curious to get to know more about this mysterious person—even if it had to be through an email interview, on his terms. Shortly after I had sent some questions into cyberspace, I received a long letter in my inbox. It was from Vilmos Kondor.

* * * *

Let me start here: What inspired you to write the Budapest Noir series?

By just simply walking around Budapest. The city is full of dark corners and secret doors, and once I started looking behind those doors and turn those dark corners, I found a city with a rich history and an uncanny ability to survive—along with her inhabitants. I was born in Budapest and grew up there. Yet I found this other face of the city later in life. I had this story in my mind about a dead girl in a dark doorway in downtown Budapest, and I was intrigued. Who is this girl? How did she get there? Why does nobody miss her? One thing led to another and today, after some ten books about Budapest, I still don't know how many more secrets she has. Cities are mysterious. People usually love where they live, and a big city can always have more surprises than a hamlet in West-Bullshitfordshire. Also, it is much easier to write a novel that takes place in a big city, since it gives so many devices to the writer. I'll always write about Budapest, and it is really okay that she never writes about me.

How do you find locations for the plots? And how were you inspired to describe the historic events in the city through the eyes of Zsigmond Gordon, the main protagonist?

Budapest has survived several wars and bloody attacks—yet she has remained surprisingly intact, so the spots were a given. The streets have looked the same for at least 150 years. Many of them even have the same names today. I just had to find out what was in those buildings 60 or 70 years ago. Hairdressers? Bars? Law firms? Old newspapers are a rich ground for a fertile mind. One article can lead to a story, and a series of articles can lead to a whole novel, as happened with *Budapest Noir*. Zsigmond Gordon, who is a crime reporter through the whole series, knows this city and likes her inhabitants, but he always wants to keep his professional—and at many times his personal—distance. He doesn't judge; he observes and reports … until something happens that shatters his closely guarded world. He spent his twenties in America, so he has a unique perspective, a special lens through which we can see this country, Hungary, in yet another, different light.

Crime novels are popular in Britain, in Scandinavia, and now also in Hungary. Was this always the case, or is the popularity of crime novels a newer trend here?

Crime fiction in particular, but popular fiction in general, was the bastard child of culture during socialism. Everybody read those novels but nobody admitted it. Do not forget that for forty-five years, there was no crime in Hungary, there were no homeless people, there was no unemployment. I mean, there was, but the system denied their existence, so that was that. I think it takes time for a society to get rid of old habits. The whole of Eastern Europe became free at the same time: in 1989 and 1990. It took ten to fifteen years for the old habits to start dying. It is not uncool anymore to read crime fiction, and the official reviewers—the people who decide what is important and what is not—have just recently declared crime fiction to be part of our literature. Sometimes I wonder why it took only seven or eight years. Before 2007–2008, nobody wanted to write Hungarian crime fiction. Nowadays, it is much different. Also, writers needed time to absorb a lot. They had to read a lot. Let's not forget that between 1945 and 1989, the works of only twenty or twenty-five crime writers from other countries existed in Hungarian translation. The Hungarian state controlled book publishing and tried to keep up with the trends, but lost track in the 1970s, and when dawn came in 1989, we had to face the fact that we'd lost twenty years or so, at least. If you add it all up, you might have an explanation as to why and when crime stories emerged.

Whereas Scandinavian crime novels are typically set in the contemporary welfare society, it is my impression that in Hungary— and in other postcommunist countries—crime novels often have more historic contexts. What are the reasons for this?

One can only understand one's present situation in life if one knows one's roots and understands them. This means hard decisions and painful discoveries. Hungary and the region in general, including even Austria, are not that great at facing the past. We Hungarians look at our history as it belongs to … somebody else: "Okay, some shameful and horrible things happened here but it is not our fault. We are just a small country and everybody wants to hurt us." The good things? "Yup, that's us. Bartok, Kodaly, Szilard, Szell, Solti—yes, they are our sons." Oh, and the ones that betrayed and killed the Jews and carried out that massacre in Yugoslavia during World War II? "Nah, it wasn't us, it was someone else. You see, we're a small country and everybody wants to hurt us."

With an attitude like that, it is hard to face reality. Modern crime fiction is about societies, crimes, and those who commit them. In order to be able to write about those, you have to understand the roots. Nobody stands alone in time and space. If you don't know the road that led to the point you're standing at, how can you know how you got there and who you are? That might be one reason why historical context is so significant in this region. World War I ended a century ago, yet we still haven't been able to talk about what happened. Crime stories set in historical context might help readers understand that we have the same roots, that we are friends and neighbors and relatives and colleagues of each other, and that the current state of affairs is our own doing.

Do you want your books to be a kind of "extraordinary history lesson"?

I want to have fun. And to show how our past is our common past, everyone's past, and that those who lived then—our parents, grandparents—were the same people as us. They lived, loved, cried, and laughed.

How would you characterize your crime fiction's typical readers, your readership? A mainstream crowd, intellectuals, or both?

If I knew the answer to this one—or if my publisher knew—then I'd be more popular, but I don't. Nevertheless, I can tell you the change I realized regarding my readers. Two or three years ago mainly older people read my novels, educated women and men above fifty. But now my readers are much younger. I mean much younger. Teenagers get my novels for graduation, youngsters in their twenties and thirties give me excellent feedback. All in all, in Hungary—as I presume all over the world—the predominant readers of crime fiction are urban women between twenty and forty. Even though I dislike the word "intellectual," I think you need some level of fluency in the world of words and history to understand and enjoy most crime novels. Right now, the tide has nevertheless turned in Hungary: it is cool to read crime fiction even if you are an inner city intellectual or a small-town pensioner or a happy hipster at a university.

Are crime novels creating a debate in Hungary and the wider region? Are audiences and writers discussing the meaning of the books in public?

That is an easy one to answer: Crime novels have not created debate in the region. Period. There is no debate at all. It has yet to be sparked. Listen, if we don't talk publicly about child abuse and rape among students and the killings of Roma, why would there be any debate about books that cover these topics? As I said before, our historical mindset is still this: When good things happen, *we* did it. When shit happens, it was done *to* us. Unless this gets resolved somehow, I don't know how a healthy exchange of views could start, let alone a debate.

Finally, I have to ask: Is Vilmos Kondor your real name, your real identity, or is it a pseudonym?

I never answer that, whether Vilmos Kondor is a pseudonym or not. People can think this or that, but I do not respond, because there would be little point in doing so. Vilmos Kondor writes the books, takes some questions, and answers them. My books aren't me, and I'm not my books. It makes no sense for me that people are so curious about who I am. I live a normal, everyday life—and typically an eventless life. My books are much, much more interesting than me. That's all I want to say to the world about that.

Andy Vajna: As Good As It Gets

One of 2018's most viral moments in Hungary's tabloid media was a photo of Arnold Schwarzenegger taking a selfie on his iPad with a smiling Viktor Orbán next to him, patting him on his shoulder. The friendship of the two strongmen goes back to the turn of the new millennium, when Viktor Orbán was first prime minister of Hungary (1998–2002), and the Austrian-born film star was preparing his candidacy as governor of California. They had been introduced by a man named Andy Vajna, the Hungarian film producer behind Hollywood blockbusters such as *Total Recall* and *Terminator3: Rise of the Machines,* some of Schwarzenegger's highest-grossing action movies of all time. Andy Vajna also appeared in Schwarzenegger's selfie, and the photo of the whole selfie session was taken by Vajna's wife—the much younger former Miss Universe model, business owner, and social media celebrity, Timea Vajna.

Now let's rewind a bit: During the crushed Hungarian Revolution of 1956, Andy Vajna, age twelve at the time, fled his native Hungary and made his way alone to Canada. He arrived having no friends and speaking no English. Later on, though, he reunited with his parents in Los Angeles. The city of Angels became Andy Vajna's home for the following five decades, where he achieved a luxurious lifestyle as a successful film producer. His close personal relationship with Orbán goes back to the 1990s, when the young Fidesz MP stayed with him during a trip to the US. Soon after Viktor Orbán's landslide election victory in 2010, the favor was to be returned. Andy Vajna moved home to Budapest, where he quickly ascended into the ranks of Hungary's oligarchs. In 2013, he became one of the few people in the country to hold a casino-operating license, and indeed he then managed to get hold of 80 percent of Hungary's casino industry. Then, in 2015, he took over the second largest TV channel in Hungary, *TV2.* That same year, the commercial channel won nearly a fifth of state advertising spending, four times more than its nearest rival. Under Vajna's ownership, TV2's editorial stance has been strongly in favor of the Orbán government, and, all in all, the film producer-turned-media mogul played a significant role in reinforcing Viktor Orbán's control of the media.

Before his death in January 2019, Andy Vajna was ranked the fifth most influential Hungarian and the nation's second most important media personality. His estimated fortune was $150 million, putting him among Hungary's twenty richest individuals.[1]

Both as a journalist and as a general follower of Hungarian affairs, I had an immense interest in the doings of this powerful man. However, I knew that I would most likely never get to talk with Andy Vajna if I contacted him for an interview about his role as an oligarch with close ties to the Orbán government. Luckily, there was another very good reason to talk to Andy Vajna: the Hungarian film industry. This was back in the summer of 2017.

When Viktor Orbán had "brought him home" to Hungary in 2011, it was officially so Vajna could become government commissioner for the entire Hungarian film industry. Since then, the industry's success speaks for itself: As the man in charge of *Magyar Nemzeti Filmalap*, the Hungarian National Film Foundation, Andy Vajna has seen foundation-supported films win more than one hundred international awards—including the Oscar triumph of *Son of Saul*, the shocking Holocaust film made by the young director László Nemes. Furthermore, the Hungarian film industry is still booming, as a result of producers from Hollywood and other nations coming to Hungary to make movies, series, and more with skilled crews and modern production facilities, as well as an attractive 25 percent tax rebate. Finally, Andy Vajna's return to Hungary contributed to the fact that more people than ever before are watching Hungarian films in the country's movie theaters. In 2017, more than one million Hungarians attended screenings of the ten most popular Hungarian feature films, compared to just under 350,000 people in 2011.

In other words, Andy Vajna's influence on the success of Hungary's movie industry was a story in itself (which you can read about elsewhere in this book). With that in mind, I contacted his press agent to get a personal interview with Vajna. Shortly after, the press agent replied that, as long as I would stick to the topic of the movie industry, Andy Vajna would be open for an interview with me. The following week, on a hot and sunny June afternoon, I took the train from central Budapest to the suburb of Zugló, the capital's District XIV. Zugló is a large and mixed neighborhood with communist-era–style high-rise apartments sprinkled between decently kept residential streets with single-family homes. Here, on the very same block, I found both the headquarters of *TV2* and the offices of the Hungarian National Film Foundation. Having the two institutions in the same place, I note, must be quite convenient for the man in charge of both. I walk past a dark blue Bentley convertible parked in front the film foundation's industrial building. Upstairs, in his 100-square-meter top floor office, wearing an orange t-shirt, Andy Vajna sits at his desk as I enter the room along with his press agent.

The roulette table next to Vajna's desk is a subtle reminder of his nationwide ownership of casinos. Behind him is a bookcase with huge block letters on the shelves spelling the famous *Terminator* catchphrase "HASTA LA VISTA BABY"—a likely homage to his old friend Arnold Schwarzenegger. Throughout the interview, Andy Vajna smokes a brown cigar. I try not to be distracted by his eccentric presence. First, I ask him about the movie industry, but then, toward the end, I smoothly squeeze in a few questions on Vajna's media ownership and his friendship with Viktor Orbán, hoping that his press agent won't interrupt our conversation.

* * * *

A few people in the film industry are worried for the future of Hungarian cinema. They say, "What happens after Andy?"

I remember when I came here for the first time. People said, "How can you hire this idiot? Who is he?" And now, suddenly, they don't want me to leave, which is a good thing, I guess. It is my job also to build an organization that survives me and I think we are very long on the way to doing that. It shouldn't be a one-man show.

You were appointed politically, is that right?

Let me tell you, I don't think so. I think I was appointed first to run this because of the prime minister's judgment of my abilities to do it. The political appointment, or the role as government commissioner of film, was a later development, only to ensure that I can get through the bureaucracy in a much more organized fashion. I am not a politician; I don't want to be a politician. I am not on any side of the political rainbow. I want to make good movies.

I have a follow-up question, if I may. Hungarian filmmakers are quite often artistic, liberal-oriented people, but they are working in a government-controlled and government-funded …

Well, it is a government-funded organization just like anywhere else in Europe. We base our decisions not on political matters. We base our decisions based on talent and story. And the filmmakers are working not in a political environment but in a very free environment. We don't have censorship. We make movies that would not be seen as promoting the country in the best light politically if that's what I wanted to do. We have total freedom of speech. If we think a movie idea has a point of view or something realistic to say, in an entertaining way, then we will make the film. We don't have to go for any kind of government clearances.

But could there be some kind of self-censorship among directors that would see them hold ideas back?

Not in my experience. If you look at a movie like *Jupiter's Moon*, if there had been political censorship, we would never have been able to make that movie. Also *The Citizen*. We have no censorship at all. We give a movie an initial go-ahead on the quality of the screenplay; that's when the first decision is made. If the script delivers, then we will make the movie. If it doesn't, we won't. We try to be as objective as possible when making that decision. Sometimes you are right, sometimes you are wrong. Let's hope we will be right more often than wrong.

But could you have a film openly criticizing the government and certain politicians?

If it is well done, yes. If it is entertaining and doesn't distort the truth, no problem.

How much do you keep in touch with politicians?

I have a few acquaintances from the political sphere. My relationship with the prime minister is excellent, and we respect each other's work. Someone will be my friend because I sympathize with him, not because he is a politician.

Do you not talk politics with them when you meet?

Maybe it is weird, but no, it's really not like that. I am no expert in politics, but I feel that the measures against illegal migration are correct. Many are supporting this approach in Europe, but not saying it out loud. People can live in peace and quiet in Hungary. In England, France, and Belgium, they are walking in the streets scared. There is no terror here. The prime minister has a vision, and he is trying to implement it. He leads his way. It may not be one hundred percent perfect all the time, but the direction is good and that's good for Hungary.

Critics have accused your TV channel, TV2, of being biased toward the government. Are you paying attention to that criticism?

Of course I take notice of it. But look at America, there are two separate worlds in news, *CNN* and *FOX*, and they work according to the owner's point of view. The same thing happens here in Hungary. *TV2* is made for my taste because I am the owner. Of course, I do not edit the news, but I tell the people who are in charge of the direction of the news program if I find it appropriate.

Fidesz politicians are constantly arguing that Hungary's media has an overwhelmingly left-wing, antigovernment bias. Do you agree?

I deal with my own interests, not whether the Left and Right media are in balance. But I think they are pretty much even.

You have been quoted as saying that the Hungary's media is "freer than anywhere else in Europe."[2] Do you really think so, and if so, why?

I think so, yes. Pick up any newspaper. The media is constantly destroying the prime minister. Where in Europe do you see that? They are constantly attacking me, too, because they think I'm somewhat associated, even though I'm not. So in fact it is fake news, as Donald Trump would say, that they are creating all the time. It is very disturbing, actually, that it is so free. You don't have to give your sources, you can invent stories, and headlines just appear. That's it. You hear all this stuff about Hungary not having freedom of speech. That's bullshit. Hungary is probably one of the most liberal countries in Europe when it comes to that.

How could that change to avoid this one-sided "fake news," as you call it?

I think the world has sort of divided into two camps. It's the same in America; it's the same in Europe—in Germany, in Hungary. I don't know about Scandinavia, but I am sure that you do have parties that the media favors and doesn't favor. I think that Hungary is as good as it can get as far as freedom of the press.

Chapter Thirteen

On Being Hungarian

Zoltán Adamecz: Freedom or Financial Stability?

To really understand the national mood of Hungary, one must leave Budapest. The thriving capital and its metropolitan area provides 40 percent of the country's GDP, though home to only about 20 percent of the country's population.[1] Having had a base in the eastern city of Debrecen over the years, and not spending my time only in Budapest, has helped me understand—at least to some degree—how it affects local people's lives when wage levels in the provinces lag behind not only the European Union but Hungarian averages as well. I have noticed a deep polarization between people in Budapest and people in the countryside, even in the way they look at each other. Nevertheless, most of them have at least one thing in common, as described by sociologist Vera Horvath: "Hungarians now have little control over their economic lives. In an open economy dominated by international companies, the vast majority of Hungarians make a living by selling the only thing they can: their labor. This puts people in a constant state of alienation as all the surplus wealth they produce during their long days is siphoned away."[2]

When "doing business" became a more legitimate activity than ever in Hungary with the fall of communism, two things happened. On the one hand, to boost competitiveness and reduce the country's crushing debt of the early 1990s, Hungary hurried to privatize state-owned companies. This immediately attracted numerous foreign investors and international companies, and the opening of the markets was so successful that outsiders today still dominate a large share of Hungary's economic life: "The biggest banks are Austrian, German, and Italian, as are the supermarkets and the IT and telecommunication companies," Vera Horvath observes. "The same goes for production: The biggest companies are Audi, General Electric, Mercedes Benz, and Bosch."[3] On the other hand, Hungary's swift adoption of capitalism meant that some people became rich very quickly, buying up businesses or land that had been state-owned "common goods" during communism. As a consequence, the cynicism Hungarians have long been known for turned its eye toward this new class of neoliberal entrepreneurs, and ever since, Hungarians generally have had a negative image of capitalists—be it George Soros or Lőrinc Mészáros, two of the richest Hungarian-born businessmen.

All this, and more, I learned from a man named Zoltán Adamecz. Through a mutual friend, I found out that he was someone I should meet. Why? "Because he is an honest, self-made man, a proud family man," my friend had told me.

Zoltán Adamecz picks me up in his silver-gray Mercedes Viano at the train station in Veszprém. This historic city in western Hungary has less than 60,000 residents and—like many other Hungarian cities of that size—is surrounded by factories of large multinational companies, including Unilever, Continental, and Haribo. Zoltán Adamecz, however, is a self-employed entrepreneur with his own company. He entered the labor market in Hungary around the transition from communism to capitalism, experiencing the public's mistrust toward people, like himself, who wanted to start up their own businesses.

His wife and some of their five children are at home this morning, so we park the car in front of his friend's house down the road. There, in the backyard, we can sit down for the interview. We end up talking for several hours, touching on topics such as Goulash

Communism, EU funding, Russia's influence on Hungary, Roma integration, and Muslim immigration.

* * * *

How do you remember life in Hungary before 1989?

We used to live very nicely then. The problem was that we had no freedom. But we had financial stability. Now it's the other way around. We have more freedom, but we have less financial stability.

You were twenty-three years old at the time. Do you look back at the time before 1989 with positive memories?

Yes, I had no bad experiences. Even though Hungary was in the communist bloc, it was perhaps in the best possible situation. We were the West of the East. The happiest barracks in the camp. Goulash Communism, as they called it. This gave people a feeling of being well off compared to other communist countries. Today we hear about all the wrongdoings of the past era, but I personally experienced nothing of that.

What was the transition like?

Before the fall of communism, I had spent three years in East Germany, and I took part in breaking down the Berlin Wall. So for me it was practically a first-hand experience. Everyone in this region—Czech, Hungarian, and East German people—envied Mercedes cars and other such goods, and we longed for Western well-being. After the fall of communism we fast developed the expectation—a misconception, as it turned out—that we'd get all this. However, the great disappointment in those first few years was that nothing came of it, and then, indeed, financial conditions deteriorated significantly. We saw public property stolen. What had once belonged to everyone—for example, the biggest factories you can think of—were bought up. The Austrians acquired all the sugar factories, for example. All were closed the same day, and people who used have jobs in them were now unemployed. Opening up to the West had a different impact on our lives than we had hoped for. Instead of opportunities and well-being, we were disappointed. That unbearable risk of changing everything is something we don't want to experience again in my generation.

In a poll conducted in 2009, 72 percent of Hungarians said they had been better off under communism.[4] *When did you start reflecting on this?*

My reflections have come gradually. From the perspective of future prospects it's worth considering this: My friends from the former East Germany who still live in that region and who, back then, found work in West Germany, they still cross the onetime border daily in the middle of the country, commuting twenty-five miles into western Germany. Why? Because salaries are higher there.

So what we hear about emigration from onetime East Bloc countries like Hungary to Western Europe, it also happens within present-day Germany, from east to west. There is still some kind of an Iron Curtain in Europe. But it is invisible?

Yes. If I look at my friends, who—thirty years after German reunification—still find differences in wages if they go twenty-five miles west in the same country, then what should I expect here in Hungary? Who can compensate me for the wage disparity? Western democracy is, in a sense, a great disappointment for many Hungarians, because this is what you experience. This is one of the downsides. Europe, both East and West, would probably have been better off had we had a so-called Marshall Plan to bolster the East after 1989. But that never happened.

How would you describe your own economic life and that of other Hungarians over the past ten years?

Personally, business has been good. I haven't really have had any difficulties. Around the turn of the millennium, people were still hoping for something better to come. As far as the 2008 financial crisis is concerned, it caught us at a bad moment. The economy was spiraling downward. We were not really prepared to take that blow, and, honestly, some effects of that crisis still linger today. For example, in my business in particular, I deal with luxury homes, and I haven't been able to reach the same figures that were attainable before 2008. The other problem is that most people have little if any chance of starting from scratch, and yet they look around and see some people who've been successful. EU support only makes the situation worse, adding to the problem, actually.

What do you mean?

All EU funding is targeted. To put it more simply, the whole system of EU subsidies is targeted at large investments, not at microinvestments. So if you as an individual want some funding, you won't get much, if anything at all. Here in Veszprém, a relatively small city, there practically isn't anyone with businesses large enough to apply for these subsidies. For instance, we had to import an Austrian company to complete the renovation of our hospital. Apart from the university, we have maybe five companies in Veszprém that have a chance of meeting the EU's funding criteria.

So it's hard for the average person in a city like Veszprém to see what EU funding is actually good for?

Yes. In sum, this complexity is why many ordinary Hungarians feel that all this talk of Western lives is nonsense. EU funding is just a trick of the business, often benefitting the German automotive industry more than Hungarian society itself. The funding has no visible impact on the everyday lives of Hungarians. If you think about how people were disappointed and bitter after the fall of communism, then you can add all the frustrations you get when you tell people how the larger EU countries take advantage of smaller countries like Hungary.

A few weeks before the April 2018 national elections, a colleague of mine asked Gergely Karácsony, the leader of the center-left opposition, this question: "A German engineer comes up with a new way to build a car. Then a Hungarian worker builds it on the cheap. A German salesperson sells the car. In a few years, robots can take the Hungarian worker's job. Where does this leave that worker?" The politician could not come up with an answer. What is your view?

The answer is obvious. In the future we will have loads of empty factories, and all the EU money that has been supporting these places will just be going to waste. To answer the question from the perspective of the people, not the machinery, these workers will be unemployed. Simple. This is one of the greatest mistakes the EU is making—a political mistake and a manageable one. The EU doesn't really support people, just large interest groups. In the long run, this system is lessening the chances for Eastern Europeans to prosper, making them impoverished instead. If you allow this to go on, you will just have more grumpy people who, in the end, will come up with the idea of leaving the EU.

You are critical of the EU bureaucracy, but you wouldn't want to leave the EU personally?

I think the discussion is larger than that. We have to accept the basic fact that all over Europe, all over the world, people who possess great wealth, they didn't get wealthy by working hard in an industry and saving up money bit by bit. This is not the formula for becoming rich. What adds to the problem and lessens my own chances of becoming rich is that every time there is a job in Hungary, then there is a foreign competitor with better technology and a better starting point. It is impossible to compete with that.

Some might say that is the core of Western capitalism, for better or for worse?

Democracy is tricky. Especially if the finances are not there to support it. The paradox is that we are unable to build a sustainable democracy if we change the government every four years. That is not the way to do it.

What, then, is the way forward? Some worry that Hungary's democracy is in decline and that its ties to Russia are ever stronger.

Regarding Russia, well, I say congratulations to Putin with his 77 percent [support in the 2018 Russian elections]. Here is a hypothetical question: What is worse, bad news for a short time or uncertainty for a long time? Disappointment with the West propels people like Viktor Orbán to go toward something else. The current state of affairs is long-term uncertainty, and it's not really sustainable.

Russia is backing the expansion of the nuclear plant in the Hungarian town of Paks, and half of Hungary's population opposes EU sanctions against Russia.[5] Furthermore, Vladimir Putin is more popular among Hungarians than any Western leader.[6] Would you support the Hungarian government if it drew even closer to Putin's Russia than it is today?

The truth is that since we are a small country, we must hold on to someone. Simply put, if the West loses its grip on Hungary for the reasons I've mentioned, we'll need to take someone else's hand. Most Hungarians don't have a bad image of Russi stemming from their personal experiences; at least I don't. Of course, those who went to POW camps there might have bad memories, but the same goes for people who were in German camps.

How do you want Hungary's future to look when it comes to its relations with Russia?

Budapest used to be the nexus between East and West in terms of Russian investment and business relationships. Vienna is now in this position. Many Hungarians think this has been taken from us and that we should rebuild and expand our relationship with Russia. The Orbán government knows that we need a strong international partner, and that if it's not the West, it should be the East.

Another topic that has been discussed a lot in Hungary in recent years is migration. What is your view on the issue?

I am against migration. I can give you an example. The mayor of Veszprém bought all the homes owned by Gypsies in the city center. Then he bought them houses in villages outside Veszprém where they could live and he modernized the center. Five Gypsy families. Around fifty people who had completely destroyed life downtown by begging in front of the cinema, beating people up, and causing other such problems. I remember being chased by a Gypsy child. Gypsies speak the same language as us, they have been living here for 500-600 years, and yet we haven't been able to convince them not to take a dump on the floor in the middle of a room. My point is that these experiences leave me afraid of immigrants who come here and *don't* know our language.

Do you have any experience with immigrants?

I myself have had no bad experiences with these Muslim people coming to Europe, but there are warning signs that make me more cautious. So I am willing to make sacrifices; for example, voting for a party, Fidesz, that I don't agree with completely. But on this matter we are on the same page. I am not inhumane toward people fleeing war. For example, we have a former barracks here in town that once housed Russian troops; immigrants could shelter there until things are settled. I see nothing wrong with providing these people shelter temporarily, and when the war is over, they can return to their countries. But the problem, as we know, is that once you have let these people in you will be unable to get them out.

Ágnes Rostás: Happy Brainwashing

Many of the Hungarians I have met over the years have told me that, in some form or another, being Hungarian is a tough job. Even on the first pages of a witty and self-critical book called *The Essential*

Guide to Being Hungarian, which I found a while ago in a small Budapest bookstore, the Magyar mind is described like this:

> The Hungarian has problems up to his ears. He loves to complain. He is convinced that he, being Hungarian, gets the most disrespect in the whole wide world. No one meets more offence and suffering than he, the Hungarian. But no one should imagine, even for a moment, that it's possible to gain any insight into a Hungarian's problems. No, the Hungarian is a true melancholic.[1]

One of these "complaining Hungarians" is Ágnes Rostás. The reason I met her was that the 2018 national elections were coming up, and that's when journalists usually take some time talking to normal people, not just politicians and pundits. Well, joking aside, I was searching various Facebook groups—a great modern tool for journalists to find normal people, by the way—and I came across a woman in her mid-thirties who would be interested in sharing her views on Hungarian politics, as well as her interpretation of her country's common mentality. "Hi Lasse, in short, I am against the government. The longer version may require two days of canned food and a large pot of coffee." I agreed to meet up with her, although just for a couple of hours to begin with—no canned food necessary.

The following day we went for a stroll along the Danube in Budapest, walking north on the Pest side, and Ágnes Rostás put her cards on the table right from the start: "As for my background, I would position myself as upper middle-class with no financial or social problems in my life. My political doubts are based on social sensitivity and moral values, not because I am personally affected." Ágnes Rostás was raised in a rural town in Zala County, in southwest Hungary, close to the Croatian border. She is an only child, and both of her parents were originally teachers working with mentally disabled children. In the 1990s, her father began what was to be a twenty-five-year tenure as the town mayor before retiring.

After moving to Budapest more than a decade ago, Ágnes Rostás graduated with a degree in economics and then worked as a translator, interpreter, teacher and real estate agent before ending up as a personal assistant for a bank manager. She quit that job recently. "I am looking for a new job where I don't get bored all the time," she says.

For the white-collar jobs Ágnes Rostás has typically applied for, the monthly salary is usually the equivalent of around $1,200 before taxes. Her considerations about leaving Hungary for a higher pay in Western Europe, though, is not about money. Rather she wants to protect her four-year-old daughter from what she calls "the hateful political culture" in Hungary. Now, without a full-time job, she gets to spend more time with her husband and their daughter. Oh, and a Danish journalist curious to hear about her life. We stopped in a café near the parliament building to get that coffee, and then we began the interview.

* * * *

You were born in 1983. What do you remember from growing up in Hungary soon before the collapse of communism?

Not much, due to my young age at the time. But I remember being in first grade. Our teachers had us all sit down to listen to a a long and boring speech by a man called Mátyás Szűrös [a former communist and Hungary's acting president in 1989–1990] about something we could not even understand. Only later did I learn what that speech was about. It was the speech that officially dissolved the one-party state, the socialist People's Republic of Hungary.

Your father was involved in politics for many years as the mayor of the town in which you grew up. What effect did that have on your views on politics?

My father was supported by MSZP, the Hungarian Socialist Party, but he was a very open-minded, diplomatic person. I never heard hatred from him toward any political party, and he spoke approvingly of the good decisions of opposing political forces, too. Sometimes I heard him talking about his job, about what he said were "meetings where old men wear suits and talk about boring stuff." Basically, that was how I interpreted these things as a child. Even though I could not understand the background, I felt the vibes of how filthy politics could be. For instance, my father told me, much later, that some contractors tried to bribe him when the town needed new asphalt. He negotiated with them as if he was buying into their scheme, but when they finally came up with an exact amount, he said: "Okay, that amount will cover two more streets in town, and you just showed your intention to do them for free. Am I right?" They did it.

What has been your relationship been with politics in Hungary more recently?

I have tried to keep a distance from politics. I never even voted until the 2018 elections. I had heard quite enough about politics from my father. When elections saw governments change from Right to Left, and vice-versa, my impression was simply that when we had a left-wing ruling party, public life was more peaceful. As soon as the Right formed a government—and yes, that means Viktor Orbán and Fidesz—everything became arrogant, dark, and fearful. Thus I sought to avoid politics as much as I could. Not watching the news, not going to vote. I did not want to participate actively in this circus.

Did your view on politics change after you became a mother?

Since having my daughter, I began worrying about the social environment she would grow up in. I'm unable to shut down all media sources, and in a couple of years she will learn how to read. For example, I'm concerned about how I could explain a billboard critical of George Soros and how to keep her out of politics at least until she is a teenager. And I'm furious that while she watches a cartoon on YouTube, hatred-soaked political campaign videos pop up right in the middle of a fairy tale, and I have to be ready to fast-forward it back to the fairy tale. All my daughter can see is an angry mother tearing the device out of her hands and then giving it back, saying "Sorry, it was a stupid commercial, I just skipped it. No, you can't watch that ad." Also, it disgusts me to see politicians—regardless of their party—using toddlers and young kids for what amounts to political paedophilia.

How does the nation's political life influence your own life these days?

I haven't really been affected by political changes in my own life. At least not economically. I always found it easy to find a job when I needed one. But I can see how the level of poverty rises, especially affecting those who are vulnerable in any sense. I can see the degradation of public education and public healthcare.

Did you experience something yourself?

Yes, the current state of public healthcare in Hungary makes me look for private doctors whenever I need a specialist. A year ago, I needed surgery for a hernia. I had a private doctor, but the operation took place at a public hospital. I was genuinely afraid that the building would simply collapse and bury us. At the beginning of the operation, I had to remind the staff that to maintain a sterile environment the window should not be open —and even more outrageous, that having a huge fly buzzing around is not a thing you want to see in an operating room. Then I watched an assistant chase the fly around with disinfectant spray.

How do you see politics influencing Hungarian society in general?

We are heading to a soft dictatorship as I see it. The leading political forces claim to be right-wing and anticommunist, but all I can see is them using the same, good old tools communism did. Propaganda is on full force, with no efforts even to hide the fact. There is the intentionally faked news. People are divided. There is "us" versus "them," not this political party or that political party. You can just read any comment section under a political news story on Facebook, let it be any side of the political spectrum. People are manipulated to be proud of things that are givens: citizenship, nationality. This keeps them passive. These manipulations make people—especially the less well educated and those who can't be bothered to process the amount of information they receive—proud that "we" defended the country from what is in fact a nonexisting threat. The immigration threat is a good way of generating fear and anxiety, allowing the government to sell itself as the ultimate warrior. People applaud from their armchairs and feel proud, as if they had won a war.

Many Hungarians would probably disagree with you on this. There seems to be a big difference in how people in Budapest see things compared to people living in outlying cities and rural areas of Hungary. How do you see this distinction?

Exactly as your question suggests. Although, even educated people in the capital city may believe in strange things. Flat Earth, homeopathy, chemtrail conspiracies. In rural areas, there is almost complete control, given not only the media there but the church. Priests talk about the government's political narrative instead of Jesus, God, and the Bible. Guess which argument belongs to a church and which does not.

How would you describe the general mentality of Hungarians?

Passive, complaining, pessimistic, suspicious, and xenophobic, due to lack of information. Those who could have been good contributors to a change of mentality, they have already left the country or will do so soon. Hungarian society is still carrying the infamous instincts from the communist era: be suspicious, don't trust even your family or close friends, report them to the authorities. Tilt your head down, do not ask questions, just work like a robot. The government will tell you what to think, so do not bother to have your own opinions. This is of course a stereotype, a generalization that is not true for each and every Hungarian. As any nation, we have nice people and bad people.

Wait, have you ever heard about the American psychologist Martin Seligman and his experiment with dogs? It's about the behavior of "learned helplessness."[2] The dogs were put in a cage where they suffered painful electric shocks and couldn't escape. After a while, the dogs learn the routine and they become uninterested, depressed. Later on, the gate is opened and the electric shocks continue. However, the dogs don't even try to escape, even though there is no more physical barrier to stop them. I think they were Hungarian dogs. Sorry for my dark humor.

Interesting. What is important to understand for outsiders who don't know Hungary as much as Hungarians? What do foreigners usually misunderstand about Hungary?

Once a Hungarian gets to know a foreigner and likes the person, the foreigner can count on overwhelming and genuine hospitality. If a Hungarian tells you to pop in whenever you are around, take it literally. The lack of proper knowledge of foreign languages, however, can intimidate many Hungarians when getting in touch with foreigners. They quickly become embarrassed and leave. This may seem to be in opposition to the things I said before. Still, the two things exist in parallel. Let's take a foreign journalist with white skin. Put him in a rural area. People will be shy, as they cannot communicate, but that's it. Now pick a colleague with dark skin. Then let him wait for the police to clear up things and assure people that he is only a journalist, not a terrorist. Happy brainwashing!

Even though you seem happy to me, words like "pessimism," "complaint," and "mistrust" are often used to describe the Hungarian mentality, both by yourself and by others. If you should look with more optimism toward the future, what would be the best way Hungary could develop in the years to come?

A leading American social psychologist named Philip Zimbardo started an experiment to try to change Hungarian society.[3] It is obviously not possible, but the idea is really welcome. His project aims at creating more everyday heroes—ordinary people who act upon the same basic moral values no matter what their social circumstances. For example, helping a homeless person in the street instead of being a bystander. When we look at history, we Hungarians are an extremely pessimistic nation. This is caused partly by the many bad things we had to endure through history. For that reason, we often face challenges with cynicism and skepticism. If these attitudes with such deep cultural and historical roots could be changed, Hungary's future could change. Just look at Slovakia. It had a similar history but has managed better. Just look at the statistics. In Hungary, theoretically, given political will, we could catch up to Western countries in ten or twenty years. Without the will to change ... well, take a look back in time and you can easily predict the future.

Tibor Tehel: Brick by Brick

"The grass is always greener on the other side." That might be one of the most worn-out clichés in the book of idioms, and for Tibor Tehel, from Veszprém, it is a total myth. He went to the other side, he tells me, but decided to come back.

On a warm day in April, I wandered around Veszprém, a handball-crazy medieval town in western Hungary. On the outskirts I walked past an industrial printing factory called OOK-Press and I noticed a group of workers crossing the street during their lunch break. I decided to follow them as they walked into a local cafeteria-style restaurant, Viadukt Étterem. This was where I met Tibor Tehel for the first time. He was one of the factory workers, and he was having a paprika-spiced fish soup. "The usual." I got one for myself and joined him at his table, curious to get to know this Hungarian working-class hero who had witnessed his country change more than once.

Tibor Tehel grew up only a few miles from here, and he lived in Veszprém his whole life—well, except for the seven years he lived in London. "I was disappointed by the development of Hungary after the fall of communism, so when we joined the EU in 2004,

I decided to go to England to work for a better salary." He stayed there only because of the money, and his experiences in London eventually made him realize that the grass is not always greener on the other side. Furthermore, while Tibor Tehel still lived in London, Viktor Orbán came to power back in Hungary, and the new prime minister soon convinced him that it was time to move home. Before leaving Hungary in 2007, Tibor Tehel had been earning €650 a month working in the printing factory. In 2014, seven years later, he returned to the same position, now earning €1,000 a month for the same job. Now he can spend his free time on things he loves: running marathons, cycling, and skiing. If he wanted to work more, he could.

The grass is green here in Veszprém—and Tibor Tehel is happier than ever before.

*　*　*　*

You grew up in the 1970s and 1980s. What memories does your childhood bring?

I always remember May 1, May Day, in Hungary. On that day, in all communist countries, every company had a spot in the processssion with a flag and information about it. After maechig for a bit, we went to the park, where we had beer and sausages. I look back at that time with positive memories.

What were your parents like?

My parents were normal people. It was a normal childhood. My father was a bus driver. I was lucky because sometimes I could go with him to West Germany, for example. I remember we had to go to Budapest to get the visas, and then I went with him to West Germany and to Yugoslavia. I have travelled a lot ever since I was little, and I saw all the differences between the countries.

Did you sense there was a support back then in your community for the communist system?

Yes and no. Opposite the bus station, where my father worked, people said, "I like this communism, I support it because, you see, we can go abroad, so it's all good." But my father's brother didn't like communism. "I hate it!," he said, and he moved to a small village nearby to live a simple life. The people who supported communism had more opportunities. Most people saw no negative effects on their lives from communism. Only if you were a singer, an artist, or, say, a priest, could you not do whatever you wanted to.

What is your assessment of the communist era?

To be honest, I have nothing negative to say. Maybe it's because I was born in 1974, and *real* communism was more associated with the era of [Soviet leader, 1964–1982] Leonid Brezhnev. I still remember when Brezhnev died. All day long on TV and radio there was sad, hushed music and sad interviews. Everyone was silent. We were supposed to be really sad, even here in Hungary. But after that, I think, things got easier. And then came Mikhail Gorbachev. I love him. He has a house in London, and his daughter used to buy goods from the company I was working for there around 2010. All Eastern Europeans should say a big thanks to Mr. Gorbachev. If he had not opened the border, we would still be in the same situation.

Then came the historic events of 1989. What do you remember from then?

I remember that I saw a young Viktor Orbán giving a speech on Heroes Square in Budapest. It was fifteen or twenty minutes long, and since I was only fifteen years old, all I remember is that Orbán was wearing white socks. Black shoes, black trousers, and white socks. That was probably not the most important, but that is what I remember. I was young and into rock music, and I was thinking that now I could probably get the Scorpions LPs more easily than ever before.

Do you remember being happy when it happened? When the Soviet troops left Hungary?

Absolutely. Close to my hometown, in a forest near Tótvázsony, there is a big military base that used to belong to the Soviet army. They would always work there. You know, most Hungarians knew that the Russians were here in Hungary, somewhere, but they couldn't see it for themselves. But here, looking into the military base from the outside, we could always see them. The area was known as "Little Moscow," and the locals knew very few details about exactly what was there. Later, after the Russians left, the site was investigated and two underground bunkers were discovered. These bunkers had stored over a hundred nuclear weapons able to reach Western Europe, should the Soviets have needed to target the democratic countries of the West. My father said that when the Soviets built it, they had to kill the guys who planned it and built it themselves instead. The place is totally abandoned now, but it was and still is a very mysterious place.

How did your life develop up through the 1990s?

I was lucky in that I started working straight away, in a printing company, and I am still working there. I have a good job and a good salary. I travelled a lot early on. In 1992 I vacationed in Spain, and later I went to Denmark to attend a handball match. I saw some differences between East and West, but they were not that great. I never had that "Oh, we're in Eastern Europe and we're poor, everyone in Western Europe is beautiful and lives good lives" sort of feeling. I saw that life can also be hard there. Salaries may be higher and some things easier, but I never felt that it was so much different. The grass is not always greener on the other side.

What has changed in Hungary since then?

If someone had told me ten years ago that in 2018, Poland, Hungary, and the Czech Republic would have some of the highest economic growth in the EU, I would not have believed them. From 2004, when Hungary became an EU member, it seemed that we were constantly being told that we were now dependent on the European

Union. People here in Hungary said, more or less,, "We need to do what the EU tells us because the EU is more qualified." I never hear that anymore. The EU is killing the real Europe. Maybe the EU is not as bad as the newspapers and the government say, but there must be something wrong.

Does your dissatisfaction with the EU have to do with its migration policies?

Not only that. Overall, in Hungary we don't really align with mainstream opinion in the EU. In Central and Eastern Europe, step by step, we are getting stronger on our own. Eventually, I think, Hungary will be strong enough to leave the EU.

How have events in Hungary in recent years shaped your political opinions?

In Hungary, we have a saying: "You need to see what he is doing, not what he is saying." For many years now, politicians on the Left have only been talking. For example, someone like Ferenc Gyurcsány [Hungary's center-left prime minister, 2004–2009]. He can say nice things and make speeches like Fidel Castro. But it's like Speakers' Corner in Hyde Park, where you can stand on a box and talk about whatever you want. Afterward, you don't do anything about it. Gyurcsány is like this. I only have to mention his so-called "lie speech" from 2006.[1]

What is your opinion of Jobbik?

I also have a problem with Jobbik. They say, "This fish needs to be Hungarian, this chair needs to be Hungarian, everything needs to be Hungarian." But these days they are not really nationalist, and they have lost many supporters.

And Fidesz, Viktor Orbán?

I support Viktor Orbán. Before 2010, Hungarians thought we cannot dream big and that we need to always depend on the EU.

Since Orbán came into office, he has shown that we can do it on our own, that we can dare to dream big again.

Do you feel that life is better than five or ten years ago?

Yes, there are more opportunities for everyone. Some people want to work just eight hours and then go home and watch TV. Others want to work more—both for their own dreams and for their workplaces. There are more jobs. If you don't like your boss, you can say, "We need to part ways," and you will be able to find another job the next day. This gives you the self-confidence to build your private life as you want. Many Hungarian people don't like Gyurcsány or Orbán or anyone, but they need to look in the mirror and ask themselves how many bricks they put into building up the country.

Russia's leader, Vladimir Putin, has visited Viktor Orbán in Hungary several times, and Russian influence seems to have increased. How do you look at that when you take into account the history you have with Russian influence here in Hungary?

Hungary is small and needs to depend on others. Now we are shouting and finding our way, but we are not strong enough for this forever. I am not wise enough about this, but I think Russia has better prospects of growth than the European Union has. If I needed to choose which way Hungary should go, I'd say that two hundred years into the future Russia will still be a flower in the vase, but no one will remember the EU. The European Union will be going down. It's just about business. Why do they fight for Ukraine? Not because they care about the Ukrainian people, but because they need this big land for political and economic reasons.

A topic that has divided the opinions in Europe is migration. Germany and Sweden had open policies to begin with, and Hungary stood on the other side. Is the Orbán government's solution the way to go, in your opinion?

I have seen for myself—in London and also in Vienna—what a very mixed population does to a society, and I don't want that here in Hungary. I think that you can do the wrong thing only once. Orbán said some weeks ago that some hundred people came here from Syria and Iraq, and they are welcome because they are Christian.[2]

Are you religious?

I believe in God, but I don't go to church every single week.

What do you think religion, and particularly Christianity, means for Hungary?

We need to save it. This is our future. For me Christianity is not just about going to church and believing in someone, it's also about the history of the country. It's the fish soup, it's this table, it's these voices from the back of the room. The love of the women. Christianity is more than just a religion."

In some other countries in Europe, religion is playing a decreasing role in society. People say they don't need it in their lives to be happy. Do you see problems with this attitude in Western Europe?

Let me just say this: I went to Poland and bicycled from village to village. In front of every house there was a cross. They really believe this. For me this was strange. But in Poland, religion is strong. In Hungary, less so. But Christianity is, for me, the Central and Eastern European lifestyle. You don't need to go to church. You believe in your way of life. You believe in your traditions.

Do you believe in democracy?

I remember when I was five or six years old, around 1980, and I was walking in a field with my father. He said, "Son, in West Germany, people sometimes go to a government building and cast a vote to allow someone to improve and organize their lives." Even though I was very young, I somehow understood what he said. At the same time, it made no sense, because the head of my country was János Kádár [communist leader of Hungary, 1956–1988], and no one had voted for him. When I got older, I came to understand what democracy is. I have zero tolerance for people who don't go and vote in a democratic country like Hungary is today. You can go to that government office, express your opinion by casting your vote, and then you can say that you have contributed with one brick to building the country.

Daniel Fabricius: Have Some Respect

People who have followed my work on social media over the years will probably recognize his name immediately. In Facebook comments, newspaper columns, and panels on TV, Daniel Fabricius, a Danish-Hungarian conservative, always appears as a relentless fighter and a stern defender of Hungary in general, and of many of Viktor Orbán's standpoints in particular. In the mainstream coverage of Hungarian politics in Danish media, his voice is one of the loudest among a relatively small and often shushed group of Orbán supporters. Nevertheless, Daniel Fabricius's insights into the culture and traditions of his second homeland provides him with a position that is hard to challenge for anti-Orbán critics who don't speak Hungarian, who don't understand Hungarian culture, and who "don't have a clue what they are talking about," as he has put it himself.

I first experienced this dynamic in February 2017, the first time I met Daniel Fabricius. At the Copenhagen Main Library, I was giving a lecture on Hungary, and about eighty people attended the event. Toward the end of the lecture, I paved the way for a debate session where the audience could ask me questions or share their own views on Viktor Orbán and Hungary. After a few shy comments, suddenly a heated debate developed between the conservative Daniel Fabricius and a far-left member of the audience. The topic was corruption, and there was literally shouting across the room, until eventually, I had to end the whole session before the two political rivals would come to blows with each other. Afterward, I had a long conversation with Daniel Fabricius in which he stated that he would often become irritated when people throw accusations at a country they barely know. That is a feeling I have often experienced among Orbán sympathizers, especially outside of Hungary, and that is why I wanted Daniel Fabricius in this book.

A famous singer once sang, "Don't criticize what you can't understand," and Daniel Fabricius recognizes the anger:

> In these situations I can become fumingly mad, thinking, *Why do people make such harsh accusations of things they barely know?* That is a very typical Hungarian reaction, something I have inherited from my mother. People can of course say what they want, but I believe that you have to know something for your opinion to hold integrity.

Again, make no mistake, Daniel Fabricius is not unbiased when speaking about Viktor Orbán's Hungary, but I was also curious to hear him reflect on the differences between his two homelands, Denmark and Hungary. Perhaps his reflections could shine light on the much-debated differences between the Eastern and Western countries of Europe? I called him up on the phone from Budapest, and this is how it went.

* * * *

What do you see as the main differences between Hungarians and Danes?

First of all, Hungarians are in many respects more direct. They don't have this political correctness and they don't hesitate by asking, "Am I allowed to say this?" Hungarians say it like it is. When Hungarians talk politics, they do it in a way that could be seen as very confrontational. Danish politicians are afraid to do certain things in politics that they would actually like to implement, because society's political correctness is blocking the way. Another thing is that in Denmark, values have become ordinary politics. In Hungary, on the other hand, people have a common set of values, which cannot be questioned politically. Those values are above politics, and they are simply just more right-leaning and conservative than in Denmark.

What are some of those values in Hungary?

Hungarians have a different approach to life, which is more family-based, more traditional. Danish society, and the Nordic countries in general, have this so-called Law of Jante, which is a code of conduct that makes the general public look with skepticism if you are doing things out of the ordinary. In Hungary, listening to Franz Liszt symphonies, going to the opera, or watching a traditional *csárdás* folk dance performance is culture. In Denmark, these things would be considered high culture, and if you tell people you like that stuff, they will think you are a snob. The respect for authorities is also quite different in Hungary than it is in Denmark. Sometimes it is too much, but Hungarians have a respect for people with authority that I don't experience in Denmark.

Are there historical events that have given rise to these differences?

The youth rebellion of 1968 in Western Europe definitely made an impact on society that was not seen in Hungary. If you go back to the 1950s or the early 1960s in Denmark, you could find a completely different set of values. The view on religion and civil society was more conservative and there was a different kind of politeness, quite similar to Hungary today. Gradually after 1968, the state has replaced the family in Denmark as the main influencer on your life. The same development has not happened in Hungary, and therefore life there remains more traditional and family-based. The Ottoman invasion, Soviet suppression, and the failed revolution of 1956 may be distant, but are still very present in the Hungarian mind today.

In some inexplicable way, Hungarians managed to survive all this, and it made them more tough-skinned than for example Danish people are today. External enemies have come again and again, compelling Hungarians to stick together and fight for each other's freedom. In the process, Hungarians have been forced to stick to certain values they were willing to give their lives to uphold. Hungary thus probably has a stronger and more broadly accepted set of values than does Denmark. Danes have been at peace for so long, so no external powers forcing them to find something to fight for—ultimately with their lives at stake.

In Denmark, we talk about being the happiest country in the world. Hungary is very low in the ranking among European countries,[1] and Hungarians often talk about being pessimists. Do you recognize this difference?

Hungarians tend to call themselves pessimists, and they are indeed. I think they should be prouder and happier for who they are than what they express. Sometimes I meet Hungarians who say that I am the proudest Hungarian they have ever met, and I don't even live in Hungary. I live in Denmark, the so-called happiest country in the world. However, this joy and happiness is very subjective. In my opinion, the *World Happiness Report* is very subjective in its understanding of happiness. Economic stability is an important but very narrow definition of happiness. In this respect, Hungary scores significantly lower than Denmark; it is one of the poorest countries in the EU, and Hungarians live less stable lives. But to say they have less happy lives, I take a very dim view of that categorization. I see more people lively and smiling on a Friday evening in Budapest than in Copenhagen.

In Danish and Western media, there seems to be a lot of criticism directed toward Hungary and especially the Orbán government. What is your take on this?

The absolutely most essential thing in international debates, when you want to criticize another country's politics, is to be able to understand the people and the culture of that country. To have the skill to say, "Now I don't look at it from a Danish perspective, but from a neutral position, from which I try to understand." There is too little understanding of Hungary in international debates. Every time someone in Denmark or in Germany or in the US voices their opinion on Hungary, they do it with Danish, German, or American lenses on. These countries are completely different than Hungary when it comes to history, language, values.

Is the international criticism of Hungary and Viktor Orbán's politics not legitimate and fair?

By and large, I don't consider it solid criticism. Yes, there are problems in Hungary, but this goes for a lot of countries. My view is that the critics see Hungary as a problem because the person in charge, who has substantial public support, is not aligned with the EU's political project and its elusive Lisbon Treaty values of tolerance and a more federalist EU. The critics want Viktor Orbán to be thrown away, so every time they have a chance to criticize him, they will. But, let me be honest, I don't think Western critics are in any moral position to educate Hungary. It is so obvious that pro-EU countries have a political agenda. You sense a desperation in their criticism of those [fellow EU member states] that resist: "Why don't they want to become progressive and adapt to our values?" Well, in Hungary's case, because Hungary does not want to.

These critics have loudly been promoting democracy, so for God's sake they should respect the choice of the Hungarian people. Instead of trying to understand Hungary, they just try to drag Hungary down. It irritates me because there are so many double standards. Just an example. If the media situation is such a big issue in Hungary, and it has been used as an argument for triggering Article 7 [of the Treaty on the European Union, on suspending member states' rights], then what about a certain former Italian prime minister who basically personally owned the whole country's media? I don't think corruption is less in Italy, either. Or the EU criticism of Hungary with its stance on Romania. The only difference is that Romania's governing party is not EU-skeptic, as is Orbán.

How do Hungarians react to this?

Hungarians do not like to be taught lessons. They are allergic to it. When Westerners say, "This is how we do it in the West, and it works well, so you should do the same, or else you lose," then they simply don't change anything at all. In fact, quite the opposite.

What should the EU have done instead in its approach to Hungary?

They called the Eastern Enlargement of the European Union in 2004 "a historical milestone." But I think this is where it first went wrong. The way that the old EU countries planned the enlargement back then was a mistaken approach. They told the Eastern countries about the Copenhagen Criteria and the EU's legal system, and then they said: "Implement this, and when you have done that, you can join the club." Instead, they should have said: "Look, we are these countries and we have this legal system and this mindset. How can we make a club where we can all fit in?' The Western countries really wanted the Eastern countries to join, but they chose the first solution, and today we are seeing the consequences: A growing political divide between East and West.

Conclusion

"If you are curious, you will find the puzzles around you.
If you are determined, you will solve them."

—Ernő Rubik, inventor of Rubik's Cube

How to Stop Polarization:
Be Curious and Listen

As we have learned through this book, the era of postpolitical consensus is over. Real politics has come alive again. This is one of the reasons for the rising polarization between liberals and conservatives, amplified by echo chambers and filter bubbles. Most of us should be able to agree that political disagreements are an unavoidable element of our society. There is no such thing as a complete and quiet consensus. Freedom of speech is one of democracy's core tenets, and in the English writer Evelyn Beatrice Hall's 1906 book *The Friends of Voltaire*, Hall wrote the famous phrase, "I disapprove of what you say, but I will defend to the death your right to say it," which is often cited to describe the principle of freedom of speech.[1]

Sober debates with our opponents are essential because they make us reflect—not only on our own values, but more importantly on our opponents' values. Debates provide understanding. If we listen, we can learn something. According to Jonathan Haidt's research, society consists of two main groups whose moral values are quite different from each other: Liberals tend to endorse values like equality, fairness, care, and protection from harm more than conservatives. Conservatives, on the contrary, tend to endorse values like loyalty, patriotism, respect for authority, and moral purity more than do liberals. Broadly speaking, these two groups thus symbolize each side of our polarized society, and since each holds deeply rooted moral values significantly different from the other's, changing this dynamic is almost impossible. In other words, the division between liberals and conservatives will certainly not be abolished just yet. It is here to stay.

However, as we have seen, a number of studies indicate that polarization is rising, that liberals and conservatives hold more negative views of one another than in the past. Some of these studies have been conducted by the American sociology professor Robb Willer. In a 2017 interview with Stanford University, where he works, he explained:

> Liberals and conservatives tend to self-segregate into ideological silos, consuming different news, associating only with like-minded others, even choosing to live in different places. What I think is most concerning is the rising animosity between the Left and Right. The fact that political polarization is associated with moral polarization is particularly concerning for the future. People's moral values are their most deeply held beliefs. Folks really struggle to understand the perspective of someone with a fundamentally different sense of right and wrong.[2]

In Willer's opinion, we must develop new approaches to politics if we are to turn the temperature down on our political conflicts and start bringing people closer together. One such approach is "moral reframing." Willer and his Stanford colleagues have conducted studies showing that if you want to move conservatives on typical liberal issues—such as same-sex marriage or national health insurance—it helps to tie those arguments to conservative values like patriotism and moral purity. Likewise, if you want to move liberals on typical conservative issues like military spending, you will be more persuasive if you find a way to tie those policies to liberal moral values like equality and fairness. Willer admits that this technique may seem intuitive, but his studies suggest that it is something most of us really struggle to do: "It turns out that when we go to persuade someone on a political issue, we talk like we are speaking into a mirror. We don't persuade so much as we rehearse our own reasons for why we believe something."[3]

To come up with those arguments, liberals and conservatives must take the time to really *listen* to one another, to understand one another's values, and to think creatively about why someone with very different political and moral commitments from their own should nonetheless come to agree with them—whether the topic is migration, inequality, family values, or climate change.

In doing so, we should be asking questions rather than arguing. According to Willer's research, arguing tends to entrench people in their own positions. We convince ourselves that our beliefs are based on logic, when in fact a great deal of our moral decisions are emotional.

Willer states that instead of arguing with our political opponents, asking them *why* they believe what they believe can be more productive. "If you ask people why do they think what they think, you will very often find that what they say is not very different from what *you* think. It is framed in a different way, or wrapped up in all of the political garbage and conflict that's there, but underneath that there's more commonality than people think."[4]

Something that both liberals and conservatives should understand is the importance of perspective. In a digital age, in which consumers themselves can decide what kind of news and points of view they see on their social media feeds, the most critical challenge is to receive a *balanced* influx of information. Why? To avoid ending up in an information bubble consisting solely of reaffirming and like-minded ideas. One way to leave your political bubble is this: Try to read commentaries or follow the news on media outlets whose political standpoint you would usually *disagree* with. As media consumers, we usually stick to our regular sources of news, and therefore we often see only one side of a story.

Such change is not an easy, because it means changing habits. Luckily, there are several applications and websites—such as the *More in Common* and AllSides—that provide different views on the same story, thereby giving you the opportunity to see things from another perspective and allowing you to form your own, informed opinion.

Furthermore, the American law professor Dan Kahan has made a spectacular finding, one rooted in psychology, that can teach us something critically important about political debate today. The phenomenon is called "politically motivated reasoning," and it suggests that people use their minds to protect the groups to which they belong from grappling with uncomfortable truths.[5] The motivation to conform is stronger than the motivation to be right. So-called belief perseverance and confirmation bias have a physiological component: It literally feels good. People in fact experience genuine pleasure—a rush of dopamine—when processing information that supports their beliefs. However, as Kahan's study shows, the more scientifically curious people are, the more they are immune to the power of partisan thinking. Curious people are more likely to seek out information that contradicts their group's beliefs. In other words, a more curious mindset could lead to better understanding on both sides in an increasingly polarized world.

So, perhaps the solution to the psychological challenge here is actually quite simple: Be curious. Search for new information. Do not consult only those news sources that confirm what you already think. Look for documentaries and books that surprise you. Talk to people who can contradict your beliefs. Don't look away when you come across facts that don't fit your own worldview.

There will be No Winner but the Endless Debate Itself

These are mostly approaches you can take on an individual level. However, even more important is what we can do on the societal level. This is where the media has an enormous responsibility. If there are no media platforms providing the content that can stimulate your curiosity and make you ask questions, then you will not learn a thing. Let's sum up the challenges: According to the Reuters Institute's *Digital News Report*, the overall trust in news media is only 31 percent in Hungary.[1] That means that only one in three Hungarian have trust in the media content they are provided. Furthermore, only 11 percent of Hungarians think that the Hungarian media is free from political influence, which puts Hungary at the bottom of the list. "In Hungary's deeply divided and distrustful society, even political neutrality is seen as bias," as one of my colleagues once put it.

Over the past few years, the Orbán government has increased its direct control over the media with changes in ownership, distribution of state advertising, and campaigns against external and internal critical voices. The conclusion from the Reuters Institute's report goes like this: "In Hungary, the public service media news is strongly progovernment, with critical voices barely present and factual errors frequent, while the online sphere is still vibrant and plural, with a wide range of political and news portals/blogs operating."[2] Most young people are consuming news online, so in theory they have a wide range of different media outlets to choose from. However, the report also states that young people often consume online news via social media platforms such as Facebook, where one's news feed is based on algorithms feeding you "more of the same" content. Thus, you might not be presented with perspectives much different from your own.

A Pew Research Center survey of news trends in various countries of the world concludes that only 18 percent of Hungarians follow their own national news closely.[3] Which means that Hungary has the world's lowest rate in this respect. In countries like Germany, the United Kingdom, and the Netherlands, approximately half the population follows national news closely. Moreover, Hungarian print media, as well as radio and television broadcasters, are either strongly progovernment or strongly antigovernment—there are barely any *independent* print or broadcasting media outlets in the country. Media outlets more or less reflect the views of their owners rather than delivering politically independent content. Instead of covering all sides of the story, entire news organizations have chosen to pick one side over another.

One example is the progovernment channel *TV2*, whose owner was the late Andy Vajna. When I interviewed him before his death, I asked him about his media ownership. He said, "Look at America, there are two separate worlds in news, *CNN* and *FOX*, and they work according to the owner's point of view. The same thing happens here in Hungary. *TV2* is made for my taste because I am the owner."

Do you remember the crying journalist I stood next to on election night in the opening of this book? Yes, she worked at Vajna's partisan *TV2* channel.

From my perspective, democratic debate is undermined when news outlets present a biased version of reality, corresponding to the owner's views. Even if the viewers are aware of the bias, it is problematic. Let me give you another example. Once I was hosting a Danish group of journalism students in Budapest, and we visited the progovernment newspaper *Magyar Hírlap*, which is owned by businessman Gábor Széles. He is the sixth-richest person in Hungary and an active supporter of Viktor Orbán and Fidesz. One of the young Danish students asked the *Magyar Hírlap* news editor this sharp question: "What if a story broke and revealed that your owner had been involved in an unforgivable scandal? Would you stay true to your journalistic integrity and publish the story, or would you protect your owner's reputation, ignore the story, and let it be?"

The editor hesitated. Her silence was striking. After a lengthy moment, she eventually admitted: "It would be difficult, but I think we would not publish the story."

In other words, the interests of media ownership outweighs those of journalistic independence. The question for the *Magyar Hírlap* editor was a hypothetical one, but it told me a lot about the media's role in Hungary.

Back in Denmark, a group of journalists at the newspaper *Berlingske* were actually once faced with a similar, real-life dilemma. In 1999, they had found out that the family of the newspaper's owner—Denmark's richest businessman at the time—had been involved in delivering weapons to German Nazis during World War II. A very damaging story for the businessman, but nevertheless an important one for the public. The dilemma: Should *Berlingske* publish the story? After much consideration, in the end the paper did publish the story, and the scandal was exposed.[4] The consequence? The long-time owner sold off the newspaper a few months later, presumably as "revenge" toward the staff. Since then, *Berlingske* has struggled financially, to say the least. But the reporters and the newspaper were widely celebrated for their decision to stand firm on their journalistic independence.

In Hungary, the Orbán government's disapproval of the critical media is no longer limited to attacks on specific news outlets. Individual journalists are directly condemned by the government and its allies. For us journalists, such attacks are beneath all contempt. But it should not stop us from reflecting upon the fact that in Hungary—and elsewhere in the world, in broad sectors of society—journalists are ranked next to politicians and car dealers on the bottom of the list of trust among those engaged in various professions. We journalists can spend a long time discussing why. Our profession is to convey information, so it goes without saying that we are preoccupied with the fact that many people generally do not really trust us.

Why is this? Some argue that the relatively low level of education among journalists means that we are not skilled enough to understand complex issues. Others point to the "New Media Reality": Time has become so scarce for journalists that we have no chance to properly live up to our standards when the media cycle is running constantly, 24/7. Conversely, others believe that economic conditions are too good for journalists, at least in Western countries. Journalists earn such good pay or are otherwise so privileged that they are out of touch with the ordinary people—the general public— they are supposed to represent.

This gives us food for thought. Today, journalists have more freedom, more reach, and more ability to share information than ever before. But with those advantages comes an even greater responsibility to the public. I fear that this responsibility is undermined by those journalists who substitute opinion for facts and emotion for neutral coverage. Some journalists even call themselves "activists." In some cases that approach *can* have certain advantages—for instance when covering local communities or when putting focus on climate change. But for the most part, journalistic activism will backlash because it becomes too easy for opponents to shrug off their coverage as "politically biased." The risk is that we become too full of our own opinions. Too emotionally offended by warranted and unwarranted criticism. Too astray from the neutral, factual voice our teachers in journalism school insisted we practice.

No, journalism is not easy—no one ever said it was—but we should nevertheless always strive to find the best achievable version of the truth. This is not done by writing "sensational" or overexaggerated, clickbait articles. A clickbait article briefly satisfies your appetite for spectacle and diversion but ultimately leaves you unsatisfied and uninformed. As journalists, instead of looking for catchy headlines, we should be looking for trends and we should be providing perspective.

According to the *Oxford Dictionary*, perspective is defined as "the true understanding of the relative importance of things; a sense of proportion."[5] There is a lot of potential in our role as journalists, if we manage to understand the responsibility of that role. The rising polarization in society is in fact the "perfect" task for us: In a polarized society, the journalist can be the public's guide, one who—with insight and knowledge about a specific terrain—can lead the public safely through that terrain. However, it is not the journalist's goal to convey complete consent among opponents; for instance, between liberals and conservatives. The goal is to convey the endless debate itself, and it is the journalist's task to ensure that this debate takes place at all.

One example of facilitating such debate is the *My Country Talks* concept, which started in Germany and has since spread across Europe under the name *Europe Talks*. Like a reversed Tinder match, the aim of the concept is to pair up liberals and conservatives and getting them to have a civil conversation in real life. About real issues. About their disagreements. According to the German journalists behind *My*

Country Talks, the ultimate goal is a less polarized debate and a more open and plural public. "But we also want to raise people's awareness of the value of joining in on the same conversation, and not splitting into different atoms," they say.[6]

Another example is the global *Human Library* concept, founded originally by one of my old friends from journalism school in Denmark. *The Human Library* aims to address people's prejudices by helping them talk to someone they would not normally meet.[7] The organization uses a library analogy of lending people rather than books—a refugee or a neo-Nazi, for example. These people have experienced prejudice, social exclusion, or stigma, and participants can ask them questions so as to learn about the other person while challenging their own prejudices as well.

I would close this book by quoting Canadian psychology professor Jordan Peterson. In one of his online lectures, Peterson reminds us that differences in intelligences are not the prime determinant of differences in political belief. As he summed it up:

> You might be talking to someone who is more conscientious and less creative than you, if you happen to be a liberal. But that does not mean that that person's perspective is not valid. That does not mean that he would not outperform you in some domains, because he would. One thing to remember is: People actually *do* see the world differently. It is not merely that they are possessed of ill-informed opinions. The whole point of a democracy is to continue the dialogue between people of different temperamental types, so that we don't move so far to the right that everything becomes encapsulated in stone and doesn't move. Or so far to the left that everything dissolves in a kind of mealy-mouthed chaos. The only way you can navigate between those two extremes is through discussion.[8]

Acknowledgments

Thinking about all the countless lonely hours I spent writing this book—sitting alone at my desk in Debrecen or in Budapest—it goes without saying that I could never have done it without the support of some very special people.

Nadía, my wonderful wife and the love of my life, I owe you eternal gratitude for the way you always tell me to follow my dreams and to never give up. You are the master of posing questions that nobody else dares to ask, and your clever comments made me reflect in ways that really helped improve this book. Ástin *mín*, your unique approach to life should be an inspiration to everyone.

Mor & Far, my lovely parents, thank you for always supporting me and for helping me strive to become the best version of myself. Both of you encouraged me to never stop searching for new knowledge and insight, and, among many other things, you taught me the importance of a good conversation.

Mormor, *min gamle ven*, you are not only my grandmother; you are basically the reason why I am writing and reading all the time. Even in your nineties, you are the sharpest observer I know, and many people could learn something from looking at the world through your eyes.

To Ida, my cool sister and my foremost supporter, and to the rest of my beautiful family in Denmark and in Iceland: Thank you for always believing in me.

To my best man and best friend Casper Christensen: Thank you for your unconditional help and moral support over the years. You really kept me going. Furthermore, your skillful proofreading improved many of the pages in this book, and I look forward to return the favor.

Huge appreciation to all my good friends in Hungary, Denmark, Iceland and the UK—you have motivated me to continue my work, assuring me that I was on the right track and providing me with alternative viewpoints that helped shape the outcome of this book.

Amina, my friend and assistant in Hungary, thank you for all the conversations over the years—you helped me better understand the perspective of the Hungarian mind.

Paul Olchváry from New Europe Books, the publisher of this book, I am really lucky to have met you; without your excellent sense of perspective, and without your patience and flexibility throughout the process, *Orbánland* would not become what it is today. Thank you, Paul. I cannot wait for our next meal at Kispiac Bisztró in Budapest. Time to celebrate!

Thanks a lot to Kurt Stengel, much distinguished art director and the man behind the cover of this book. Great job!

Nick Thorpe from the *BBC*, one of the most experienced journalists in this part of the world, thank you so much for taking the time and effort to write the foreword to this book.

To my editors back in Denmark, I owe you big thanks for giving me free rein to do the kind of insightful and independent foreign journalism that I find to be most important for readers.

To the legendary Tony Dabbous Láng, Melinda Zacher and the rest of the team from the Bestsellers bookshop in Budapest, thank you for your continuous interest in my book.

To Bastiaan Ober, the most helpful Dutchman I have ever come across: *Hartelijk bedankt*! Your immense knowledge of Hungarian affairs and the English language contributed to the quality of this book.

To my old colleagues from the Danish organization for foreign journalism, *Korrespondenterne*—Rasmus, Janne, Katrine, Lena, and the rest of you—I am grateful for your inspiration and support. You were the ones who first encouraged me to write a book about Hungary, and from each of your corners of the world, you have improved the level of foreign journalism in Denmark and beyond.

Thank you to the members of HIPA, the Hungarian International Press Association, who taught me everything about politics and media in this country, and who helped me gain access to some of Hungary's key political leaders.

Additional thanks to all the curious people who have followed my work through social media and have participated in the many debates that ensued, I have learned a lot from these debates. Also, I would like to thank the teachers, students, organizations, and other visitors who came to Hungary to meet me and listen to my lectures. The feedback I received from you has helped me to become a better journalist and a better public speaker.

Last but not least, a very special thanks to each and every one of you who backed the initial crowdfunding campaign on Kickstarter and thereby helped fund the making of *Orbánland*.

I am truly grateful for all your support.

Notes

History In The Making (And A Journalist In Tears)

1. National Election Office. Parliamentary Election Results. April 8, 2018. http://www.valasztas.hu/dyn/pv18/szavossz/hu/l22.html

2. Ipsos MORI, *BBC Global Survey: A World Divided?* Ipsos MORI. April 23, 2018. https://www.ipsos.com/ipsos-mori/en-uk/bbc-global-survey-world-divided

3. Federico Vegetti, *The Political Nature of Ideological Polarization: The Case of Hungary.* Central European University. December 20, 2018.

4. Quartz, *European politics is more polarized than ever, and these numbers prove it.* Quartz. March 30, 2016. https://qz.com/645649/european-politics-is-more-polarized-than-ever-and-these-numbers-prove-it/

Welcome To Orbánland

1. Bálint Magyar, *Post-Communist Mafia State* (Central European University Press, 2016)

2. Igor Janke, *Forward* (Aeramentum, 2016)

3. Matthew S. Levendusky, *Why Do Partisan Media Polarize Viewers?* American Journal of Political Science. February 23, 2013.

4. Foreign Affairs, *Wrong way down the Danube*. Foreign Affairs. July 10, 2012. https://www.foreignaffairs.com/articles/hungary/2012-07-10/wrong-way-down-danube

5. Ferenc Gyurcsány, Speech at MSZP party congress in Balatonőszöd, May 26, 2006. Leaked and broadcast on Magyar Radio. September 17, 2006.

Part I: Essays

Chapter One: Arrivals in Europe

The Memory Wars

1. Rutger Bregman, *Utopia for Realists* (Bloomsbury, 2016).

2. Ivan Krastev, *After Europe* (University of Pennsylvania Press, 2017).

3. Christian Welzel, *Freedom Rising* (Cambridge University Press, 2013).

4. Pew Research Center, *End of Communism Cheered but Now with More Reservations*. November 2, 2009. http://www.pewglobal.org/2009/11/02/end-of-communism-cheered-but-now-with-more-reservations/

5. Frank Furedi, *Populism and the European Culture Wars* (Routledge, 2018).

6. Paul Lendvai, *Orbán—Europe's New Strongman* (C Hurst & Co., 2017).

Migration Broke the Camel's Back

1. Asylum In Europe, *Country Report: Hungary*. August 8, 2018. https://www.asylumineurope.org/reports/country/hungary

2. The Hungarian Helsinki Committee, *What you need to know about the refugee crisis in Hungary*. September 30, 2015. https://www.opensocietyfoundations.org/voices/what-you-need-know-about-refugee-crisis-hungary

3. Heinrich Böll Stiftung, *Why Hungarian voters are turning away from Fidesz and toward Jobbik*, June 2, 2015. https://www.boell. de/en/2015/06/02/why-hungarian-voters-are-turning-away-fidesz-and-toward-jobbik

4. Index, *Orbán: Gazdasági bevándorlóknak nem adunk menedéket*. January 11, 2015. https://index.hu/belfold/2015/01/11/orban_gazdasagi_bevandorloknak_nem_adunk_menedeket/

5. Gábor Török, *Orbán's motives*. January 11, 2015. https://www.facebook.com/torokgaborelemez?fref=nf

6. László Szekély, *Az eljárás megindulása*. Office of the Commisioner for Fundamental Rights, April 2015. https://www.ajbh.hu

7. Index, *Orbán eltökélte, bezáratja a debreceni menekülttábort*. May 18, 2015. https://index.hu/belfold/2015/05/18/orban_eltokelte_bezaratja_a_debreceni_menekulttabort

8. Die Bundesregierung, *Sommerpressekonferenz von Bundeskanzlerin Merkel*. August 31, 2015. https://www.bundesregierung.de/breg-de/aktuelles/pressekonferenzen/sommerpressekonferenz-von-bundeskanzlerin-merkel-848300

9. Index, *Orbán: A menekültügy Németország problémája*. September 3, 2015. https://index.hu/kulfold/eurologus/2015/09/03/orban_a_menekultek_nemetorszag_problemaja/

10. Altinget, *Løkke: Vi er blevet overhalet af virkeligheden*. Altinget. September 7, 2015. https://www.altinget.dk/artikel/loekke-vi-er-blevet-overhalet-af-virkeligheden

11. Viktor Orbán press conference. September 15, 2015. http://www.kormany.hu/en/the-prime-minister/the-prime-minister-s-speeches/interview-with-prime-minister-viktor-orban-on-commercial-station-tv2-s-facts-evening-television-programme

12. International Organization for Migration, *Migration Issues in Hungary*. June 29, 2018. http://www.iom.hu/migration-issues-hungary

13. Wikipedia overview, *Opinion polling for the 2018 Hungarian parliamentary election*. April 3, 2018. https://en.wikipedia.

org/wiki/Opinion_polling_for_the_2018_Hungarian_parliamentary_election

14. Nézőpont Institute, *Political Poll 2015*. July 2015. https://nezopontintezet.hu

15. Politico.eu, *Orbán wins the migration argument*. September 15, 2017. https://www.politico.eu/article/viktor-orban-migration-eu-has-won-the-argument/

A Clash of Solidarities

1. Ivan Krastev, *After Europe* (University of Pennsylvania Press, 2017).

2. Ibid.

3. Ibid.

4. EU Statistics, *Average Salary in the European Union 2018*. March 15, 2018. https://www.reinisfischer.com/average-salary-european-union-2018

5. Ivan Krastev, *After Europe* (University of Pennsylvania Press, 2017).

6. OECD report, *Labor Force Statistics 2018*. https://www.oecd-ilibrary.org/employment/oecd-labor-force-statistics-2018/hungary_oecd_lfs-2018-15-en

7. Ivan Krastev, *After Europe* (University of Pennsylvania Press, 2017).

8. Ibid.

Chapter Two: Another Side to the Story

Is This the End of the End of History?

1. Francis Fukuyama, *The End of History?* in the *National Interest*, 1989.

2. Samuel P. Huntington, *The Clash of Civilizations?* in *Foreign Affairs*, 1993.

3. Francis Fukuyama, *Huntington's Legacy* in the *American Interest*. August 27, 2018. https://www.the-american-interest.com/2018/08/27/huntingtons-legacy/

4. The National Review, *Events, Dear Boy, Events*. July 18, 2011. https://www.nationalreview.com/corner/events-dear-boy-events-charles-c-w-cooke/

5. The Guardian, *One In Four Europeans Vote Populist*, November 20, 2018. https://www.theguardian.com/world/ng-interactive/2018/nov/20/revealed-one-in-four-europeans-vote-populist

6. Ivan Krastev, *After Europe* (University of Pennsylvania Press, 2017).

7. Ken Jowitt, *New World Disorder* (University of California Press, 1992).

8. Jesper Vind, *Merkel-tiden Er Ovre*. Weekendavisen. February 23, 2018.

9. The New York Times, *Clinton's Economic Plan*. February 18, 1993. https://www.nytimes.com/1993/02/18/us/clinton-s-economic-plan-speech-text-president-s-address-joint-session-congress.html

10. Anthony Giddens, *The Third Way* (Polity, 1998).

11. Tony Blair, Speech in Chicago. April 22, 1999. https://www.globalpolicy.org/component/content/article/154/26026.html

12. Theresa May, Speech in Birmingham. *Telegraph*. October 6, 2016. https://www.telegraph.co.uk/news/2016/10/05/theresa-mays-conference-speech-in-full/

The Anywheres Versus the Somewheres

1. David Goodhart, *The Road To Somewhere: The Populist Revolt and The Future of Politics* (C Hurst & Co., 2017).

2. Eurostat, *People in the EU: Statistics on Geographic Mobility*. December 2017. https://ec.europa.eu/eurostat/statistics-explained/index.php?title=People_in_the_EU_-_statistics_on_geographic_mobility

3. Viktor Orbán, Speech on Kossuth Square. March 15, 2018. http://www.kormany.hu/en/the-prime-minister/the-prime-minister-s-speeches/orban-viktor-s-ceremonial-speech-on-the-170th-anniversary-of-the-hungarian-revolution-of-1848

4. Paul Lendvai, *Orbán—Europe's New Strongman* (C Hurst & Co., 2017).

5. Ibid.

6. Bloomberg, *Orbán accuses Soros of stoking refugee wave to weaken Europe.* October 30, 2015. https://www.bloomberg.com/news/articles/2015-10-30/orban-accuses-soros-of-stoking-refugee-wave-to-weaken-europe

7. George Soros, Here's my plan to solve the asylum chaos. MarketWatch. September 30, 2015. https://www.marketwatch.com/story/george-soros-heres-my-plan-to-solve-the-asylum-chaos-2015-09-29

8. Douglas Murray, *The Strange Death of Europe* (Bloomsbury, 2017).

9. Dimitris Avramopoulos, *Europe's migrants are here to stay.* Politico. December 18, 2017. https://www.politico.eu/article/europe-migration-migrants-are-here-to-stay-refugee-crisis/

10. Douglas Murray, *The Strange Death of Europe* (Bloomsbury, 2017).

11. United Nations, *Universal Declaration of Human Rights.* December 10, 1948.

12. UNHCR, *UN Refugee Convention. The 1951 Refugee Convention and 1967 Protocol.* July 28, 1951, and January 31, 1967.

13. United Nations, *Global Compact for Migration.* December 18, 2018.

14. Viktor Orbán, Press conference in Prague. November 30, 2018.

We Need To Talk About Populism

1. Information, *Thomas Piketty: Venstrefløjen har ladt de fattige i stikken.* Information. July 20, 2018. https://www.information.dk/udland/2018/07/thomas-piketty-venstrefloejen-ladt-fattige-stikken

2. Frank Furedi, *Populism and the European Culture Wars* (Routledge, 2018).

3. Ibid.

4. Ibid.

5. Paul Lendvai, *Hungary: Between Democracy and Authoritarianism* (Oxford University Press, 2012).

6. Viktor Orbán, Speech at the 28th Bálványos Summer Open University. July 22, 2017. http://www.kormany.hu/en/the-prime-minister/the-prime-minister-s-speeches/viktor-orban-s-speech-at-the-28th-balvanyos-summer-open-university-and-student-camp

7. Frank Furedi, *Populism and the European Culture Wars* (Routledge, 2018).

8. Viktor Orbán, Speech at Hungarian Diaspora Council. November 30, 2016. http://www.miniszterelnok.hu/prime-minister-viktor-orbans-speech-at-the-6th-meeting-of-the-hungarian-diaspora-council/

Chapter Three: Stuck In The Moral Matrix

The Tables Have Turned

1. Lasse Skytt, *Orbáns sejr viser, hvorfor det liberale Vesten har misforstået nationalkonservatismens appel*. Information. April 10, 2018. https://www.information.dk/udland/2018/04/orbans-sejr-viser-hvorfor-liberale-vesten-misforstaaet-national konservatismens-appel

2. Viktor Orbán, Speech after swearing the prime ministerial oath of office. May 10, 2018. http://www.kormany.hu/en/the-prime-minister/the-prime-minister-s-speeches/prime-minister-viktor-orban-s-address-after-swearing-the-prime-ministerial-oath-of-office

3. Ibid.

4. Viktor Orbán, Speech at the 29th Bálványos Summer Open University. July 28, 2018. http://www.kormany.hu/en/the-

prime-minister/the-prime-minister-s-speeches/prime-minister-viktor-orban-s-speech-at-the-29th-balvanyos-summer-open-university-and-student-camp

5. The Rubin Report, *Steven Pinker on the Case for Reason, Science, Humanism, and Progress*. YouTube. March 23, 2018.

6. Magyar Nemzet, *A Fideszben nem javasolják Orbán Viktornak a miniszterelnöki vitát*. Magyar Nemzet. November 3, 2017. https://www.magyarnemzet.hu/archivum/belfold-archivum/a-fideszben-nem-javasoljak-orban-viktornak-a-miniszterelnoki-vitat-3858820/

7. Ibid.

8. Index, *Hungarian PM calls leading news website fake*. Index, May 30, 2018. https://index.hu/english/2018/05/30/hungarian_pm_calls_country_s_leading_news_website_fake/

9. Index, *PM Orbán's much-awaited press conference*. Index, January 10, 2019. https://www.index.hu/english/2019/01/10/orban_press_conference_migration_soros_corruption_europe_media/

10. Ibid.

11. Central European Press and Media Foundation. www.cepmf.hu

How Should The Left Fight Back?

1. Chantal Mouffe, Populists are on the rise but this can be a moment for progressives too. The Guardian. September 10, 2018. https://www.theguardian.com/commentisfree/2018/sep/10/populists-rise-progressives-radical-right

2. Ibid.

3. Ibid.

4. John O'Sullivan, *The Second Term of Viktor Orbán* (The Danube Institute, 2015).

5. Ibid.

6. Nolan, Daniel: "Meet the Conservative who Could Unseat Viktor Orbán." Open Democracy, January 14, 2022. https://

www.opendemocracy.net/en/peter-marki-zay-viktor-orban-hungary-opponent-election-interview

Why Nationalism Is Here To Stay

1. Dana R. Carney, *The Secret Lives of Liberals and Conservatives.* New York University Psychology, 2008.

2. Mark Brandt, *The Ideological-Conflict Hypothesis: Intolerance Among Both Liberals and Conservatives.* Tilburg University, 2014.

3. Jonathan Haidt, *The Righteous Mind: Why Good People Are Divided by Politics and Religion* (Vintage Publishing, 2012).

4. Ibid.

5. Ibid.

6. Ibid.

Part II: Features

Chapter Four: What Does Viktor Orbán Really Want?

One Solution: Orbán's Solution

1. Peter Krasztev, *The Hungarian Patient* (Central European University Press, 2015)

2. Viktor Orbán, Speech on March 15, 2016. http://www.kormany.hu/en/the-prime-minister/the-prime-minister-s-speeches/speech-by-prime-minister-viktor-orban-on-15-march

3. Bálint Magyar, *Post-Communist Mafia State* (Central European University Press, 2016).

How Liberals Misunderstand The Appeal Of Conservatism

1. Jonathan Haidt, *The Righteous Mind: Why Good People Are Divided by Politics and Religion* (Vintage Publishing, 2012).

2. W.E.B. Du Bois, *The Souls Of Black Folks* (Bantam Classics, 1989, originally published in 1903).

Can Hungarians Save Their Country By Having More Children?

1. Viktor Orbán, Speech at Budapest World Congress of Families. May 25, 2017. http://www.miniszterelnok.hu/prime-minister-viktor-orbans-opening-speech-at-the-2nd-budapest-world-congress-of-families/

2. Hír TV, *Szilard Nemeth: Aki teleszüli, azé a világ.* May 24, 2017. https://hirtv.hu/ahirtvhirei_adattar/nemeth-aki-teleszuli-aze-a-vilag-1395766

3. United Nations Reproductive Rights. Conference on Population, 1994. http://www.un.org/en/development/desa/population/theme/rights/index.asp

4. Euronews, *Hungary leads way in EU family policy, but motives suspect.* May 27, 2016. https://www.euronews.com/2016/05/27/hungary-leads-way-in-eu-family-policy-but-motives-suspect

5. Hungarian Free Press, *Viktor Orbán's deal for women and a plan to increase the birth rate in Hungary.* April 23, 2018. http://hungarianfreepress.com/2018/04/23/viktor-orbans-deal-for-women-and-a-plan-to-increase-the-birth-rate-in-hungary/

6. Index, *Novák Katalin: Mondjuk ki a nyilvánvalót, akkor is, ha homofóbnak tartanak majd.* June 30, 2018. https://index.hu/belfold/2018/06/30/novak_katalin_mondjuk_ki_a_nyilvanvalot_akkor_is_ha_homofobnak_tartanak_majd_csalad_allamtitkar/

A Superstar Conservative Comes To Town

1. Time Magazine. *Talking With Tucker Carlson, the Most Powerful Conservative in America.* Time Magazine. July 15, 2021. https://time.com/6080432/tucker-carlson-profile/

2. Balkan Insight. *Orbán tries to give illiberalism a makeover.* Balkan Insight. July 30, 2019. https://balkaninsight.com/2019/07/30/hungarys-orban-tries-to-give-illiberalism-a-makeover/

3. FOX News. *Hungarian prime minister hits back at Biden calling him a 'thug' on 'Tucker'.* FOX News / YouTube. August 6, 2021. https://www.youtube.com/watch?v=s01ZL5TnBNY&t=5s&ab_channel=FoxNews

4. Benjamin Novak. *Hungarian govt sent out a transcript to reporters of @TuckerCarlson's interview with PM Orban. The transcript with "anti-communist" Orban does not include any mention of China or Xi Jinping.* Benjamin Novak on Twitter, August 6, 2021. https://twitter.com/b_novak/status/1423727185634934784

5. János Szilárd Tóth. *Öt ok, amiért a nyugati konzervatívok nem értik, mi történik Magyarországon.* Válasz Online. August 11, 2021. https://www.valaszonline.hu/2021/08/11/tucker-carlson-douglas-murray-jordan-peterson-magyarorszag/

Chapter Five: Attacking The Opponents

The Man Who Became the Symbol of Europe's Polarization

1. Karl Popper, *The Open Society and Its Enemies* (Princeton University Press, 2013, originally published in 1945).

2. George Soros, Speech given to the Los Angeles World Affairs Council. September 20, 2006. http://www.lawac.org/speech-archive/pdf/2006/Soros_612.pdf

3. Viktor Orbán, Speech on Kossuth Square. March 15, 2018. http://www.kormany.hu/en/the-prime-minister/the-prime-minister-s-speeches/orban-viktor-s-ceremonial-speech-on-the-170th-anniversary-of-the-hungarian-revolution-of-1848

4. Viktor Orbán interview on Kossuth Radio. June 8, 2018. http://www.kormany.hu/en/the-prime-minister/news/transformation-of-populations-is-taking-place-in-europe

5. George Soros, *Here's my plan to solve the asylum chaos.* MarketWatch. September 30, 2015. https://www.marketwatch. com/story/george-soros-heres-my-plan-to-solve-the-asylum-chaos-2015-09-29

6. Foreign Policy, *George Soros: This Is Europe's Last Chance to Fix Its Refugee Policy.* July 19, 2016. https://foreignpolicy. com/2016/07/19/this-is-europes-last-chance-to-fix-its-refugee-policy-george-soros/

7. Financial Times, *George Soros attacks "hate-mongering" of Viktor Orban's Hungary.* November 20, 2017. https://www.ft.com/content/c4fc5fc0-cccc-11e7-b781-794ce08b24dc

Is Academic Freedom In Decline In The Old East Bloc?

1. Central European University, *CEU Disagrees with Decision to Sign Legislation, Plans Immediate Legal Action.* March 31, 2017. https://www.ceu.edu/article/2017-04-10/ceu-disagrees-decision-sign-legislation-plans-immediate-legal-action

2. Hungary Today, *CEU Enjoyed Unfair Advantage Over Hungarian Universities.* March 31, 2017. https://hungarytoday. hu/pm-orban-ceu-enjoyed-unfair-advantage-hungarian-universities-63942/

3. George Soros, *The Soros Lectures At The Central European University* (Public Affairs, 2010).

4. Viktor Orbán, Speech at the 25th Bálványos Summer Free University. July 26, 2014. http://www.kormany.hu/en/the-prime-minister/the-prime-minister-s-speeches/prime-minister-viktor-orban-s-speech-at-the-25th-balvanyos-summer-free-university-and-student-camp

5. Viktor Orbán, Speech at the 29th Bálványos Summer Free University. July 28, 2018. http://www.miniszterelnok.hu/prime-minister-viktor-orbans-speech-at-the-29th-balvanyos-summer-open-university-and-student-camp/

6. Reuters, *Hungary to stop financing gender studies courses.* August 14, 2018. https://www.reuters.com/article/us-hungary-government-education/hungary-to-stop-financing-gender-studies-courses-pm-aide-idUSKBN1KZ1M0

A Wound That Keeps Bleeding

1. Zoran Milanović, President of Croatia. *Povodom karte/globusa na kojemu se vidi hipertrofirana Mađarska (…).* Facebook post. May 7, 2020. https://www.facebook.com/ZoranMilanovic/posts/2553630018235956

2. Viktor Orbán. *Orbán Viktor's ceremonial speech on the 170th anniversary of the Hungarian Revolution of 1848.* About Hungary. March 21, 2018. https://abouthungary.hu/speeches-and-remarks/orban-viktors-ceremonial-speech-on-the-170th-anniversary-of-the-hungarian-revolution-of-1848

3. Kafkadesk. *Has the Trianon centenary brought a divided Hungary one step closer to unity?* Kafkadesk. June 8, 2020. https://kafkadesk.org/2020/06/08/has-the-trianon-centenary-brought-a-divided-hungary-one-step-closer-to-unity/

4. Ibid.

5. France24. *Hungary's Orbán Courts Diaspora for Election Boost.* France24. March 28, 2018. https://www.france24.com/en/20180328-hungarys-orban-courts-diaspora-election-boost

Chapter Six: A Colorful Past

Hungarian Film In the Spotlight

1. Viktor Orbán, Speech in Miskolc. April 11, 2016. http://www.miniszterelnok.hu/sport-restores-hungarys-self-respect/

2. Hungarian National Film Fund. Magyar Nemzeti Filmalap. https://www.mnf.hu/en/industry

3. Ibid.

Licking the Wounds of Communism

1. Vilmos Kondor, *Budapest Noir* (Harper Paperbacks, 2012, published in Hungarian in 2008)

2. Marek Krajewski, *Death in Breslau* (MacLehose Press, 2008, first published in 1999)

3. Bogdan Hrib, *Kill the General* (Profusion, 2011)

4. Zygmunt Miłoszewski, *A Grain of Truth* (Bitter Lemon Press, 2011)

5. Zygmunt Miłoszewski, *Entanglement* (Bitter Lemon Press, 2007)

When the Pope Came By

1. Vatican News. *Cardinal Erdö: The Eucharistic Congress is a symbol of hope.* Vatican News. September 27, 2021.

   https://www.vaticannews.va/en/pope/news/2021-09/cardinal-erdo-eucharistic-congress-hope-pope-budapest.html

2. Magyar Kurír. *Orbán Viktor: Magyarországon a kereszténység nem választás, hanem előre meghatározottság kérdése.* Magyar Kurír. June 18, 2021.

Chapter Seven: Silenced Voices—Should We Be Listening?

The Politically Incorrects (and the Downfall of the West)

1. Douglas Murray, *The Strange Death of Europe* (Bloomsbury, 2017).

2. Steven Pinker, *Enlightenment Now* (Viking, 2018).

3. Dave Rubin, *The Rubin Report.* YouTube.

4. Bari Weiss, *Meet the Renegades of the Intellectual Dark Web.* The New York Times. May 8, 2018. https://www.nytimes.com/2018/05/08/opinion/intellectual-dark-web.html

5. Russell Brand And Jordan B. Peterson. *Under the Skin #52.* YouTube.

6. Jordan B. Peterson, *12 Rules for Life* (Random House, 2018).

7. Mark Lilla, *The Once And Future Liberal: After Identity Politics* (Harper, 2017).

Roma Minority Takes Back Control Of Its Own Destiny

1. István Zoltán Pásztor, *The number and spatial distribution of the Roma population in Hungary*. University Of Debrecen. July 2016.

Welcoming Nationalists From All Over Europe

1. Le Figaro, *Ces Allemands qui fuient leur pays pour s'installer en Hongrie*. Le Figaro. October 23, 2016. http://www.lefigaro.fr/international/2016/10/23/01003-20161023ARTFIG00110-ces-allemands-qui-fuient-leur-pays-pour-s-installer-en-hongrie

2. Viktor Orbán, State of the Union speech. February 10, 2017. http://www.kormany.hu/en/the-prime-minister/the-prime-minister-s-speeches/prime-minister-viktor-orban-s-state-of-the-nation-address-20170214

3. 444.hu, *Magyarországra költözik a brit szélsőjobboldali vezető, Nick Griffin*. 444.hu. March 18, 2017. https://444.hu/2017/03/18/magyarorszagra-koltozik-a-brit-szelsojobboldali-vezeto-nick-griffin

4. Handelsblatt, *Runaway German Holocaust Denier Seeks Asylum in Hungary*. Handelsblatt. May 15, 2017. https://www.handelsblatt.com/today/politics/nazi-refugee-runaway-german-holocaust-denier-seeks-asylum-in-hungary/23569678.html?ticket=ST-332220-UAGnhw1etTvBN0G7EB7D-ap3

5. Horst Mahler, *We are fighting to win*. Original source removed. Spring 2017. http://www.germanvictims.com/2017/03/we-are-fighting-to-win/

6. Magyar Narancs, *Hivatalos: kiutasították Magyarországról a putyinista hátSquareembert, James Dowsont*. Magyar Narancs. May 24, 2017. https://magyarnarancs.hu/kismagyarorszag/hivatalos-kiutasitottak-magyarorszagrol-a-putyinista-hatterembert-james-dowsont-104334

7. Viktor Orbán, Interview on Kossuth Radio. November 23, 2018. http://www.kormany.hu/en/the-prime-minister/news/pro-immigration-forces-look-upon-european-institutions-as-transport-agencies

Chasing Rainbows

1. LXXIX 2021. Law on stepping up the fight against pedophile offenders and amending certain laws to protect children. Hungarian Parliament, June 23, 2021.

   https://mkogy.jogtar.hu/jogszabaly?docid=A2100079.TV

2. Viktor Orbán's commemoration speech on the 65th anniversary of the 1956 Revolution. October 23, 2021. https://abouthungary.hu/speeches-and-remarks/prime-minister-viktor-orbans-commemoration-speech-on-the-65th-anniversary-of-the-1956-revolution-and-freedom-fight

3. The 9th amendment to Hungary's constitution, stipulating that a mother is a woman and a father a man. December 15, 2020.

   https://www.parlament.hu/irom41/13679/13679.pdf

4. LGBT+ Pride Global Survey 2021. IPSOS. https://www.ipsos.com/sites/default/files/ct/news/documents/2021-06/lgbt-pride-2021-global-survey-ipsos.pdf

5. Telex: *Závecz: A magyarok 56 százaléka elfogadó a melegekkel szemben.* Telex. July 14, 2021.

   https://telex.hu/kult/2021/07/14/rtl-klub-zavecz-kutatas-homoszexualitas-megitelese-magyarorszag

6. Global Attitudes Toward Transgender People 2018. IPSOS. https://www.ipsos.com/en/global-attitudes-toward-transgender-people

7. Index: *Speaker of Hungarian Parliament: Fighting for LGBT adoption is morally equivalent to pedophilia.* Index. May 17, 2019. https://index.hu/english/2019/05/17/speaker_of_hungarian_parliament_a_normal_homosexual_does_not_regard_himself_as_equal/

Chapter Eight: Under the Carpet

Corruption in the VIP Stands

1. Four Four Two Magazine. *The 12 most beautiful football stadiums in the world.* Four Four Two Magazine. November 12, 2015. https://www.fourfourtwo.com/features/12-most-beautiful-football-stadiums-world

2. The Guardian. *Viktor Orbán's reckless football obsession.* The Guardian. January 11, 2018. https://www.theguardian.com/news/2018/jan/11/viktor-orban-hungary-prime-minister-reckless-football-obsession

3. Miklós Ligeti and Gyula Mucsi. *Corruption in Sports. Opening the door to corruption in Hungary's sport financing.* Transparency International Hungary, 2016. https://www.transparency.org/files/content/feature/1.12_OpeningTheDoor_LigetiMucsi_GCRSport.pdf

4. Transparency Hungary. *Jogerős: nem lehet titkolni, honnan jöttek a tao-pénzek.* Transparency Hungary. March 23, 2017. https://transparency.hu/hirek/jogeros-nem-lehet-titkolni-honnan-jottek-a-tao-penzek/

5. Atlatszo. *The Meszaros empire won public tenders worth 826 million euros last year.* Atlatszo. January 17, 2019. https://english.atlatszo.hu/2019/01/17/the-meszaros-empire-won-public-tenders-worth-e826-million-last-year-93-percent-of-which-came-from-european-union-funds/

6. Financial Times. *Viktor Orban's oligarchs: a new elite emerges in Hungary.* Financial Times. December 20, 2017. https://www.ft.com/content/ecf6fb4e-d900-11e7-a039-c64b1c09b482

7. The Guardian. *Viktor Orbán's reckless football obsession.* The Guardian. January 11, 2018. https://www.theguardian.com/news/2018/jan/11/viktor-orban-hungary-prime-minister-reckless-football-obsession

8. Hungary Today. *Orbán dismisses corruption claims.* Hungary Today. January 11, 2019. https://hungarytoday.hu/orban-dismisses-corruption-claims/

9. DW. *Hertha Berlin sack goalkeeping coach over controversial comments.* DW. April 8, 2021. https://www.dw.com/en/hertha-berlin-sack-goalkeeping-coach-over-controversial-comments/a-57107713

10. Reuters. Hungary PM Orban: Taking knee is 'provocation', 'has no place on pitch'. Reuters. June 10, 2021. https://www.reuters.com/lifestyle/sports/hungary-pm-orban-taking-knee-is-provocation-has-no-place-pitch-2021-06-10/

Surrounded by Dishonesty

1. United Nations. *Global Cost of Corruption at Least 5 Per Cent of World Gross Domestic Product, Secretary-General Tells Security Council.* United Nations and World Economic Forum. September 10, 2018. https://www.un.org/press/en/2018/sc13493.doc.htm

2. Transparency International. Global Corruption Index. Transparency International. 2020. https://www.transparency.org/en/cpi/2020/index/nzl

3. Ibid.

4. K-Monitor. K-Teszt. K-Monitor. 2020. http://k-teszt.hu/k-teszt-2015/?lang=en

Last Stop on the Silk Road

1. Index. *Megnyitja első londoni* üzletét *a Nanushka.* Index.hu. May 28, 2021. https://index.hu/gazdasag/2021/05/28/szijjarto-peter-nanushka-london-divat-bruton-street-orban-viktor/

2. Budapest Business Journal. *Orbán: if EU doesn't pay, Hungary will turn to China.* Budapest Business Journal. January 11, 2018. https://bbj.hu/politics/foreign-affairs/visits/orban-if-eu-doesn-t-pay-hungary-will-turn-to-china

3. Index.hu. *Orbán: Keleti szél fúj.* Index.hu. November 5, 2010. https://index.hu/belfold/2010/11/05/orban_keleti_szel_fuj/

4. Direkt36. *Hungary revoked 16 Golden Visa holders' residence permit. It seems that the moneyman of the Syrian president and the family of Russian SVR chief were not among them.* Direkt36. December 6, 2018. https://www.direkt36.hu/en/tizenhat-kotvenyes-papirjait-vontak-vissza-utolag-ugy-nez-ki-hogy-a-szir-diktator-penzembere-es-az-orosz-kemfonok-csaladja-nincs-kozottuk/

5. Direkt36. *How Orbán's Eastern Opening brought Chinese spy games to Budapest.* Direkt36. March 14, 2021. https://www.direkt36.hu/en/kemjatszmakat-hozott-budapestre-orban-kinai-nyitasa/

6. Xinhuanet. *Budapest Airport sees record cargo turnover thanks to China's Alibaba.* Xinhuanet. July 22, 2021. http://www.xinhuanet.com/english/europe/2021-07/22/c_1310076065.htm

7. Direkt36. *Huge Chinese loan to cover the construction of Fudan University in Budapest.* Direkt36. April 6, 2021. https://www.direkt36.hu/kinai-hitelbol-keszul-a-magyar-felsooktatas-oriasberuhazasa-a-kormany-mar-oda-is-igerte-egy-kinai-cegnek/

8. Quartz. *A top Chinese university stripped "freedom of thought" from its charter.* Quartz. December 18, 2019. https://qz.com/1770693/chinas-fudan-university-axes-freedom-of-thought-from-charter/

9. Reuters. *Hungarians protest against planned Chinese university campus.* Reuters. June 6, 2021. https://www.reuters.com/world/china/hungarians-protest-against-planned-chinese-university-campus-2021-06-05/

10. Ibid.

Chapter Nine: At the Crossroads

The Mother of Corona Vaccines

1. Reuters. Budapest mural pays tribute to Katalin Kariko, Hungarian-born pioneer behind COVID-19 vaccine. Reuters. August 28, 2021. https://www.reuters.com/lifestyle/budapest-

mural-pays-tribute-katalin-kariko-hungarian-born-pioneer-behind-covid-2021-08-28/

2. University of Pennsylvania School of Medicine. *Penn Study Finds A New Role For RNA In Human Immune Response.* Science Daily. August 24, 2005. https://www.sciencedaily.com/releases/2005/08/050824082351.htm

Living on the Edge

1. Népszava. *Robotokat vetne be a kormány a déli határnál.* Népszava. August 28, 2019. https://nepszava.hu/3047972_robotokat-vetne-be-a-kormany-a-deli-hatarnal

2. Transparency International. *Borders Without Borders: How the EU is Exporting Surveillance in Bid to Outsource its Border Controls.* Transparency International. November 10, 2020. https://privacyinternational.org/long-read/4288/borders-without-borders-how-eu-exporting-surveillance-bid-outsource-its-border

Cold War Comeback

1. Richard H. Cummings. *Cold War Radio: The Dangerous History of American Broadcasting in Europe, 1950-1989.* McFarland & Company, 2009.

2. Radio Free Europe. *Reporting On Prague Demonstrations Was A 'Fire That Spread'.* Radio Free Europe. November 10, 2014. https://pressroom.rferl.org/a/pavel-pechacek-interview-25-year-anniversary/26683830.html

3. Deutsche Welle. *Radio Free Europe rebrands in Bulgaria, Hungary and Romania.* DW. April 2, 2020. https://www.dw.com/en/radio-free-europe-rebrands-in-bulgaria-hungary-and-romania/a-53000510

4. Freedom House. *Freedom In The World 2021. Hungary.* Freedom House, 2021. https://freedomhouse.org/country/hungary/freedom-world/2021

PART III: Conversations

Chapter Ten: On Politics

Zoltán Kovács: Viktor Orbán's Right-Hand Man

Zoltán Kovács biography: Government spokesperson for the Orbán government. He was born in 1969 in Abaújszántó, a town of 3,000 people not far from the Slovak border. Kovács did his undergraduate degree in the eastern city of Debrecen before moving to Budapest in 1992 to pursue first an MA and then a PhD in history at the Central European University, the university that has recently been in the government's sights. Kovács joined the Fidesz party in 1997 after Orbán had transformed the once-liberal party into a right-wing force. According to himself, getting involved in politics at first "obviously was about friendship… and most definitely about anticommunism." Kovács returned to Debrecen to teach history and there he met Lajos Kósa, one of the founders of Fidesz, who later helped bring him into national politics.

1. Lasse Skytt, *Orbáns omrejsende talerør*. Berlingske. October 9, 2017. https://www.berlingske.dk/internationalt/orbans-omrejsende-taleroer

2. Politico, *Juncker slaps down Orbán over border funding request*. Politico.eu. September 5, 2017. https://www.politico.eu/blogs/playbook-plus/2017/09/juncker-slaps-orban-over-border-funding-request/

3. Zoltán Kovács, *Dear New York Times Editors: You just don't get it, do you?* AboutHungary.hu. March 14, 2017. http://abouthungary.hu/blog/dear-new-york-times-editors-you-just-dont-get-it-do-you/

4. George Soros, *Here's my plan to solve the asylum chaos*. MarketWatch. September 30, 2015. https://www.marketwatch.com/story/george-soros-heres-my-plan-to-solve-the-asylum-chaos-2015-09-29

Ferenc Gyurcsány: Should I Stay or Should I Go?

Biography: Leader of the center-left party Democratic Coalition and former Prime Minister of Hungary (2004-2009). He was born in 1961 in Pápa, a historic town in western Hungary. In 1984, he became a teacher from the University of Pécs where he later studied economics before getting his degree in 1990. In the 1980s, Gyurcsány was politically active in KISZ, the Organization of Young Communists, but after the political change in 1989, he moved to the private sector as a businessman. During the 1990s, he was the CEO at Altus, a holding company, and by 2002, Gyurcsány had become the 50th richest person in Hungary. Then he returned to politics for the socialist party, MSZP. Two years later, in 2004, he was voted to become prime minister of Hungary after the resignation of Péter Medgyessy. At the 2006 elections, he was re-elected as prime minister, but the consequences of a leaked confidential speech as well as growing financial problems for Hungary made him resign his position in 2009. After Viktor Orbán's landslide victory in 2010, Gyurscány decided to leave the socialists and form his own party, the Democratic Coalition. Today, he is a MP in the Hungarian parliament as one of the leading figures for the leftist opposition.

1. Ferenc Gyurcsány, Speech at MSZP party congress in Balatonőszöd, May 26, 2006. Leaked and broadcast on Magyar Radio. September 17, 2006. https://en.wikipedia.org/wiki/%C5%90sz%C3%B6d_speech

2. Paul Lendvai, *Orbán—Europe's New Strongman* (C Hurst & Co., 2017).

Bernadett Szél: Women are Different

Bernadett Szél biography: Bernadett Szél is politician and a former copresident of the green-liberal party Lehet Más a Politika (LMP, in English: Politics Can Be Different). She was born in Pécs in 1977 and became an economist, working for both corporate firms and human rights organizations before joining Hungarian politics around 2010. Bernadett Szél was elected copresident of LMP in 2013 and stayed in the position until 2018 when she was forced out of the party. She remains an independent member of the parliament.

1. 444.hu, *Orbán elárulta, miért nem enged nőket a politika csúcsára.* 444.hu. October 6, 2015. https://444.hu/2015/10/06/orban-elarulta-miert-nincsenek-nok-a-magyar-politika-legfelso-szintjein/

2. ATV, *Hazarendelik a washingtoni nagykövetet.* ATV. April 4, 2017. http://www.atv.hu/belfold/20170404-hazarendelik-nyaron-szemerkenyi-rekat-washingtonbol

3. The World Bank, *Proportion of seats held by women in national parliaments.* 2019. https://data.worldbank.org/indicator/SG.GEN.PARL.ZS

4. 4Liberty.eu, *Women in Politics: Hungarian Attitudes, They Are A'Changin.* May 15, 2017. http://4liberty.eu/women-in-politics-hungarian-attitudes-they-are-achangin/

5. Index, *Egyvalakit látok, aki majd megküzdhet Orbánnal.* Index. July 11, 2017. https://index.hu/belfold/2017/11/07/medgyessy_peter_interju_orban_gyozni_fog_a_baloldal_csak_jobbikkal_gyozhetne/

6. Hungarian Spectrum, *Sexism in the Hungarian parliament.* Hungarian Spectrum. September 12, 2013. https://hungarianspectrum.wordpress.com/2013/09/12/sexism-in-the-hungarian-parliament/

7. The Independent, *Hungarian Prime Minister Viktor Orbán bans gender studies programmes.* The Independent. October 24, 2018. https://www.independent.co.uk/news/world/europe/hungary-bans-gender-studies-programmes-viktor-orban-central-european-university-budapest-a8599796.html

Márton Gyöngyösi: Political Theft on the Right

Biography: Márton Gyöngyösi is a politician and one of the leaders of Jobbik. He was born in 1977 in Kecskemét, a city between Budapest and Szeged. As the son of a Hungarian diplomat, he grew up in different countries around the world, including Egypt and India, and he studied economy and business at Trinity College in Dublin,

Ireland. In 2004, he moved back to Hungary and started working as a tax consultant in the Budapest office of KPMG, and later at Ernst & Young, before being elected into parliament for Jobbik in 2010. Since then he has been Jobbik's intellectual architect and today he serves as the party's Executive Vice President.

1. Reuters, *Anger as Hungary far-right leader demands lists of Jews.* Reuters. November 27, 2012. https://www.reuters.com/article/ us-hungary-antisemitism/anger-as-hungary-far-right-leader-demands-lists-of-jews

2. Reuters, *Hungary's Jobbik ditches far-right past to challenge Orbán in 2018.* Reuters. January 11, 2017. https://www.reuters.com/ article/us-hungary-jobbik/hungarys-jobbik-ditches-far-right-past-to-challenge-orban-in-2018

András Fekete-Győr: My Generation

Biography: Founder of the Momentum Movement. Born in 1989 in Budapest where he attended a German-Hungarian bilingual school. He then studied drama and history at Buda's Told Ferenc Academic High School, where his interests came to focus on social studies. Finally, he decided to study law at the ELTE university in Budapest. After obtaining his diploma, he joined a multinational company. Quickly he got tired of working in a law firm, and instead he wanted to obtain political experience abroad. First, he got a position in the legal committee at the European Parliament; then he moved to Berlin to work as an assistant to German CSU politician Hans-Peter Friedrich. When returning home to Hungary, András Fekete-Győr decided to establish a new political youth organisation, Momentum Movement, which later became a political party after leading a successful campaign against the Orbán government's plan to make Budapest host the 2024 Olympics. Momentum Movement did not receive enough votes to get any parliament seats in the 2018 national elections.

1. The Independent, *Ervin Zador: Blood on the water.* The Independent. December 2, 2006. https://www.independent.co.uk/ sport/olympics/ervin-zador-blood-on-the-water-426695.html

2. Viktor Orbán, Speech about the Olympics in Budapest. August 22, 2016. http://www.kormany.hu/en/the-prime-minister/news/prime-minister-viktor-orban-believes-that-budapest-is-the-right-city-for-2024-olympic-games

3. 444.hu, *Ahogy elköltötték a budapesti olimpiai első hétmilliárdját, azt bizonyítja, hogy most kéne abbahagyni az egészet.* 444.hu. September 2, 2016. https://444.hu/2016/09/02/ahogy-elkoltottek-a-budapesti-olimpiai-elso-hetmilliardjat-azt-bizonyitja-hogy-most-kene-abbahagyni-az-egeszet

4. Reuters, *Hungary's Olympic dream 'killed' by political upstarts, says PM Orban.* Reuters. February 24, 2017. https://www.reuters.com/article/us-olympics-2024-budapest-orban

5. 24.hu, Fekete-Győr: Gyurcsány eltakarodhatna már. 24.hu. March 7, 2017. https://24.hu/belfold/2017/03/07/fekete-gyor-gyurcsany-eltakarodhatna-mar/

Chapter Eleven: On Activism

Márton Gulyás: The Unorthodox Protester

Biography: Márton Gulyás is a leftist political activist and internet star in Hungary. He was born in 1986 in Budapest as the third child of a middle-class family. In his teenage years, he was involved in theatre, directing plays and making films. Later, he started the YouTube channel Slejm, which in 2018 evolved into the current weekly internet show Partizán. Márton Gulyás took initiative to the Country for All Movement in an attempt to change the nonproportional Hungarian electoral law. The movement also was active during the April 2018 elections, coordinating which local candidates had the best chance of beating Fidesz.

1. 444.hu, *Kilóra eladják az országot az oroszoknak, és én vagyok a nemzetbiztonsági kockázat?* 444.hu. September 12, 2017. https://444.hu/2017/09/12/kilora-eladjak-az-orszagot-az-oroszoknak-es-en-vagyok-a-nemzetbiztonsagi-kockazat

Daniel Friberg: A Western Refugee

Biography: Daniel Friberg is a Swedish alt-right activist, publisher and writer with close ties to Hungary. He was born in 1978 and grew up in Gothenburg in a politically left-leaning family, but in his teenage years he became involved with the Swedish white nationalist culture of the 1990s. Friberg earned an MBA in business from Gothenburg University in 2006 and later worked as a business man. At the same time, he founded several publishing and media companies, including the AltRight.com website, to promote nationalist and far-right political views. In 2014, he moved to Budapest where he wrote and published the book *The Real Right Returns*, which is considered a manifesto and a handbook for alt-right activists.

1. Viktor Orbán, Speech after swearing the prime ministerial oath of office. May 10, 2018. http://www.kormany.hu/en/the-prime-minister/the-prime-minister-s-speeches/prime-minister-viktor-orban-s-address-after-swearing-the-prime-ministerial-oath-of-office

2. Newsweek, Richard Spencer's "White Supremacist' Website AltRight.com Taken Offline. Newsweek. May 4, 2018. https://www.newsweek.com/richard-spencers-white-supremacist-website-altrightcom-goes-offline-910320

3. Viktor Orbán, State of the Union speech. February 10, 2017. http://www.kormany.hu/en/the-prime-minister/the-prime-minister-s-speeches/prime-minister-viktor-orban-s-state-of-the-nation-address-20170214

János Szűcs: Roma, Fight For Your Rights

Biography: János Szűcs is a political activist with Roma background. He was born in 1987 and grew up in a poor Roma family in eastern Hungary. Through his childhood, his mother encouraged him to spend time with both fellow cigánys and ethnic Hungarians because, as she told him, they were all equal human beings. János Szűcs did well in school and later studied finance and HR management. After graduating university, he moved abroad and had internships in the European Parliament and at the US Embassy in Budapest before returning back to his home region to make a difference for the country's poorest. Together with his mentor, the long-time Roma politician István Kamarás, he founded the political party Opre Roma Párt, which is, among other issues, working on establishing the world's first independent Roma province in north-eastern Hungary.

1. István Zoltán Pásztor, *The number and spatial distribution of the Roma population in Hungary*. University Of Debrecen. July 2016.

2. Joanna Kostka, *Financing Roma Inclusion with European Structural Funds: Why Good Intentions Fail* (Routledge, 2018)

Chapter Twelve: On Culture

Éva S. Balogh: Hunting For Historical Justice

Biography: Éva S. Balogh (1936-2021) was a historian and publisher of the daily news blog, Hungarian Spectrum. She was born in Pécs where she spent her childhood, until she moved to Budapest at age eighteen to study at the ELTE university. After the failed Hungarian revolution in 1956, she left for Canada and later moved to the United States. At Yale University, Éva S. Balogh graduated in history, got a PhD degree and continued to work there for many years as a history professor. In 2007, she started the Hungarian Spectrum blog from her home in the States, and wrote more than 4,000 articles on Hungary's political life.

1. Budapest Beacon, *Meet Hungarian Spectrum's Éva Balogh*. Budapest Beacon. November 7, 2014. https://budapestbeacon. com/meet-hungarian-spectrums-eva-balogh/

Mária Schmidt: A New Era Has Arrived

Biography: Mária Schmidt is a historian and former Chief Advisor to Prime Minister Viktor Orbán. She was born in 1953 in Budapest and graduated as a secondary school teacher of history and German language. She earned a doctorate and later a PhD in history and worked as a professor at the Catholic Pázmány University. In 1998, she became Orbán's advisor, and today she has close ties with Hungary's political leader. Furthermore, Mária Schmidt is the director of the House of Terror museum and since 2016 the owner of the progovernment, conservative business magazine Figyelő. She is included on Forbes's top 50 list of richest Hungarians with a total wealth of €66 million.

1. Francis Fukuyama, *The End of History?* in The National Interest, 1989.

2. The Jerusalem Post, *Yad Vashem: Hungarian Holocaust museum is a 'falsification of history."* The Jerusalem Post. September 21, 2018. https://www.jpost.com/Diaspora/Yad-Vashem-publicly-criticizes-controversial-Hungarian-Holocaust-Museum-567692

Vilmos Kondor: The Burden on Budapest

Biography: Vilmos Kondor is the author of the *Budapest Noir* crime novel series. His person is shrouded in mystery as he never appears in public and only does written interviews. According to his publisher's press material, he was born in 1954 and attended university in Szeged before continuing his studies in Paris. He graduated in chemical engineering from the Sorbonne and then returned to Hungary. Currently, while writing the popular crime novel books, he teaches mathematics and physics at a high school. He lives with his wife, daughters and dog in a small village near Sopron in Western Hungary. In 2017, his bestselling book *Budapest Noir* was adapted into a movie.

1. Vilmos Kondor, *Budapest Noir* (Harper Paperbacks, 2012, published in Hungarian in 2008)

Andy Vajna: As Good As It Gets

Biography: Andy Vajna was a film producer, media owner and a close friend of Viktor Orbán. He was born in 1944 in Budapest, but fled Hungary at the age of 12 during the 1956 uprising. He ended up in Los Angeles, and after an eventful early career as a photographer and barber, he moved to Hong Kong where he established a wig manufacturing company. After returning to California in the mid-1970s, Andy Vajna became a film producer in Hollywood. With huge success, he produced box office action hits like *Rambo*, *Die Hard* and *The Terminator* before returning to his native Hungary in 2011 to become government commissioner in charge of the country's film industry. Through his connections with Viktor Orbán, Vajna also became owner of *TV2* and other media outlets, as well as the majority of Hungary's casinos. Before his death, Andy Vajna ranked 18th on *Forbes Magazine's* list of the richest Hungarians with an estimated total wealth of €210 million. Andy Vajna died in his home in Budapest on January 20, 2019. He was 74 years old.

1. Forbes Magazine Hungary, *Magyarország 50 leggazdagabb embere—már nem Csányi az első*. Forbes Magazine. December 28, 2018. https://forbes.hu/a-magazin/magyarorszag-50-leggazdagabb-embere-mar-nem-csanyi-az-elso/

2. Financial Times, *Orbán tightens grip on Hungary's media*. Financial Times. August 16, 2016. https://www.ft.com/content/50488256-60af-11e6-ae3f-77baadeb1c93

Chapter Thirteen: On Being Hungarian

Zoltán Adamecz: Freedom or Financial Stability?

Biography: Zoltán Adamecz is a self-employed business owner living with his wife and five children in Veszprém, a middle-sized city close to Lake Balaton in the western part of Hungary. He was born in 1967 and grew up in Veszprém in a lower-middle class family under the communist Kádár regime. His parents worked as a military major and a housewife. Before the system change in 1989, Zoltán Adamecz worked in East Germany for a few years before returning to Hungary to start his own company in the service sector within trade. Since then he has been an entrepreneur and managed his own company with more than twenty employees.

1. Portfolio.hu, *We produce 40% of the country's GDP in Budapest.* Portfolio.hu. May 24, 2012. https://www.portfolio.hu/users/elofizetes_info.php?t=cikk&i=167708

2. Jacobin Mag, *What Orbán Knows and His Enemies Don't.* Jacobin Mag. March 9, 2018. https://www.jacobinmag.com/2018/03/viktor-orban-hungary-fidesz-authoritarian-opposition

3. Ibid.

4. Pew Research Center, *End of Communism Cheered but Now with More Reservations.* November 2, 2009. http://www.pewglobal.org/2009/11/02/end-of-communism-cheered-but-now-with-more-reservations/

5. Daily News Hungary, *Almost half of Hungarians oppose EU sanctions against Russia.* Daily News Hungary. February 1, 2017. https://dailynewshungary.com/almost-half-hungarians-oppose-eu-sanctions-russia/

6. Index, *A magyarok jobban szeretik Putyint, mint Merkelt.* Index. February 2, 2017. https://index.hu/belfold/2017/02/02/putyint_jobban_szeretik_a_magyarok_merkelnel_de_nagyon_megoszto/

Ágnes Rostás: Happy Brainwashing

Biography: Ágnes Rostás is an economist and a mother living in Budapest with her husband. She was born in 1983 in an upper middle-class family and grew up in a town near the Croatian border. Her father was the mayor of the town, but she has never been active in politics. At a university in Budapest, she studied economy and later found jobs in different sectors, including teaching and real estate, but she quickly got bored with the tasks or unsatisfied with the salary. At the time of the interview, April 2018, she was looking for a job.

1. István Bori, *The Essential Guide To Being Hungarian* (New Europe Books, 2012).

2. M.E.P. Seligman, *Learned Helplessness* (Annual Review of Medicine, 1972)

3. McDaniel College, *Philip Zimbardo shows how we all can practice everyday heroism.* McDaniel College. April 27, 2015. http://mcdaniel.hu/heroes-square/

Tibor Tehel: Brick by Brick

Biography: Tibor Tehel is a printing worker at a factory outside of Veszprém in western Hungary. He was born in 1974 and grew up close to where he lives now, in a village called Zirc. His father was a bus driver, sometimes taking his son with him on weeklong bus trips to West Germany and Yugoslavia. Tibor Tehel never got an education, but soon after the fall of communism, he landed a job at the printing factory. He still works there today, but between 2007 and 2014, he lived and worked in London, delivering goods to hotels and restaurants. Back in Veszprém, Tibor Tehel lives with his dog in a one-bedroom apartment.

1. Ferenc Gyurcsány, Speech at MSZP party congress in Balatonőszöd, May 26, 2006. Leaked and broadcast on Magyar Radio. September 17, 2006. https://en.wikipedia.org/wiki/%C5%90sz%C3%B6d_speech

2. AboutHungary.hu, *Hungary Helps: 2 million USD to re-build community in Iraq.* AboutHungary.hu. May 29, 2017. http://abouthungary.hu/blog/hungary-helps-2-million-usd-to-re-build-community-in-iraq/

Daniel Fabricius: Have Some Respect

Biography: Daniel Fabricius is a Danish-Hungarian economist living in Copenhagen. He was born in 1993 and grew up in the western part of Denmark with his Hungarian mother and Danish father. His parents had met each other in Budapest and worked, respectively, as a school teacher and at the Royal Danish Post. From a young age, Daniel Fabricius was politically active, and later he became a notable member of the Young Conservatives, an affiliated youth party of Conservative People's Party in Denmark. Throughout his childhood, he has visited his family in Hungary on a regular basis, and in his early 20s, he lived in Budapest for some time, establishing a wine exporting company and working for a civil organization. Before graduating from Copenhagen Business School, Daniel Fabricius studied in Vienna for a semester. Today he works in a Nordic investment bank in the Danish capital.

1. John F. Helliwell, *World Happiness Report 2018*. United Nations. 2018.

Conclusion

How to Stop Polarization: Be Curious and Listen

1. Evelyn Beatrice Hall, *The Friends of Voltaire* (Cornell University Library, 2009, originally 1906).

2. Stanford News, *Empathy, respect for one another critical to ease political polarization*. Stanford University. January 20, 2017. https://news.stanford.edu/2017/01/20/empathy-respect-critical-ease-political-polarization-sociologist-says/

3. Ibid.

4. Ibid.

5. Dan Kahan, *The Politically Motivated Reasoning Paradigm*. Yale University, 2015.

There will be No Winner but the Endless Debate Itself

1. Reuters Institute, *Digital News Report 2017*. Oxford University, 2017.

2. Ibid.

3. Pew Research Center, *Publics Globally Want Unbiased News Coverage, but Are Divided on Whether Their News Media Deliver*. Pew Research Center, 2018.

4. Berlingske, *Våbenfabrik handlede ulovligt med Nazityskland*. Berlingske. November 19, 1999. https://www.berlingske.dk/samfund/vaabenfabrik-handlede-ulovligt-med-nazityskland

5. Angus Stevenson, *Oxford Dictionary of English*. Oxford University Press, 2010.

6. NiemanLab, *In Germany, a news site is pairing up liberals and conservatives and actually getting them to (gasp) have a civil conversation*. NiemanLab. August 8, 2018. http://www.niemanlab.org/2018/08/in-germany-a-news-site-is-pairing-up-liberals-and-conservatives-and-actually-getting-them-to-gasp-have-a-civil-conversation/

7. The Human Library Organization. www.humanlibary.org

8. David Fuller, *A Glitch in the Matrix: Jordan B. Peterson, the Intellectual Dark Web and the Mainstream Media*. YouTube. February 17, 2018.

Index

About the Author

Lasse Skytt is a Danish foreign correspondent who has covered Hungary and Central Europe for nearly a decade. Previously based in Copenhagen, London, and New York City, he graduated with journalism degrees from The New School and the University of Southern Denmark and has lived in Hungary since 2013.

CPSIA information can be obtained
at www.ICGtesting.com
Printed in the USA
JSHW051236070322
22928JS00001B/1

9 780999 541678